Achieving an
Abortion-Free
America
by 2001

Thomas A. Glessner

MULTNOMAH

Portland, Oregon 97266

Scripture quotations are from the Holy Bible: New International Version, ©1973, 1978, 1984 by International Bible Society. Used by permission of Zondervan Bible Publishers.

Cover design by Durand Demlow

Edited by Rodney L. Morris

ACHIEVING AN ABORTION-FREE AMERICA BY 2001
© 1990 by Thomas A. Glessner
Published by Multnomah Press
Portland, Oregon 97266

Multnomah Press is a ministry of Multnomah School of the Bible, 8435 NE Glisan Street, Portland, OR 97220

Printed in the United States of America

Library of Congress Cataloging-in-Publication Data

Glessner, Thomas A.

    Achieving an abortion-free America by 2001 / Thomas A. Glessner.

      p.   cm.
    ISBN 0-88070-361-X (paper)
    1. Abortion—Government policy—United States. 2. Pro-life movement—United States. I. Title.
    HQ767.5.U5G58   1990   90—6550
    363.4'6'0973—dc20   CIP

90 91 92 93 94 95 96 97 98 99 - 10 9 8 7 6 5 4 3 2 1

Dedication

This book is dedicated to the greatest blessings in my life—my wife and children. First, to Laura, my wife, whose uncompromising pro-life stand is helping us together build a legacy of unmeasurable wealth to pass on to our children. Second, to our children, Joshua, SaraLynn, and Brannan, who, I pray, will inherit a world free of the death ethic of abortion and the destruction it brings to so many lives. And finally, to our tiny unborn baby who now resides in the womb and has yet to see the light of day. May your future, little one, be filled with a divinely inspired love of life which comes from the Author of life.

Contents

Foreword

When Curt Young, the second executive director of the Christian Action Council, announced his intention to step down after ten years' labor, members of the Council's board of directors asked themselves whether anyone could ever fill his shoes. In addition to building the CAC from a tiny broom-closet of an office in Washington's National Press Building into the nation's foremost Christian pro-life organization, and in the process launching a crisis pregnancy ministry that now has over four hundred centers nationwide, he produced an important pro-life book, *The Least of These: What Everyone Should Know about Abortion* (1983). Curt's nominee as his successor, young Seattle attorney Thomas A. Glessner, had already posted some impressive accomplishments in crisis pregnancy work, and after moving to the Washington, D.C., area, he quickly demonstrated that he could not merely carry on the established work, but could build it and launch new initiatives. The present work, *Achieving an Abortion-Free America by 2001*, illustrates this.

In 1983 *Roe* v. *Wade*, the infamous Supreme Court decision permitting abortion on demand, was ten years old, and the number of aborted unborn children in the United States was approaching fifteen million. Since that time, seven more years have passed, twenty-five million babies have ended up in the abortionists' garbage pails, and abortion has become a "way of life" for millions—or, better said, a "way of death" for one baby in three conceived in the United States.

If you were offered a position in which you had one chance in three of being dead before nine months were out, would you be likely to accept? Those are the odds facing babies conceived in America during the nine months when, abortion (and accidental miscarriage) apart, they occupy a "position" in a mother's womb.

With its 1989 decision, *Webster* v. *Reproductive Health Services*, a rejuvenated Supreme Court challenged—but did not overturn—the assumption that abortion on demand is a constitutionally guaranteed right in the United States. Even this slight setback has provoked a frenzy on the part of those for whom liberty to abort at will is a necessary corollary to their claim to sexual license without discipline or restraint, as well as to those financially powerful interests for whom abortion is not merely a business but an ever-reliable source of increasing wealth. In consequence, they have launched a series of vehement attacks, not only against those who would change the law to create at least a semblance of protection for unborn children, but even against those who do not directly challenge the liberty of abortion but only seek to help pregnant women find a better way to deal with problem pregnancies instead of the one in which, as Hans Millendorfer puts it, "killing represents a solution."

Although some—a few—in the mass media make an effort to be balanced, abortion advocates can almost always count on their collaboration, or even their collusion, in presenting the pro-abortion cause in the most charming light, while systematically ignoring, if not actively misrepresenting, its pro-life opponents.

In such a situation, those for whom "killing" does not "represent a solution," who are not comfortable with the thought that one baby in three, or perhaps even more, will wind up "terminated" before birth every year, need information, exhortation, and a sound strategy for the future. Tom Glessner's *Achieving an Abortion-Free America by 2001* is an invaluable resource for all who are not content lamely to accept the ongoing violation, through mass abortion, of human dignity, justice, and the law of God. This solid, well-documented book is not journalistic pabulum but solid fare, no "uncertain sound" but a clear summons to commitment and to action. It will be hated and maligned by those for whom abortion is either a precious license or a lucrative occupation, but cherished by those who value the dignity of human life, and gratefully remembered, twenty years hence, by some whose lives it helped to spare.

Harold O. J. Brown
Forman Chair of Ethics in Theology
Trinity Evangelical Divinity School
Deerfield, Illinois

Preface

There is seldom a book that I can enthusiastically endorse without some qualifications. Moreover, there are very few books from a pro-life perspective that are compelling and readable and serve in a timely manner to give clear direction for the future. In *Achieving an Abortion-Free America by 2001*, Thomas Glessner has provided us with such a book.

Most books begin with post-*Roe* v. *Wade*. Glessner begins with an insightful analysis of post-*Webster* and the opportunities leading up to *Webster*, followed by an appraisal of where we need to go from here. He covers the importance of reaching the hearts of Americans (not just the minds through education), of reaching out to women with crisis pregnancies, of following a clear legislative strategy for the 1990s (which he provides), and of becoming involved in different aspects of pro-life activism. His general insights as well as practical how-to's are a welcome stimulus for achieving an abortion-free America.

Glessner is a Christian lawyer and executive director of the Christian Action Council in Washington, D.C. (The CAC is the major evangelical pro-life organization with both a pastoral and a political outreach.) As a Christian well-versed in Scripture, Glessner motivates us to be concerned about every aspect of the abortion issue. As a knowledgeable lawyer, Glessner guides us through the maze of past legal action and provides a lucid and forward-looking legislative strategy for the 1990s. As executive director of the CAC, Glessner shows his leadership by providing us directions and a map for the future. As a pro-life activist, Glessner is able to portray specific how-to's of personal involvement—how to picket, how to carry out local projects, how to fight Planned Parenthood and more. His helpful insights on how to win a political campaign and how to frame the issue should be read by all pro-life politicians. Glessner also gives us his appraisal of the Rescue Movement.

Glessner's style is captivating for the average reader, with extensive footnotes and appendices for those interested in pursuing specific points further. Great profit will be gained from a careful reading and studying of *Achieving an Abortion-Free America*, which provides for the pro-life movement in general, and for Christian pro-lifers in particular, a clear direction for the 1990s.

Paul B. Fowler, Ph.D., pastor
St. Andrew's Presbyterian Church
Hollywood, Florida

A New
Opportunity Emerges

July 3, 1989, was an historic day for the pro-life movement. On that day I was privileged to be sitting in the front row of the courtroom in the Supreme Court when the decision in *Webster* v. *Reproductive Health Services* was handed down.

The mood was tense as the packed courtroom anxiously awaited the decision. Sitting in the courtroom were well-known activists on both sides of the abortion issue, each one nervously awaiting the entrance of the justices into the court chambers. The Court had been asked by the State of Missouri and the Bush Administration to use the *Webster* case to overturn its landmark case of *Roe* v. *Wade*, which opened the door for abortion-on-demand in America. How would the justices of the Court respond to this request?

As I awaited the entry of the justices into the courtroom I was acutely aware of the historic magnitude of this day.

The nine justices of the most powerful court in the history of the world were about to render a decision that many hoped would play a significant role in ending abortion-on-demand in America. These mere mortals—eight men and one woman—have been given by our government power over life and death. And on this day the fate of the most helpless and vulnerable of our human family—the unborn—lay in their hands.

I thought of a similar time in American history when the Court discarded the 1896 precedent of *Plessy* v. *Ferguson*, which kept black Americans relegated to an inferior status through the "separate but equal doctrine." I further reflected on the Court's disastrous decision in *Dred Scott* v. *Sanford* in 1857, which dehumanized black slaves and helped usher in a bloody civil war. Would *Roe* v. *Wade* on this day take its deserved place with such discredited legal relics? Would the Court admit the terrible mistake it had made on January 22, 1973, and bring forth a decision in which justice would prevail?

I prayed, "Dear God, may this decision be one of true justice. May unborn babies be once again protected under the law and may America be spared from the impending judgment which will surely come if the abortion holocaust is not ended."

Emotion swelled within me when it was announced that Chief Justice William Rehnquist would read the majority opinion of the Court. Rehnquist had been an original dissenter in *Roe* v. *Wade* and has severely criticized it in every abortion case heard subsequently by the Court. As the Chief Justice read his decision it became clear to me that a new opportunity was being given to God's people. While not expressly overturning *Roe* v. *Wade*, the *Webster* decision essentially cut the heart out of *Roe* by granting the states a compelling interest to protect preborn human life "throughout pregnancy." This decision issues an open invitation for state legislatures to severely restrict and even ban abortion.

For years the conventional wisdom in the pro-life movement has been that abortion will be ended through a constitutional amendment. Our elected politicians in Washington D.C. were looked to as the ones who would end the killing. Yet the *Webster* decision permanently changes such conventional wisdom. This decision now opens the door for the abortion holocaust to be ended state by state, city by city, and community by community. Now, more than ever, involvement by activists at the local level will make a difference in stopping the slaughter of the unborn.

This truth hit me hard as I listened intently to the Chief Justice read the opinion of the Court. And as I realized that the people of God were being given a second chance to respond to the cries for life, I asked myself whether we had the vision and the resolve to meet the challenge and opportunity the Court was laying before us.

Afterwards, the scene outside the Supreme Court building resembled a carnival. Hundreds of abortion opponents and supporters had gathered to demonstrate and respond to the decision. Abortion proponents were screaming rehearsed chants, such as "Go ahead, kneel and pray, *Roe* v. *Wade* is here to stay!" while hundreds of pro-lifers prayed and sang hymns of thanksgiving. Reporters from both the secular and Christian media were seeking interviews and responses to the decision which seemed at first to be a major defeat for the pro-abortion movement.

As I spoke to reporters, I emphasized that the decision was a major victory for the pro-life movement. However, I cautioned that while it was a victory, the battle for the sanctity of human life was far from over. I immediately thought of the words of Winston Churchill after a major victory in World War II. Churchill then said, "This is not the end. It is not even the beginning of the end. But it is, perhaps, the end of the beginning."

How true those words of that great English statesman have proven to be in the war to save the lives of unborn babies. Perhaps it is more accurate to speak of the *Webster* decision not as a victory, but rather as an opportunity. The door has been opened by this decision for the people of God to act decisively and once again bring protection to those helpless little ones who reside in the womb. As in Queen Esther's day, it is "for such a time as this" that Christians have been called in the 1990s to speak out and end a holocaust that has, to date, taken the lives of more than twenty-three million unborn children in the United States.

However, the question that remains to be answered is: "Will the people of God respond to this challenge?" I firmly believe America is at a crossroads. Whichever road we, as a nation, choose to take will embark us on a journey of no return. One path, if taken, will continue us on the road to destruction and judgment. The second path will lead this once great nation down the road to restoration, reconciliation, healing, and revival. I pray we will choose the second road, the road of restoration. I believe the people of God hold the key to which road our nation travels during the next decade. If we respond to the moving of the Spirit of God, revival will heal our land and we will see an abortion-free America by 2001.

The intense activity in the immediate weeks following the *Webster* decision has verified my initial assessment. During this period, the pro-life movement suffered some initial setbacks in the legislatures of the states of Florida, Illinois, and Texas. In addition, state court decisions in California and Florida invalidated parental consent laws, and Congress made efforts to liberalize federal funding of abortion. The national media joined the pro-abortion frenzy by daily reporting its assessment that the *Webster* decision had galvanized pro-abortion forces. The media seemed to gloat over politicians who had consistently voted pro-life but were changing their positions in fear of the perceived majority that allegedly supports abortion.

The *Washington Post*, in an editorial dated October 11, 1989, probably best stated the post-*Webster* sentiment of the media when it said:

> There is a pattern developing. State officials, who for years had heard only from anti-abortion forces, are learning that there would be obstacles to limiting or criminalizing the procedure even if *Roe* were overturned. There are substantially more pro-choice voters than there were before *Roe*, and though they have been relatively quiet since 1973, they are organizing now. There is a far greater appreciation of privacy rights among the public than there was in 1973. And there is a new interest in state constitutions, some of which already have strong privacy provisions that would conflict with abortion regulation. No matter what the U.S. Supreme Court may say states can do to restrict abortions, governors and legislators will find it increasingly difficult to turn back the clock.

The battle lines have been drawn. On one side stand the pro-abortion forces supported by a sympathetic media, endorsed by a secular humanist establishment, and led by such organizations as Planned Parenthood, the National Organization of Women (NOW), the National Abortion Rights Action League (NARAL), People for the American Way (PAW), and the American Civil Liberties Union (ACLU). Countering these modern-day Goliaths are the people of God, determined to win this battle for the heart and soul of America.

Against tremendous odds, the people of God must stand firm and take action. We must stand firm against the spiritual forces of death at work in this country destroying countless lives and relationships through abortion. And we must stand firm in the political arena as representatives of a kingdom to come, where the Lord of life will reign everywhere.

From the beginning of the American experience our laws have protected the unborn from destruction by abortion. Our legal system erected a wall of protection to guarantee the right to life of the unborn. Yet the erosion of this wall and its eventual demolition became complete in 1973. Moreover, respect for born human life has been severely eroded to the point where America is now seriously discussing the feasibility of euthanasia.

It is the responsibility of the people of God to rebuild this wall of protection. The *Webster* decision has given us a new opportunity to act, and the decade of the 1990s will be determinative in deciding this crucial issue. If, however, we commit this cause to the Lord of life and unify under his banner, I believe we will see an abortion-free America by 2001.

The Wall
of
Protection
for the Unborn

CHAPTER ONE

The Destruction of the Wall

The wall of protection for the unborn child in America came tumbling down on January 22, 1973. On this date, the United States Supreme Court issued its infamous *Roe* v. *Wade* decision which opened the door for unrestricted abortion-on-demand throughout all nine months of a woman's pregnancy.

Since this decision was rendered, more than 23 million unborn children have been destroyed in the United States. Today, one out of every three babies conceived in America is aborted. In more than fourteen metropolitan areas, abortions outnumber live births.[1] Each year 1.6 million unborn children die by abortion. Abortion claims the lives of 131,520 children each month, 4,384 each day, 183 each hour, 3 each minute, and 1 every 20 seconds.[2] Such staggering statistics clearly indicate that the wall of protection for the unborn has been demolished since the issuance of *Roe*.

SUPPORT FOR THE WALL OF PROTECTION

Although abortion was sanctioned in some pre-Christian societies, such as the Roman empire, opposition to this practice also existed in pagan civilizations. Dr. Harold O. J. Brown, professor at Trinity Evangelical Divinity School and chairman of the Christian Action Council, writes:

> Even in pagan antiquity, abortion, although widely practiced, was by no means universally approved, and was indeed explicitly condemned as immoral, dangerous, and harmful to the general welfare, by the most important pre-Mosaic law codes and by some of the most celebrated thinkers, philosophers, and moralists of pagan Greece and Rome.[3]

The earliest known laws on abortion are in the Code of Hammurabi in Babylon, adopted around 1728 B.C.[4] Such laws dealt only with an unintentional act causing a woman to miscarry. The perpetrator of the act was fined. However, if the woman also died, and she was a noblewoman, the perpetrator's daughter would also be put to death.[5]

Ancient laws against abortion also existed through the reign of King Tiglath-Pileser I of Assyria in the twelfth century B.C. Such laws punished the woman who caused herself to miscarry and penalties were also prescribed for accessories to the act.[6]

The Hittites also proscribed abortion with prohibitions applying to all persons, means used, and circumstances. Financial penalties were additionally rendered against perpetrators of the act.[7]

Ancient condemnation of abortion was not limited to the Near East. Opposition to abortion was widespread in ancient Indian religious writings, such as the Vedas and the Vinaysas of the Buddhists. Condemnation was also contained in one of the ancient Indian legal codes, the Code of Manu which dates back to A.D. 100. However, the laws it brings together go back hundreds of years prior to that date.[8]

In later Hindu tradition, abortion is ranked with the murder of a husband or a learned Brahman. Only these acts make women outcasts, while penances can expiate other sins such as adultery.[9]

In Zoroastrian literature, when a guilty couple "destroy the fruit in her womb . . . the murder is on both the father and herself; both the father and herself shall pay the penalty for willful murder." Abortion is considered a murder under all marital conditions.[10]

The ancient Jews also opposed abortion. Father John Connery, professor of theology at Loyola University in Chicago, explains that:

> The attitude of the Jews toward barrenness as a curse, the regard for fertility as one of God's greatest blessings, the mandate to increase and multiply, the hope of the Jewish maiden that she might bear the Messiah, all militated against any easy attitude toward self-induced abortion, or even any deliberate attitude. And there is no positive evidence of such an attitude.[11]

Ancient Jewish tradition was based on Exodus 21:22-25, which addresses only abortion caused by a third party.[12] However, the books of the Maccabees represent the thought of some substantial parts of the Jewish community not long before the time of Christ. In 2 Maccabees 7:22-23 (REB), a mother says to her sons:

> "You appeared in my womb, I know not how; it was not I who gave you life and breath, not I who set in order the elements of your being. The Creator of the universe, who designed the beginning of mankind and devised the origin of all, will in his mercy give you back again breath and life, since now you put his laws above every thought of self."

Perhaps the most famous of all ancient proscriptions on abortion is in the Oath of Hippocrates. Hippocrates, known as the father of modern medicine, lived in the fifth and fourth centuries B.C. and strongly condemned abortion. The pertinent part of the Oath states:

> "Neither will I administer a poison to anybody when asked to do so, nor will I suggest such a course. Similarly, I will not give to a woman a pessary [something introduced into the womb] to cause abortion."[13]

As the Court acknowledged in *Roe*, the advent of Christianity brought about a universal embracing of the Hippocratic Oath. The acceptance of the Oath in relation to abortion was unquestioned in American society until the time leading up to the fateful day of January 22, 1973. This widespread recognition of the oath's proscription of abortion is shown in the historical roots of the American legal system—the English common law.

Common Law Support for Abortion Prohibitions

The common law is that body of law and theory which was originated, developed, and formulated in England. Developed essentially through case law (as opposed to statutory law) the common law is composed of decisions of courts in specific cases. Each decision or ruling sets a precedent to be followed by future courts in similar circumstances. That portion of the common law of England (including such acts of parliament as were applicable) which had been accepted at the time of the American Revolution constitutes the common law in authority in the United States today. Unless an aspect of that common law has been specifically abrogated by a state legislature, it is recognized today as an organic part of the laws of most of the United States.

Two English jurists who wrote extensively on the

common law, Sir William Blackstone and Sir Edward Coke, expressed opposition to abortion. Coke referred to abortion in his *Third Institute* as a "misprision." Blackstone defines "misprisions" as "generally understood to be all such high offenses as are under the degree of capital, but nearly bordering thereon." Such an offense could be equated to some felonies today which are not punished with death.[14]

Blackstone in particular was acknowledged as a supreme authority on the common law, and his *Commentaries on the Laws of England* were heavily relied upon by United States Supreme Court Chief Justice John Marshall and other early American jurists in building the American legal system. In Book I of his *Commentaries*, Blackstone discusses abortion under a section titled "On the rights of Persons." In this section Blackstone proclaims life to be "the immediate gift of God" which begins in the womb. He continues with the declaration that the destruction of the unborn child is "homicide or manslaughter."[15]

This right to life of the unborn child, according to Blackstone, is an "absolute" right. Such a right is in contrast to "relative" rights which Blackstone believes are secondary, artificial, and only come into play as a part of legally established relationships with other individuals. According to Blackstone, it is the first and primary end of human laws to maintain and protect "absolute" rights.[16]

Statutory Prohibitions of Abortion

Beginning in the nineteenth century, statutes began appearing which criminally punished abortion. It is likely that the law was responding to the scientific discovery of the ovum in 1827. It was at this time that we learned how conception occurs. A greater appreciation developed for the unborn child who was understood to be a separate, distinct, and living being from the moment of conception. Prior to this, the common law had made a distinction between prenatal life before and after quickening, the point in a pregnancy when movement from the child can first be felt. The common law protected prenatal life after quickening because it is at this stage that there is actual evidence of life within the womb.

The first English statutory prohibition on abortion was Lord Ellenborough's Act enacted in 1803.[17] This law made abortion after quickening a capital offense and for the first time clearly made pre-quickening abortion a punishable offense.

American states also began to respond to this greater understanding of biology. Legislation outlawing abortion accelerated after the 1827 discovery, and by 1860 thirty-one of the eventual fifty states had adopted statutes punishing abortion. Between 1849 and 1875, twenty-four states and territories enacted anti-abortion statutes for the first time.[18]

In 1859 the American Medical Association issued a significant report through its Committee on Criminal Abortion. Under the leadership of Dr. Horatio R. Storer of Boston, this report recommended that the AMA at its national convention "condemn the procuring of abortion, at every period of gestation, except as necessary for preserving the life of either mother or child [and] request the zealous cooperation of the various State medical societies in pressing this subject upon the legislatures of their respective States."[19]

Storer wrote a book with Franklin F. Heard in 1868 titled, *Criminal Abortion: Its Nature, Its Evidence and Its Law*, in which they state:

> Physicians have now arrived at the unanimous opinion, that the foetus in utero is alive from the very moment of conception. . . . [T]he wilful killing of a human being, at any stage of its existence is murder. . . . [A]bortion is, in reality, a crime against the infant, its mother, the family circle, and society.[20]

Such statements put to rest the claim from modern-day abortion proponents that the anti-abortion laws of the nineteenth century were designed only to protect the woman from exposure to unsanitary surgery. While it is true (and ironic) that the pioneers of the feminist movement during this time opposed abortion as an act which exploits women, the motivating factor behind the AMA's push for tighter abortion laws was its concern for the life of the unborn child.

Concern for the unborn by the international medical community in the twentieth century was consistent with this early opinion of the American Medical Association. In 1948, the World Medical Association adopted the Declaration of Geneva which said, "I will maintain the utmost respect for human life, from the time of conception; even under threat, I will not use my medical knowledge contrary to the laws of humanity."[21] In October 1949, the WMA adopted the International Code of Medical Ethics which stated, "A doctor must always bear in mind the importance of preserving human life from the time of conception until death."[22]

Hence, up until the end of World War II, the wall of protection for the unborn was well established and the humanity of the unborn child was unquestioned. Yet the foundation of the wall began to erode shortly thereafter.

THE ASSAULT ON THE WALL

With the close of World War II, attempts were made to change the anti-abortion laws in America. The impetus for this change came from an increasing acceptance by American society of a humanist world view which considers mankind self-sufficient and not in need of a God who intervenes in human affairs. With man seen as self-sufficient, the medical and intellectual communities began to discuss the need to control the uncontrollable, including the ability to control one's reproductive capacities, once a hushed topic.

By the early 1950s a movement was afoot to rescind the anti-abortion laws then in existence in all fifty states. Led by Dr. Alan Guttmacher, a leading figure in Planned Parenthood, the movement advocated a slow approach, utilizing education and the gradual acceptance by the American public of abortion in the hard cases—rape, incest, and severe fetal handicap.

Stopping illegal abortions by reforming existing state laws became a common topic at medical conferences during the 1950s. Illegal abortion was discussed as a problem that could not be solved by the existing laws. It was typically suggested that legal commissions be formed to study the abortion laws in the different states and determine how those laws could be revised. The goal was to frame a model abortion law which could be presented for the consideration of the different state legislatures.

In response, the American Law Institute (ALI) in 1959 published a proposed model statute on abortion. The ALI statute proposed that abortion not be considered the killing of another human being, but rather an "offense against the family." The proposal introduced various exceptions where abortion would be legal, such as in cases where the pregnancy would "gravely impair the physical or mental health" of the mother, in cases where the unborn child possessed a "grave physical or mental defect," or in cases where the pregnancy was due to rape. These exceptions have vague and elastic terms that allow for abortions in other cases by stretching the definition of the exception.

During the 1960s the push for a change in the abortion laws gained tremendous momentum. In 1964 the Association for the Study of Abortion was created. According to Dr. Bernard Nathanson, a former abortionist now turned pro-lifer, this organization was "an immaculately respectable and strictly academic" group that included physicians, lawyers, sociologists, and clergymen.[23] This organization aimed its efforts primarily at professionals. Its first president was Dr. Robert E. Hall of Columbia University's College of Physicians and Surgeons, who called upon obstetricians to lead the battle for legalized abortion.[24]

The movement for legalization was noticeably accelerated in 1965. At this time the national Federation of Temple Sisterhoods, a Jewish group, called for liberalization of abortion laws. In addition, the Union of American Hebrew Congregations backed a change in the law regarding abortion.[25] The New York Civil Liberties Union became actively involved by proposing the repeal of that state's criminal abortion law. The parent organization, the ACLU, followed suit the next year, becoming the first national organization to "assert the right of all women to obtain abortions."[26]

Portions of the religious community also raised their voices for the liberalization of abortion laws. The New York State Council of Churches, the state's largest interdenominational organization, called for the New York legislature to rescind the state's abortion law. Joining in this call was the Protestant Council of New York and the Episcopal Diocese of New York.[27] In California, the late Episcopal bishop James Pike called for a change in the laws on abortion.[28]

The media finally took up the campaign for liberalization in 1965 with the *New York Times* issuing editorials on three separate occasions. In each editorial the *Times* proclaimed that compassion required a change in the law. In one editorial the New York state law was called "barbarous," and in another the paper referred to "the high cost in human misery" caused by the law.[29] Such an emotional appeal from one of the country's top newspapers carried weight in the shaping of public opinion.

In 1966, the medical profession began to join in the call for a repeal of existing abortion laws. The Association for the Study of Abortion issued a poll which allegedly showed "the nation's psychiatrists . . . overwhelmingly in favor" of easing abortion restrictions.[30]

Early in 1967 the medical journal *Modern Medicine* printed a survey that purported to show that 87 percent of physicians overall, 84 percent of obstetrician-gynecologists, and 95 percent of psychiatrists favored a change in the abortion laws.[31] Finally, in June 1967, the AMA's House of Delegates departed from its policy of more than a hundred years and endorsed liberalization of abortion laws.

The American Medical Association (AMA) and the American College of Obstetricians and Gynecologists adopted resolutions that were to contribute to the change in public perception of abortion and in the eventual change in the law. The AMA resolution opposed induced abortion except in cases where (1) continuation of the pregnancy would threaten the health or the life of the mother; (2) there is documented medical evidence that the infant may be born with an incapacitating physical deformity or mental deficiency; or (3) there is documented medical evidence that the continuation of a pregnancy resulting from legally established statutory or forcible rape or incest may constitute a threat to the mental or physical health of the patient.

The American College of Obstetricians and Gynecologists adopted a resolution in May 1968 listing three conditions where abortion should be acceptable. They are: (1) when the continuation of the pregnancy may threaten the life of the woman or seriously impair her health, broadly defined; (2) when the pregnancy has resulted from rape or incest; or (3) when continuation of the pregnancy is likely to result in the birth of a child with grave physical deformities or mental retardation.

THE WALL IN RUINS

The complete collapse of the wall of protection occurred on January 22, 1973, with the Supreme Court's decision in *Roe* v. *Wade* and its companion case, *Doe* v. *Bolton*. At issue in these two cases were the criminal abortion statutes of Texas and Georgia. The Texas statute banned the performance of abortion, except where necessary to save the life of the mother. The Georgia statute, modeled after the ALI proposal, allowed for abortions in cases of rape, fetal deformity, or threat to the life of the mother.

A class action suit challenging the constitutionality of the Texas law was brought by a pregnant single woman, identified by the pseudonym Jane Roe. (Roe, later identified as Norma McCorvey, claimed that her pregnancy resulted from a rape. Years later McCorvey admitted that she invented the claim of rape in order to obtain sympathy for her case.) The Georgia statute was attacked by a woman identified by the pseudonym Mary Doe and twenty-three other individuals (nine described as Georgia-licensed physicians, seven as nurses, five as clergymen, and two as social workers).

In rendering its decision in favor of the plaintiffs and voiding the Texas and Georgia statutes, the Court stated that a constitutional right to privacy, while not expressly mentioned in the Constitution, exists and is broad enough to include a woman's personal decision to "terminate her pregnancy." Such a right could be found, according to the Court, in the Fourteenth Amendment, which declares that no state shall deny liberty to any person without due process of law. This constitutional liberty was interpreted to include the right to an abortion.[32]

The ultimate effect of this decision was to void the anti-abortion statutes then in existence in all fifty states. The particular details from the Court's opinion leave no doubt that the United States of America has the most permissive abortion law in the Western world. It is important to understand some of the societal ramifications that have come from *Roe* and its demolition of the wall of protection for innocent human life.

The Court's Decision and Its Ramifications

1. Abortion is legal throughout pregnancy.

In rendering its decision, the Court discussed the right to abortion during the three trimesters in a woman's pregnancy. In the *first trimester* abortion is a matter of the right to privacy. According to the Court, during the first trimester the abortion decision must be left to the sole judgment of the pregnant woman in consultation with her attending physician.[33]

In the *second trimester*, up to the point of viability, the state has no interest in protecting the unborn. Rather, the state may promote its interest in the health of the mother, if it chooses, by regulating the abortion procedure only in ways that are reasonably related to maternal health. Measures passed with the sole intent of protecting the unborn from abortion are not allowable at this stage. The viability of the unborn child is that point in the child's development when he or she can survive outside the womb, albeit with artificial technological means. The Court stated that viability occurred generally between twenty-four and twenty-eight weeks of gestational development.[34]

After the point of viability and into the *third trimester*, abortion must still be allowable to protect the "health" of the mother. At this point, according to the Court, a state "may, if it chooses, regulate and even proscribe abortion except where it is necessary, in appropriate medical judgment, for the preservation of the life or health of the mother."[35]

The language of the Court regarding abortions after viability seems, at first glance, to restrict late-term abortions. However, the two important phrases, "if it chooses" and "health of the mother," pave the way for unrestricted abortion in the third trimester.

"If it chooses" makes it clear that states do not have to prohibit abortions after viability. Unless individual states enact legislation that prohibits abortion in the third trimester, those abortions are allowable. Most states have not regulated or prohibited the performance of abortions after viability.

The phrase "health of the mother" is even more permissive and raises the question as to what factors justify an abortion for health reasons in the third trimester. In the companion case of *Doe* v. *Bolton*, the Court answered this by stating "that the medical judgment may be exercised in the light of all factors—physical, emotional, psychological, familial, and the woman's age—relevant to the well-being of the patient. All these factors may relate to health. This allows the attending physician the room he needs to make his best medical judgment."[36] Such a broad definition of *health* means that any stress upon a pregnant woman may justify an abortion. Therefore, abortion-on-demand is allowable even after the unborn child is viable.

Those who favor abortion as a social policy agree with this analysis. Yale law professor John Hart Ely, a supporter of legalized abortion, states that the effect of *Roe* and *Doe* on the ability of states to restrict abortion means that "the statutes of most states must be unconstitutional *even as applied to the final trimester* . . . [for] even after viability the mother's life *or health* (which presumably is to be defined very broadly indeed, so as to include what many might regard as the mother's convenience . . .) must, as a matter of constitutional law, take precedence over . . . the fetus's life."[37]

2. Life must be "meaningful" to be protected.

In drawing distinctions at the three different trimesters in a woman's pregnancy, the Court stated that a state's interest in protecting the life of the unborn child becomes "compelling" only at the point of viability. "This is so," stated the Court, "because the fetus then presumably has the capability of *meaningful life* outside the mother's womb."[38]

This type of language is referred to in legal circles as "dictum" or language used by the Court which is not necessary or essential to the ultimate determination of the case before it. In other words, the Court could have rendered a decision having the same effect without making this particular statement. However, such language is troubling. By stating that a state's interest in protecting human life is compelling only when such life is "meaningful," the Court has opened a Pandora's box that has sweeping ramifications.

If life must be "meaningful" before it can be protected, then who sets the criteria to determine which lives are meaningful? If the life of an unborn child prior to viability is not deemed "meaningful," what about the life of a severely handicapped newborn? What about the lives of the terminally ill, the infirm, the elderly, and others whose contributions to society are seen by some as minimal? Who decides which lives are "meaningful" and therefore worthy of protection?

In using this language the Court opened the door for the practice of infanticide (the deliberate killing of a handicapped newborn) and euthanasia. Indeed, reported cases of handicapped newborns being set aside to die are becoming more commonplace. Likewise, cases where terminally ill patients are denied food and water are becoming more and more accepted under a quality-of-life ethic which demands that a life be "meaningful" before it can be protected.

Several states now allow a genetically handicapped person to file a "wrongful life suit." In these cases the plaintiff, usually represented by a court-appointed guardian, alleges that had his or her parents been given the proper genetic screening tests during the pregnancy, they would have opted for an abortion instead of bringing a handicapped infant into the world. The birth of the handicapped infant is deemed "wrongful," and the plaintiff seeks damages against the obstetrician.

The acceptance of the Court's language that life can only be protected if is "meaningful" has paved the way for the killing of other members of the human family merely because they, like the unborn child from an unplanned pregnancy, are inconvenient. American society now believes that there is such a thing as a life not worthy to be lived. This is a huge departure from the traditional belief in the sanctity-of-life ethic which holds that all human beings are made in the image of God and deserve protection under the law.

3. The unborn child is not a person.

It is surprising to most people to learn that the humanity of the unborn child was not an issue which concerned the Court in *Roe*. Yet the Court stated on page 159 of its opinion:

> We need not resolve the difficult question of when life begins. When those trained in the respective disciplines of medicine, philosophy, and theology are unable to arrive at any consensus, the judiciary, at this point in the development of man's knowledge, is not in a position to speculate as to the answer.

In other words, the fact that abortion kills a living human being was not relevant to the Court in rendering its final decision. Rather, the legal technicality discussed by the Court was whether the unborn child should be considered a person under the Fourteenth Amendment to the U.S. Constitution.

The Fourteenth Amendment says in part that no state shall "deprive any *person* of life . . . without due process of law." The Court freely acknowledged that if an unborn child is a person then abortion cannot be allowed under this amendment. The ultimate decision of the Court was that the unborn child should not be considered a person under the Constitution.

By ruling in this manner the Court issued a legal precedent holding that not all human beings are persons with the right to life and, therefore, not all human beings need be protected under the law. This reasoning is similar to a previous Court blunder in the nineteenth century. In 1857, the U.S. Supreme Court issued a ruling in *Dred Scott* v. *Sanford* which denied constitutional protection to black slaves holding that they were not "citizens" under the preamble of the Constitution. No credible scholar, historian, or lawyer today would dare attempt to justify the decision of the Court in the *Dred Scott* case. Yet, the holding in *Roe* which denies the personhood of the unborn child, irrespective of the clear humanity of that child, is a similar error which must be corrected.

The ultimate irony of the Court's personhood ruling in *Roe* is that the Court has, in the past, held that corporations are persons under the Fourteenth Amendment. Under *Roe* humanity apparently has nothing to do with constitutional protection. According to the Supreme Court some nonhumans, such as corporations, are protected by the Constitution while some humans, such as the unborn, are not.

A Brave New World upon Us?

1. Fetal tissue research

Recent scientific research projects provide further evidence that the wall of protection for the unborn has been destroyed. In his famous novel *Brave New World*, twentieth-century writer Aldous Huxley wrote of a future society where human life is disposable and can be manipulated, abused, and even destroyed for what is perceived as the greater societal good. The Pandora's box opened by *Roe* v. *Wade* now gives us the medical procedure of implantation of tissue from aborted babies for the treatment of certain diseases. Is Huxley's Brave New World upon us?

Recent medical advances mean that the unborn child is a prime source of fresh, living cells to treat certain diseases such as diabetes, Parkinson's disease, Alzheimer's disease, nerve degeneration, bone marrow diseases, and even some skin disorders. The potential demand for fetal tissues and organs is sizable. The use of tissue from aborted children is intriguing to medical researchers because these cells are soft and pliable and easy to use in transplants. Fetal tissues also have strong regenerative abilities and develop rapidly in a recipient's body.

Medical research using the fetal tissue of animals for transplants into adult animals has been conducted since the 1800s. However, in 1985 two Denver researchers, Everett Spees and Kevin Lafferty, used pancreatic tissue from aborted human babies and transplanted them into an adult diabetic. By the end of 1987, fifteen other diabetics had received similar transplants. Others have reportedly received fetal liver cells as a treatment for a blood disorder.[39]

In September 1987, doctors in Mexico reported a successful treatment for Parkinson's disease by transplanting tissue from the brain and adrenal gland of a thirteen-week-old aborted baby into the brains of two patients.[40] The report set off a wave of controversy regarding the ethics of the research and the implications it holds for the future. The prospects for this technology make it apparent that marketing in fetal tissue and organs may become a lucrative business. It has also led to some bizarre incidents.

In 1987 a Minnesota woman with diabetes said that she wanted to get pregnant, have an abortion, and then transplant insulin-producing islet cells from her baby into her own body in hopes of curing her disease. A California woman wanted to become pregnant by her father through artificial insemination, abort the baby, and transplant its brain cells into her father who is suffering from Alzheimer's disease. In still another reported case from Rochester, New York, a woman searched among participants at an international conference on brain implants for a surgeon who would use fetal cells to treat her husband's severe Parkinson's disease. Since the woman was too old to conceive, her daughters were willing to produce a fetus to help.[41]

For fetal tissue to be most useful, the cells must be sufficiently mature, at least sixteen to twenty-four weeks into the pregnancy. Since the vast majority of miscarriages occur within the first eight weeks of pregnancy, the pool of available fetal tissue must come from babies slated for late-term abortions.

If fetal tissue transplants become routinely accepted, then one can easily envision a black market for the tissue of aborted babies and the exploitation of women as fetal organ farms. Financial encouragement for women to abort late in their pregnancies or to become pregnant for the purpose of aborting will become commonplace under this new field of medicine. Former abortionist Dr. Bernard Nathanson, now a pro-life activist, says:

> And where would it end? Now it is proposed these organs be used for treatment of disease, but tomorrow these abhorrent practices will certainly be proposed for failing sexual function (transplantation of fetal testicular tissues, probably costing $10,000 or so) and the day after tomorrow for cosmetic purposes (fetal skin probably $20,000 an ounce).[42]

Because of the controversy, in 1988 researchers at the National Institutes of Health (NIH) were refused permission to treat patients with implants of fetal tissue until the legal and ethical issues could be studied by an expert committee. Later in the year that committee recommended that the research be allowed to proceed with federal grants. However, the temporary ban on these federally funded projects was continued in November 1989 by Secretary of Health and Human Services Louis W. Sullivan who stated: "After carefully reviewing all of the materials, I am persuaded that one must accept the likelihood that permitting the human fetal research at issue will increase the incidence of abortion across the country."[43]

Whether federal funds will eventually be used in fetal research remains to be seen, but the acceptance of this practice by the medical community and the public has staggering implications. It is a terrible irony that we can destroy unborn children on the pretense that they are not human, but then extract their brains, bone marrow, and other organs for research and transplants because they are so very human.

In *Roe* v. *Wade* the Supreme Court said no one knows when human life begins and only "meaningful life" can be protected under the law. The advent of transplants using fetal tissue exposes this nonsense from the Court. If the use of the tissues of unborn babies to treat disease becomes acceptable, then we are acknowledging that these little ones are human, that they are living and have value. However, if the only value we place on the unborn is in their utility as spare parts for other humans, then we have indeed become an exploitative society that abuses its most vulnerable and helpless members, the unborn.

2. *"Selective reduction" of multiple fetuses*

The demolition of the wall of protection has led to another bizarre practice in the medical profession. Women who are unwillingly pregnant with more than one baby can now "reduce" their pregnancy by aborting some of the unborn children while allowing the rest to proceed to birth. This practice is described by an Orwellian euphemism— "selective reduction."

The practice is made possible by ultrasound techniques developed in the last few years that allow a doctor to guide a needle into the chest cavity of an unborn child. Injected into the child's heart is a potassium chloride solution, and the fetal heart is then monitored. If heart activity continues, a sterile saline solution is injected next to the heart to destroy it by extrinsic pressure.

After the child's cardiac functions cease, the procedure is then repeated in one or more additional fetuses. Before being discharged from the hospital the mother undergoes a second ultrasound scanning. If cardiac activity is observed in a child that was to be killed, the mother is scheduled to undergo the procedure again.[44]

The practice is generally performed on women who have become pregnant with multiple fetuses through the use of fertility drugs. In some cases the practice is used in a multiple pregnancy to abort a fetus with a genetic handicap. In one case a test revealed that a woman would give birth to twin boys—one normal and one afflicted with Down's syndrome. The woman said she would abort both of the children rather than rear a retarded child. But Drs. Thomas D. Kerenyi and Usha Chitkara at Mt. Sinai School of Medicine in New York successfully killed the handicapped child and later reported: "It was a very gratifying experience in such an endangered pregnancy to follow the normal fetus to full term and through vaginal delivery."[45]

Proponents of "selective reduction" defend the practice by arguing that it increases the chances of survival for the children that are left in the womb. Dr. Joseph Schulman, director of the Genetics and IVF Institute in Fairfax, Virginia, once observed another doctor reduce quadruplets to twins. "It was not a pleasant sight," he said. "No one's proud of doing it, but doctors see it as a medical necessity."[46]

Regardless, this practice should be uniformly condemned since it kills an innocent child to improve the chances of another child surviving. Such *selective execution* (as it should properly be called) allows a doctor to play God and determine who can and cannot be born.

3. Sex selection abortions

Modern technology now has provided us with tests that will indicate the gender of a child prior to birth. Through amniocentesis and a more recent test called chorionic villi sampling (CVS), a determination of the gender of the unborn child may be made in utero. Amniocentesis is performed when the pregnancy is at least sixteen weeks along, while CVS can determine the sex of a child in the first seven to nine weeks.

Some women from ethnic groups that value males above females may want to abort a female baby to try again for a male, and there are doctors willing to perform the test to enable such sex selection abortions to occur. In a recent survey of 295 geneticists in the U.S., nearly two-thirds said they would perform prenatal diagnosis for the sole purpose of determining the sex of the child so the parents could choose to abort if the child is the undesired gender.[47] In 1973, the year of *Roe* v. *Wade*, only 1 percent of the medical geneticists surveyed approved of prenatal diagnosis for sex selection. In a similar survey conducted sixteen years later, nearly 20 percent approved of the practice.[48]

There is growing evidence that this is exactly what some parents are opting for. Dr. Laird Jackson, director of the medical genetics division at Thomas Jefferson University in Philadelphia, stated in 1987 that about 10 of the 2,500 pregnant women tested there have opted for an abortion solely because the baby was the undesired sex.[49] Officials of the Baylor University medical school in Houston have said that 4 of the 320 women who have undergone CVS procedures have had abortions for sex selection purposes, and officials at Michael Reese Medical Center in Chicago and the University of California at San Francisco each state that about 1 out of 1,000 women in the testing programs abort for gender selection.[50]

Internationally, the idea of aborting for gender selection is not new. In India, some women undergo the test for the sole purpose of discovering whether the child is a girl.[51] If it is, the child is promptly aborted. The reasons given are painfully familiar—the expense of marrying a daughter off, the need for sons to help in the family business and to carry on the family name. In short, the age-old preference of boys over girls.

Following reports of sex selection abortions in Britain, some laboratories that test for fetal abnormalities are withholding information about the sex of the unborn child from the parents. Michael Ridler, of the Kennedy Galton Center, says: "I and my staff do not want to contribute to the killing of normal babies, so we have stopped routinely reporting sex and have reverted strictly to our contract, which is to screen for abnormalities."[52]

In response to this growing practice, Senator Gordon Humphrey (R-NH) has introduced in the United States Senate a bill appropriately called the "Civil Rights of Infants Act." The bill, which has not been passed by the Congress, would amend Title 42 of the U.S. Code which contains most of the civil rights statutes. In the legislation, the right not to be aborted on the basis of sex would be a civil right, thus invoking a series of remedies for civil rights violations. The scope of the civil remedies would be as broad or narrow as the remedies for other civil rights violations.

This noble effort from Senator Humphrey is not only a correct legislative response to the issue, but it points out the moral bankruptcy in the law as long as *Roe* v. *Wade* is the law of the land. Only *persons* have civil rights to be protected, and under *Roe* the unborn are not persons. Thus, the use of the civil rights statutes of the United States probably would not be enforced as long as the unborn are considered nonpersons. Senator Humphrey's legislation, if passed, will likely be rendered unconstitutional by some federal judge unless *Roe* is reversed.

The growing practice of sex selection abortions is another indication of the collapse of the wall of protection. To their credit even some feminists oppose this practice, correctly calling it an atrocity and "feticide."[53] However, such pious denunciations ring a bit hollow since these same feminists assert that abortion must be safeguarded so that women can control their own lives.

Without denying in any sense the depravity of killing unborn baby girls, I submit that the feminist position is morally bankrupt. They cannot have it both ways. Once the abortion of any child for any reason is permitted, the abortion of all children becomes permissible. Once the wall of protection is demolished, as it is in modern-day America, then all unborn children are subject to abortion for any reason—including gender selection. If society and feminists believe it is acceptable to kill a child because the child is handicapped or because the mother is unmarried or because it is a third child in a family that only wanted two, then that same faulty logic allows the killing of a child because she is a girl.

While the process of aborting little girls when little boys are wanted is termed "selective abortion," every abortion is a selective one and must be opposed with every ounce of energy we have. Only the values of the parents make one abortion different from another. Parents who value only physically and mentally normal children might reject a child who is retarded. Parents who value education and want to provide their children with it might reject a third child if their resources can only educate two. Parents who value their time and freedom might reject any children they produce, and parents who value boys might well reject a girl.

4. The abortion pill—RU486

The emergence of the abortion pill RU486 is a further example of the destruction of the wall of protection for the unborn and raises new questions in the abortion debate. Dr. Etienne Beaulieu, a researcher for Roussel-Uclaf laboratories in France, discovered the drug in 1982. The drug company has agreed with the World Health Organization to provide the abortion pill at low cost to developing nations. The U.S. Food and Drug Administration (FDA) has not yet given its approval for the drug to be marketed in the United States. However, proabortion advocates are applying intense pressure upon government officials to allow the drug to come into this country.

The drug is taken orally and works on the lining of the uterus to prevent implantation of the human embryo.

The maintenance of this lining is essential to human reproduction. Progesterone, a hormone produced by the ovaries, prepares the uterus for the implantation of the fertilized egg. RU486 interacts with progesterone receptors in the woman to block the effects of the progesterone. The resulting chemistry makes the womb hostile to the implanted embryo and induces abortion.[54] A U.S. team of medical researchers report that RU486 induces abortion in nine out of ten women who are less than seven weeks pregnant.[55] Dr. Beaulieu suggests that a complementary dosage of prostaglandin given early after the dose of RU486 could push the effectiveness rate to 95 percent.[56]

Dr. David Elia, a Paris gynecologist, has organized clinical tests of RU486 and claims that its use has significant advantages over surgical abortions. States Elia: "We imagine there will be less infection, less injuries for the uterus and the cervix." Another advantage, according to Elia, is that "a lot of women prefer the methodology because they don't want the physician to touch their bodies. A lot of women prefer to do it like a natural spontaneous abortion, or miscarriage, and they don't want to have anesthesia and to be hospitalized or in a private clinic. It seems to them it's less offensive to their bodies."[57]

Elia's patients understand that using RU486 is an abortion procedure; avoiding a surgical abortion does not cover over this reality. "To my patients it felt the same in their minds and in their hearts. This is always an abortion. They don't experience it like some natural bleedings. When they want this compound, it is not because they want to hide from the abortion, but because they prefer the method. They experience it like an abortion. There is no ambiguity on that point."[58]

A pregnant woman wanting to use RU486 must obtain the drug early in her pregnancy, since after the first few weeks she produces too much of her own progesterone for it to be neutralized by the drug. Two days after taking the pill the woman may receive a dosage of prostaglandin, either in the form of a vaginal suppository or injection. Within three hours abdominal cramps begin and she may be given a painkiller. In the next one to three days, the unborn child will be expelled. Another visit to the clinic is required to verify that the abortion has been successful. If it has not been, then the woman has a choice of other abortion methods.[59]

RU486 is now being trumpeted as an alternative to surgical abortion. A 1986 article appearing in the *New England Journal of Medicine*, coauthored by Dr. Beaulieu, states: "RU486 offers a reasonable alternative to surgical abortion, which carries the risks of anesthesia, surgical complications, infertility, and psychological sequelae."[60] In response, Dr. Joseph R. Stanton, a prominent Boston physician, states:

> For 14 years, the American populace has been told that "surgical" abortion is a medical procedure, safe, easy, without significant complications. How often have we not heard preached from impeccable medical auspices that abortion is safer than having a baby? Those who have raised caution or caveat have been imperiously swept aside by the purveyors of abortion as the safe new freedom. One wonders as Homer nods, did the editorial board of the *New England Journal of Medicine* perhaps give the game away when it printed on its pristine paper that surgical abortion has "complications," "infertility," and "psychological" sequelae? [61]

The new development of RU486 is a step towards a longtime goal of the abortion industry—to reduce abortion to a private act, a pill taken at home. Pro-abortionists argue that since American society accepts contraception, there should be no significant moral problems in accepting abortifacients and early induced abortions through RU486. They argue further that until the human embryo "looks like a human," its evident biological humanity is not of moral significance. Hence, abortion advocates are arguing strenuously that abortion in the early stages of pregnancy should be a free fire zone, and the abortion pill will be a tool to accomplish this.

CONCLUSION

The emergence of RU486 is just another indication that the wall of protection and respect for the sanctity of human life has been demolished. If abortion, the deliberate killing of an unborn child, can be reduced to a private act at home through the taking of a pill, then our efforts to rebuild the wall must go beyond a mere change in the law. We must reach the very hearts and minds of the American people to be successful. To accomplish this we must pursue a biblical model for rebuilding the wall that will not only bring about a change in the law but will also convict of sin and bring revival throughout the land.

As I have shown in this chapter, the historical wall of protection for the unborn and respect for the sanctity of human life was demolished in 1973 by the Supreme Court. Without the wall of protection, bizarre bioethical issues such as fetal experimentation and selective reduction have raised their ugly heads. Without the wall of protection, abortion-on-demand has become an accepted part of American life.

We are living in the midst of the ruin and rubble of our own decadence and selfishness. The effort to successfully rebuild the demolished wall compels us to look to the Word of God for answers, for only through a divinely inspired plan will this wall be restored. We find just such a plan in the life and story of a great man of God—Nehemiah.

Notes

1. U.S. Department of Health and Human Services, Center for Disease Control, Abortion Surveillance Report, May 1983.

2. Ibid.

3. Harold O. J. Brown, "What the Supreme Court Didn't Know: Ancient and Early Christian Views On Abortion," in *The Human Life Review* 2 (Spring 1975):6.

4. Ibid.

5. Ibid., 7.

6. Ibid., 7-8; Eugene Quay, "Justifiable Abortion—Medical and Legal Foundations," *Georgetown Law Review* 49 (1961):395, 420.

7. Quay, "Justifiable Abortion," 402-3.

8. Ibid., 403-5.

9. George Buhler in *Sacred Books of the East,* ed. F. Max Muller (Oxford: Clarendon Press, 1879-1910), 42:165.

10. Ibid.

11. John Connery, *Abortion: The Development of the Roman Catholic Perspective* (Chicago: Loyola University Press, 1977), 14.

12. The scriptural passage states: "If men who are fighting hit a pregnant woman and she gives birth prematurely but there is no serious injury, the offender must be fined whatever the woman's husband demands and the court allows. But if there is serious injury, you are to take life for life, eye for eye, tooth for tooth, hand for hand, foot for foot, burn for burn, wound for wound, bruise for bruise."

This passage has been used by some to suggest that the unborn child has less value than a born person. However, a clear understanding of this passage leads one to a contrary conclusion.

The Thirty-eighth General Assembly of the Orthodox Presbyterian Church issued its "Report of the Committee to Study the Matter of Abortion" on 24-29 May 1971. The report states in part:

> This passage clearly deals with a case of accidental killing. If even such accidental killing of an unborn child is punished by a fine, we must surely assume

that the intentional killing of an unborn child is at least as serious as (in all probability more serious than) the offense in view in verse 22. How can we then defend the intentional destruction of the unborn on the basis of a passage which condemns even its accidental destruction? . . . We conclude, therefore, that Exodus 21:22-25 does not suggest that the unborn child is anything less than a human person from the point of conception. Any attempt to make the passage teach such a thesis results in insuperable difficulties of exegesis, logic and application. Since this is the only passage alleged to provide proof of such a thesis, we conclude that there is no Scriptural basis for such arguments and that unless better arguments are forthcoming we cannot regard Scripture as even remotely suggesting such a view.

13. Hippocrates, *Works* (London: Loeb Classical Library, 1923-27), 1:291-92.

14. Edward Coke, *Third Institute* 50 (1644); and William Blackstone, *Commentaries on the Laws of England* (Birmingham, Ala.: The Legal Classics Library, 1983), 4:119.

15. Blackstone, *Commentaries on the Laws of England*, 1:125

16. Ibid.

17. Stephen M. Krason, *Abortion, Politics, Morality and the Constitution* (Washington, D.C.: University Press of America, 1984), 149.

18. For a listing of these states see note 1 to the dissenting opinion of Justice William Rehnquist in Appendix A, *Roe* v. *Wade*.

19. Transactions of the American Medical Association (1859), 12:75

20. Horatio R. Storer and Franklin F. Heard, *Criminal Abortion: Its Nature, Its Evidence and Its Law* (Boston: Little, Brown and Co., 1868), 28-29.

21. *World Medical Association Bulletin* 1 (April 1949):22.

22. *World Medical Association Bulletin* 2 (January 1950):6-34.

23. Bernard Nathanson, *Aborting America* (Garden City, N.Y.:

Doubleday, 1979), 30. It is my intent only to give a brief synopsis and not a detailed historical account of the movement to legalize abortion in America. However, for further reading about the history of the pro-abortion movement, I recommend Dr. Nathanson's book, which is an excellent account of this time period and the forces behind the movement for liberalization of abortion laws in America.

24. Krason, *Abortion and the Constitution*, 20.

25. *New York Times*, 19 November 1965, 15.

26. Krason, *Abortion and the Constitution*, 20.

27. Ibid., 24-27.

28. Ibid., 24.

29. *New York Times*, 13 February 1965, 20; and *New York Times*, 8 December 1965, 46.

30. *New York Times*, 31 March 1966, 13.

31. *Modern Medicine* 9 (April 1967):12-13.

32. *Roe* v. *Wade*, 153.

33. Ibid., 164.

34. Ibid.

35. Ibid., 164-65.

36. *Doe* v. *Bolton*, 192.

37. John Ely, "The Wages of Crying Wolf: A Comment on *Roe* v. *Wade*," *Yale Law Journal* 82 (1973):920, 921 n19.

38. *Roe*, 163.

39. David Andrusko, "Harvesting the Living" in *A Passion for Justice* (Washington, D.C.: National Right to Life Committee, 1988), 87-88.

40. Ibid., 88.

41. Larry Thompson, "Fetal Tissue: Should Fetal Tissue from Abortions Be Available for Treatment of Patients with a Range of Diseases?", *Washington Post Health Magazine*, 26 January 1988, 11.

42. Bernard Nathanson, "Obscene Harvest: Selling Fetal Body Parts for Profit," *Liberty Report*, January 1988.

43. *Washington Post*, 31 November 1989.

44. Richard L. Berkowitz et al., "Selective Reduction of Multifetal Pregnancies in the First Trimester," *The New England Journal of Medicine* 318 (April 1988):1043-47.

45. *Houston Chronicle*, 18 June 1981, 12.

46. Gina Kolata, "Multiple Fetuses Raise New Issues Tied to Abortion," *New York Times*, 25 January 1988, A1.

47. Dorothy C. Wertz and John C. Fletcher, "Fatal Knowledge? Prenatal Diagnosis and Sex Selection," *The Hastings Report*, May-June 1989, 21-27.

48. John Leo, "Baby Boys to Order," *U.S. News and World Report*, 9 January 1989, 59.

49. Joyce Price, "Prenatal Test of Sex Sometimes Triggers Abortion Decisions," *Washington Times*, 13 February 1987.

50. Ibid.

51. Jo McGowan, "In India, They Abort Females," *Newsweek*, 30 January 1989, 12.

52. Judith Perea, "Sex Seals the Fate of Fetuses in Britain," *New Scientist*, 22 January 1987.

53. McGowan, "They Abort Females," 12.

54. Joseph Stanton, "Mifepristone RU 486: The Latest Chapter of Chemical Warfare on the Human Unborn" (unpublished article).

55. "French Abortion Pill 90% Effective," *Medical World News*, 12 October 1987, 82.

56. Stanton, "Mifepristone RU 486."

57. Robin Herman, "In France, A New Method of Abortion," *Washington Post Health*, 27 September 1988.

58. Ibid.

59. Ibid.

60. B. Couzinet et al., "Termination of Early Pregnancy by the Progesterone Antagonist RU486 (Mifepristone)," *The New England Journal of Medicine* (1986):1569.

61. Stanton, "Mifepristone RU 486," 2.

CHAPTER TWO

Rebuilding the Wall

Since 1973 the wall of protection for the unborn has been demolished. The destruction of this wall has left other members of the human family, such as the handicapped and the elderly, vulnerable to assault. In order to reconstruct the wall and guarantee protection for innocent human life, we need to establish a biblical model for our rebuilding efforts. Such a model can be found in the book of Nehemiah, which gives a divine blueprint for action to restore the moral foundation of our nation.

THE NEHEMIAH PRINCIPLES

In this book we are told how Nehemiah rebuilt the walls of the city of Jerusalem after the exile of the children of Israel and the subsequent destruction of the city. The efforts of this great man of God give clear insight into a divinely inspired plan for the rebuilding of a city which, due to the apostasy of the children of Israel, had been destroyed as an act of divine judgment. This great book of the Bible sets forth what I call the *Nehemiah Principles* which, if understood and followed, will guide us in restoring the sanctity of human life in America.

Principle one: The rebuilding of the wall will not be successful unless it is preceded by repentance, prayer, and fasting by God's people.

At the beginning of this book, Nehemiah receives a disturbing report about the condition of the Jewish remnant that survived the exile, and especially about the condition of Jerusalem, whose walls have been broken down and its gates burned. Nehemiah is heartbroken over the plight of his beloved city: "When I heard these things, I sat down and wept. For some days I mourned and fasted and prayed before the God of heaven" (Nehemiah 1:4). In his moving prayer of intercession for his nation, Nehemiah confesses Israel's sins and asks God's favor upon him as he seeks to go about the task of rebuilding the wall.

Nehemiah's attitude is instructive for us today. How many times have the people of God been so moved by the condition of our country resulting from the abortion holocaust that we have wept, fasted, and prayed? Have we become so secure and comfortable that the condition of the wall is of no concern to us? God did not allow Nehemiah to rebuild the wall of Jerusalem until he exhibited a contrite spirit and sought the Lord's favor with all his heart.

God's people should be grieved over the bloodshed in our land. We must spend time in fasting and prayer for an end to abortion. Like Nehemiah, we need to seek the Lord's favor with all our hearts and then commence the awesome task of rebuilding the wall of respect for the sanctity of innocent human life.

Principle two: The rebuilding of the wall is the responsibility of God's people. We cannot expect others to accomplish what we have been called to do.

In chapter 2, Nehemiah tells how he asked King Artaxerxes for permission to travel to Jerusalem for the specific purpose of rebuilding her walls. Nehemiah did not ask for a regiment of the king's army to accompany him to provide labor for his task. He did not seek to compel others to do the job that belonged to God's people. Rather, he merely asked for the opportunity to rebuild the wall, and then he sought help from the children of Israel.

The *Webster* decision has given the people of God in America the opportunity to rebuild the wall of protection for innocent human life. However, as in Nehemiah's day, the wall will not be rebuilt until God's people commit themselves to its reconstruction; it is our responsibility. Nonbelievers may help in the process and may even play roles of significance in this battle, but the responsibility to be "salt" and "light" belongs to the church. We are the ones commanded to "speak up for those who cannot speak for themselves" and to "defend the fatherless." To ignore these commands of Scripture is to seriously shirk our responsibilities as followers of the Lord of life. As in Nehemiah's day, the people of God must take the primary role in rebuilding the wall or its reconstruction will not be accomplished.

Principle three: The rebuilding of the wall will not be successful unless Christians in every locality build the section of the wall in their communities.

When Nehemiah began to oversee the wall's reconstruction, he directed Jerusalem's families to rebuild the section of the wall closest to their own homes. In chapter 3 we are told how the builders of the wall each worked on their assigned section in their own communities. Inspired by the wisdom of God, Nehemiah realized that people care most about that which affects them directly.

According to Nehemiah's plan, each family would have a personal stake in seeing that its assigned duty was not only completed but done well. Nehemiah knew that the rebuilding project would not be accomplished in a day. Yet, through the diligence and commitment of God's people, the wall of Jerusalem was rebuilt.

In the same way that Nehemiah directed the citizens of Jerusalem, the Lord's people should now begin to rebuild the wall of protection for innocent human life within their own communities. As the *Webster* decision has shown, the solution to the abortion problem will not come from Washington D.C., as many have believed in recent years. Rather, abortion will end in America when Christians in every community rise up and say abortion will not be tolerated in our cities and towns. When abortion is made a scandal in every community of the nation, it will cease. Only then will politicians respond to the will of the vast majority of Americans who believe that abortion-on-demand is not a good to be promoted.

Through local pro-life activism, preceded by a contrite spirit and prayer and fasting, abortion in America will be ended.

Principle four: The rebuilding of the wall will be met by fierce opposition which will only be defeated through intense spiritual warfare.

Nehemiah met with fierce opposition to his rebuilding project, beginning with ridicule and contempt (Nehemiah 4). It escalated to slander (Nehemiah 6) and ended with attempts at intimidation by threats to Nehemiah's life. Yet each attempt to stop the reconstruction was met by Nehemiah with intense prayer for strength.

Nehemiah understood that his enemies did not merely oppose the rebuilding of a city but opposed the very God of the universe, and he prays accordingly: "Hear us, O our God, for we are despised. Turn their insults back on their own heads. Give them over as plunder in a land of captivity. Do not cover up their guilt or blot out their sins from your sight, for they have thrown insults in the face of the builders" (4:4-5).

Nehemiah met every attack with fervent prayer, calling out to God for deliverance and protection from the enemies who opposed the rebuilding of the wall. Those enemies understood that the rebuilding of the sacred city of the Israelites would unify God's people and bring him glory. This was the last thing the enemies of Israel wanted.

Likewise today, the last thing the enemies of the faith want is a united body of Christ. Efforts are continually being made to divide believers and render the gospel ineffective. The battle over the sanctity of human life is no different. Abortion breaks the heart of God. Psalm 139 tells us of a God who is actively involved in the procreative process. The destruction of these little ones through abortion not only grieves our heavenly Father but is a direct assault on his sovereignty as the Creator of life. Those who oppose the building of the wall of protection are opposing the very God of creation. Hence, as in Nehemiah's day, we too can expect fierce opposition to our building efforts.

Many in the pro-life movement are under direct assault from pro-abortion adversaries. Crisis pregnancy centers have been maligned in the media through concerted efforts to discredit them in the eyes of the public. Lawsuits have been filed around the nation against pro-life activists for their courageous opposition to the killing centers in their communities. Some courts have even rendered monetary judgments against activists for disrupting the "business" of the abortion clinics.

The media has also joined in the assault on the integrity of pro-life activists. During the summer of 1989, immediately after the *Webster* decision, the public was deluged with pro-abortion propaganda on television. Two made-for-television movies—*Roe* v. *Wade* on NBC and *Choices* on

ABC—promoted the virtues of "choice" and the necessity of keeping abortion-on-demand legal. On Ted Turner's WTBS cable channel, a "documentary" produced by the pro-abortion advocacy organization Fund for a Feminist Majority was shown with a panel discussion following. The two movies were emotional and sentimental pleas for legalized abortion-on-demand. The viewing audience was manipulated into believing that the option of abortion must remain available to women with crisis pregnancies. The Ted Turner program was an out-and-out attack, complete with name calling from Mr. Turner, who called people who hold the pro-life position "bozos" and "idiots."

As the abortion issue heats up in our communities we must expect these attacks to intensify. However, like Nehemiah, we must understand the nature of these attacks and respond appropriately. Ephesians 6:12 reminds us that "our struggle is not against flesh and blood, but against the rulers, against the authorities, against the powers of this dark world and against the spiritual forces of evil in the heavenly realms." Our battle is primarily a spiritual one. Our enemies are not the people who oppose us politically and philosophically. Such people need to be freed from their spiritual blindness and bondage. They should be seen as potential allies to be won over. Rather, the real enemy is Satan and the forces of his kingdom.

To successfully rebuild the wall in America today, the people of God must be prepared to enter into intense spiritual warfare against the principalities and powers that oppose us. As with Nehemiah, we must meet our opposition with fervent prayer to our heavenly Father who alone can provide us with the cover and the strength necessary to be victorious. And we must thoroughly comprehend the necessity every day to "put on the full armor of God" that we may be able to withstand the attacks of the devil.

Yes, fierce opposition will come, but let us take this occasion and seize the opportunity before us. Through prayer, fasting, and local involvement, the church can make a difference in the final outcome of this intense struggle for the lives of God's little ones who reside in the womb.

Principle five: The successful reconstruction of the wall will lead to the restoration and healing of our nation.

It took fifty-two days to rebuild the wall of Jerusalem. The completion of this project brought glory to God and placed fear into the hearts of Nehemiah's enemies. Nehemiah reports: "When all our enemies heard about this, all the surrounding nations were afraid and lost their self-confidence, because they realized that this work had been done with the help of our God" (Nehemiah 6:16).

The rebuilding of the wall accomplished much more than just the physical reconstruction of the city of Jerusalem. While the city had indeed been restored, the people of Israel also returned to the God of Jacob confessing their sins. The rebuilding of the wall led to national repentance and restoration. The Book of the Law was read and the hearts of the people returned to the Lord Jehovah (Nehemiah 9:1-3).

In our day there is a great need for the hearts of the people of God to return to their first love—the Lord Jesus Christ. I believe that rebuilding the wall of protection for innocent human life made in the image of God will result in revival across the land and the restoration and healing of our nation.

As in Nehemiah's day, the complete restoration of the wall will, I believe, convict God's people of sin and lead to national repentance. As the Holy Spirit convicts and the rebuilding is accomplished, respect for life under the law will be restored. This will lead to an acknowledgment of the Creator of life as the source of all provisions and will pave the way for a spiritual revival in the 1990s that will heal our land.

CONCLUSION

The five Nehemiah Principles set forth in this chapter give a divine blueprint for the restoration of the wall of protection for the unborn and for a return to the sanctity of human life ethic that has been obliterated in American society. The present decade is a crucial time in the life of our nation in determining the outcome of this battle for human life.

As the Lord's vessels, we can accomplish much, but ultimate victory in this cause will come only when revival occurs in our own lives and throughout the church in America. When revival comes, God will use us as special instruments to protect his little ones. As in Nehemiah's day, the reconstruction of the wall will take time, but through the grace of God and the commitment of his people, the wall shall be rebuilt!

CHAPTER THREE

The Foundation for the Wall

The foundation for the wall of protection will be established when our legal system acknowledges that the unborn child is a person under the Constitution and deserves legal protection. Under the precedent of *Roe* v. *Wade* the legal classification of *person* is not synonymous with *human being*. The Fourteenth Amendment grants protection only to a legally recognized person. Under the Constitution, as interpreted by the Supreme Court, only persons have value. The failure of the Court to acknowledge the personhood of the unborn means that these human beings have no value under the law and cannot be protected.

With this ruling, the Court destroyed the very foundation upon which respect for life has traditionally been based. The Judeo-Christian ethic, which respects the sanctity of human life regardless of stage of development or condition of dependency, rests upon the recognition that all human life is made in the image of God and is therefore valuable. Under this biblical view, a human being is to be protected under the law, irrespective of whether that life is devalued in the eyes of others. This foundation of personhood, upon which all other legal rights and privileges are derived, must be rebuilt in America.

A reversal of *Roe* v. *Wade* by the Court without an acknowledgment of the personhood of the unborn child will create an intolerable social climate. The mere reversal of *Roe* only returns the abortion issue to the individual states for further deliberation. In such an event, some states will undoubtedly prohibit abortion while others will allow it. The same state legislature which, like Missouri, declares that human life begins at conception may, with a change in the composition of its legislators, declare that life begins at birth. The lives of the unborn will be held hostage to the changing political climates in each state. We will avoid this scenario only through the recognition of the constitutional personhood of the unborn.

At the height of the Civil War, President Abraham Lincoln said this nation could not continue to exist half slave and half free. To allow a social and political climate to persist where abortion is legal in some states and illegal in others means that we are half slave and half free. The importance of this point was not lost on former President Ronald Reagan: "Abraham Lincoln recognized that we could not survive as a free land when some men could decide that others were not fit to be free and should therefore be slaves. Likewise, we cannot survive as a free nation when some men decide that others are not fit to live and should be abandoned to abortion or infanticide."[1]

As an inalienable right, life is a gift coming solely from God. It is not a right to be awarded or taken away by a vote of elected officials. The great words from the Declaration of Independence that "all men are created equal, that they are endowed by their Creator with certain unalienable rights, that among these are life, liberty and the pursuit of happiness," still hold true today. The right to life is an inalienable right, derived from the Creator, which every human being enjoys. This right, given to us by God, may not be denied to some by the political process.

Natural Law, Personhood, and the Right to Life

The right to life and the personhood of the unborn are absolute principles derived from God, the source of all law. In the early part of American history, our legal system acknowledged that rights are valid only to the extent that they originate from the "natural law." The natural law is that system of rules and legal principles which are of divine origin and are discovered by the rational intelligence of man. The precepts of the natural law are derived from God, and if any man-made laws are contrary they are not legitimate.

Twentieth-century writer and Christian philosopher C.S. Lewis wrote of the natural law, which he called the "Tao":

> It is the sole source of all value judgments. If it is rejected, all value is rejected. If any value is retained, it is retained. The effort to refute it and raise a new system of value in its place is self-contradictory. There never has been, and never will be, a radically new judgement of value in the history of the world. What purport to be new systems or (as they now call them) 'ideologies,' all consist of fragments from the Tao itself, arbitrarily wrenched from their context in the whole and then swollen to madness in their isolation, yet still owing to the Tao and to it alone such validity as they possess.[2]

The natural law, according to Lewis, is:

> the reality beyond all predicates. . . . It is Nature,

it is the Way, the Road. It is the Way in which the universe goes on, the Way in which things ever-lastingly emerge, stilly and tranquilly, into space and time. . . . It is the doctrine of objective value, the belief that certain attitudes are really true, and others really false, to the kind of thing the universe is and the kind of things we are. Those who know the Tao can hold that to call children delightful or old men venerable is not simply to record a psychological fact about our own parental or filial emotions at the moment, but to recognize a quality which demands a certain response from us whether we make it or not.[3]

Perhaps the best legal perspective of the natural law comes from Sir William Blackstone, the great eighteenth-century English jurist and commentator on the common law. Blackstone wrote extensively about the natural law in volume one of his *Commentaries on the Laws of England*. He says that mankind, created in the image of God, is subject to the laws of the universe set up by the Creator. These laws are both physical and moral. The moral laws, to which all civilizations are subject, are derived from God and are just in the same manner that God is just. These moral principles are discoverable by reason and through the holy Scriptures which Blackstone calls the "revealed law" of God. All man-made law derives its legitimacy from the natural law.[4]

In short, natural law is that body of objective truth, ordained by God from the foundation of the world, to which all of creation is subjected. If governments ignore the natural law and pass man-made laws to the contrary, those laws are invalid and not binding. Governments may compel compliance with those laws through the use of brute power, but since they are outside the natural law they are illegitimate and without moral foundation.

Blackstone states that among the absolute rights stemming from the natural law is the right to life which originates inside the mother's womb.[5] This right to life, cannot be destroyed merely upon the discretion of another and "whenever the constitution of a state vests in any man, or body of men, a power of destroying at pleasure, without the direction of laws, the lives or members of the subject, such constitution is in the highest degree tyrannical."[6]

The legal personhood of an infant in utero was unquestioned by Blackstone. In addition to the right to life, the unborn infant enjoys other rights as well, such as inheritance rights. In short, the unborn child, according to Blackstone, enjoys the basic legal rights which are enjoyed by those born.[7]

Another voice who spoke eloquently of the natural law and the right to life was seventeenth-century political philosopher John Locke. The influence of Locke was significant in shaping the viewpoints of the founding fathers of the American Republic toward the nature of law and government.[8] In his essay, "Of Civil-Government," Locke spoke eloquently of the natural law, its divinely ordained premises, and the right to life.[9]

The writings of both Locke and Blackstone supply persuasive evidence that the right to life, which commences in the womb, is a necessary maxim of the natural law. Accordingly, any government that denies this absolute right is, as Blackstone puts it, "tyrannical." Certainly the decision of *Roe* v. *Wade*, which allows the destruction of unborn human life for any reason whatsoever, must come under such a judgment. Indeed, the right to life given by God, and absolute under the natural law (from which all legitimate laws are derived), cannot be extinguished by a decision from nine mortal and fallible human beings. That Supreme Court decision violates the natural law of God and is therefore illegitimate.

The Revealed Law and Personhood

Blackstone believed there could be no law without God, and that the role of a judge is not to make new law but to discover and implement those laws that already exist through the divine order. As a scientist probes the universe to discover and to proclaim its physical laws, likewise a judge's role is to scrutinize mankind and pronounce the natural laws of the universe which are ordained by God. A judge can no more invent a law governing robbery, murder, or adultery than can a scientist invent the law of gravity. These laws come from God and exist independently of man.

For a judge or legislator to be qualified to discover and then proclaim these laws of nature, he must have a philosophical and theological basis consistent with the fundamental premises of the natural law. A person of reprobate mind can no more understand the workings of the natural law than can one born blind comprehend the color green. For a judge to operate within this framework, he must be one who operates and makes decisions within the Judeo-Christian ethic. As C.S. Lewis put it, "Those who understand the spirit of the Tao and who have been led by that spirit can modify it in directions which that spirit itself demands. Only they can know what those directions are. The outsider knows nothing about the matter."[10]

To help the judge or legislator ascertain those natural laws that govern the conduct of mankind, he should look to the "revealed law" under which all human laws find legitimacy. This "revealed law" is, according to Blackstone, "to be found in the holy scriptures."[11] The revealed law is a part of the natural law and its moral precepts are of the same origin. However, it is superior to all other canons in the natural law. Nothing in the natural law is contrary to that found in the revealed law—the Word of God.[12]

Does Scripture, the revealed law, confer personhood on the unborn child and thus condemn abortion? Some abortion proponents argue that since abortion is not specifically mentioned in the Bible, Scripture is therefore neutral on the issue. Dr. Harold O. J. Brown, chairman of the Christian Action Council, responds as follows:

The Bible does not deal specifically with abortion. For that matter, it does not deal specifically with infanticide, the killing of babies. Nor does it talk about parricide, fratricide, uxoricide (killing of one's wife), nor genocide (the killing of a whole race). Examples of such crimes are mentioned, but not singled out for special treatment. In fact, the Bible does not even discuss suicide (self-killing). There are specific provisions against homicide—the deliberate taking of human life ("killing" or "slaying" is the usual expression). The Bible prohibits the taking of innocent human life. If the developing fetus is shown to be a human being, then we do not need a specific commandment against feticide (abortion) any more than we need something specific against uxoricide (wife-killing). The general commandment against killing covers both.[13]

The humanity of the unborn child is crucial to the ultimate determination of the abortion issue. If the unborn child is a human being, then the issue is resolved; a civilized society cannot tolerate the intentional killing of helpless innocent human beings. In *Roe* the Supreme Court stated that the humanity of the unborn child need not be resolved in order to determine the legality of abortion. Rather, the only relevant issue to the Court was whether such a child, irrespective of its humanity, is a "person" and thus has value under the Constitution.

However, such a distinction between humanity and personhood cannot be found in Scripture. While the Court stated that legal personhood and value belong only to those capable of "meaningful life outside the womb,"[14] Scripture does not place superior worth on postnatal life. Rather, every human being is valuable to God from the moment of conception. The revealed law of God is full of examples which show that the unborn child is precious in the sight of the Creator.

In Luke's Gospel, we are told a beautiful story about the pregnancies of Mary and her cousin, Elizabeth. Elizabeth was barren and well along in years, but God blessed her and her husband, Zechariah, with a child. This child was filled with the Holy Spirit while yet in his mother's womb, according to Luke 1:15. Likewise, the angel Gabriel told Mary that she too was to be the mother of a child—Jesus Christ the Lord.

After Mary was told that her cousin was pregnant, she made a trip to visit Elizabeth and an interesting event occurred:

> At that time Mary got ready and hurried to a town in the hill country of Judea, where she entered Zechariah's home and greeted Elizabeth. When Elizabeth heard Mary's greeting, the baby leaped in her womb, and Elizabeth was filled with the Holy Spirit. In a loud voice she exclaimed: "Blessed are you among women, and blessed is the child you will bear! But why am I so favored, that the mother of my Lord should come to me? As soon as the sound of your greeting reached my ears, the baby in my womb leaped for joy. Blessed is she who has believed that what the Lord has said to her will be accomplished!" (Luke 1:39-45)

Luke, the author of this Gospel, was a physician, and one of the more common physical conditions he would have treated was pregnancy and childbirth. Luke's description of John the Baptist jumping for joy in the womb is a medical observation of prenatal life, with which he was exceedingly familiar.

Today, medical science can actually give us an ultrasound picture of what John the Baptist's leap for joy must have looked like. The first ultrasound I saw was a four-minute videotape of a baby jumping inside his mother's womb. The child was bouncing up and down like a gymnast on a trampoline. I viewed a similar scene when my wife was expecting our first child. When our doctor focused the ultrasound equipment on our son, he exclaimed, "Look, he's dancing." My wife and I could clearly see our preborn child, Joshua, moving his legs and performing an impressive tap dance. (He's now six years old and hasn't slowed down yet!) It must have been something like this when John the Baptist jumped for joy in the presence of Jesus, who also was then an unborn child.

Luke, a man of science and medicine, also calls John the Baptist inside the womb a *baby.* The Greek word used is *brephos,* which can be translated unborn child, baby, or infant. This is the same word Luke uses in 2:12, when the angel says to the shepherds, "This will be a sign to you: You will find a baby [*brephos*] wrapped in cloths and lying in a manger." The good doctor employs the same word to describe John in the womb that he uses to describe the newborn Jesus. They are both babies.

Does an unborn child have value in the eyes of God? Does Scripture, the revealed law of God, grant personhood to the unborn? The answer is an impassioned *yes*! If not, why would God choose an unborn baby, John the Baptist, to be the first person to whom the presence of Jesus the Messiah was revealed?

When John the Baptist jumped for joy in utero, Elizabeth was six months pregnant. However, Scripture plainly shows that the unborn child has human value (and hence, personhood) from the earliest moments of pregnancy. Psalm 139:13-16 states:

> For you created my inmost being;
>   you knit me together in my mother's womb.
> I praise you because I am fearfully and
>   wonderfully made;
>   your works are wonderful,
>   I know that full well.

My frame was not hidden from you when I was
made in the secret place.
When I was woven together
in the depths of the earth,
your eyes saw my unformed body.

This passage clearly states that God's love and concern for the unborn exists at the earliest point of development. The Hebrew term *golem*, meaning embryo or fetus, is used here and translated as "unformed body." This is indeed an awesome thought. When we were embryos, before our mothers even knew they were pregnant, the sovereign God of the universe cared for us and was intimately involved in our development; he saw our unformed bodies and loved us.

I often wonder how marvelous it would be to be able to remember back to our initial days after conception when each of us was daily changing in development through the creative design of God. There will probably not be another time period in our lives this side of heaven when we will experience the intimacy and communion with our Creator that we enjoyed in those early days in the womb.

The revealed law of God refers to individuals even before their conception in language used to describe persons already born. In Jeremiah 1:5 the Lord says:

"Before I formed you in the womb I knew you,
before you were born I set you apart;
I appointed you as a prophet to the nations."

God knew Jeremiah not only after he was conceived but prior to conception as well! Likewise Jesus, the Son of God, was given his name by the angel before his conception (Luke 2:21), and Levi is said to have paid tithes to Melchizedek while still "in the body of" his great-grandfather

Abraham (Hebrews 7:10). Such things are true from God's perspective because the sovereign God has no beginning or ending and is not bound by time constraints. Each of us, even before we were physically alive, already existed as a thought in the mind of the eternal God. Because of this wondrous truth, I believe we can say with boldness that every unborn child has value to our heavenly Father, and therefore has personhood under the revealed law of God.

Constitutional Law and Personhood

Under the natural law and the revealed law of God, personhood and value belong to all human beings because they are made in the image of God. This value and worth can neither be earned nor forfeited because they are based not upon what we accomplish but upon who we are. The right to life and the personhood of all human beings, including the unborn, is a God-given right granted to us by virtue of being created in the image of God.

In *Roe* v. *Wade*, the Supreme Court interpreted the Constitution to deny personhood to the unborn. Yet a proper reading of our Constitution gives ample room to apply the Fourteenth Amendment's protection of persons to the unborn.

As I indicated earlier, the founding fathers of the Republic and the framers of the Constitution were schooled in the beliefs of Blackstone and Locke in the natural law and the absolute right to life. Thomas Jefferson's eloquent declaration of the inalienable rights of "life, liberty and the pursuit of happiness" was nothing more than a recitation from Blackstone's discussion on the natural rights of man. The chief architect of the Constitution, James Madison, explained his belief that the founding of the American Republic rested on the natural and revealed law of God when he said: "We have staked the whole of all our political institutions upon the capacity of mankind for self-government, upon the capacity of each and all of us to govern ourselves, to control ourselves, to sustain ourselves according to the Ten Commandments of God."[15] The superior status of the right to life, an absolute right emanating from the natural law, was an accepted maxim of the law to the founding fathers and the framers of the Constitution.

With this in mind, the Preamble to the Constitution gives us a starting place for a proper understanding of the constitutional personhood of the unborn. The Preamble says:

> WE THE PEOPLE of the United States, in order to form a more perfect Union, establish justice, insure domestic tranquility, provide for the common defence, promote the general welfare, and secure the blessings of liberty to ourselves and our *posterity*, do ordain and establish this Constitution for the United States of America (my emphasis).

Black's Law Dictionary defines "posterity" as "all the descendants of a person in a direct line to the remotest generation." It includes those born and those yet to be born, which obviously includes the unborn. Hence, if our Constitution was established to secure "the blessings of liberty" to our "posterity" then the Constitution must grant protection to the unborn.

The Supreme Court made a grievous error in *Roe* v. *Wade* when it stated that the right to privacy which allows for abortion-on-demand is derived from the Fourteenth Amendment of the Constitution. This Amendment states in part: "nor shall any State deprive any person of life, liberty, or property, without due process of law." In this decision the Court combined the right to liberty found in this Amendment with its denial of personhood to the unborn to allow for abortion-on-demand. Yet, a fair reading of the historical period at the time this Amendment was adopted shows clear inaccuracies in the Court's reasoning and understanding of history.

The Fourteenth Amendment was ratified in 1868. Along with the Thirteenth and Fifteenth Amendments, this Amendment was intended to give full legal status and equal rights to the freed black slaves. As we saw in chapter 1, during this time period the American Medical Association, led by Dr. Horatio R. Storer of Boston, took a strong stand against human abortion. In addition, during the first half of the nineteenth century many states adopted tough anti-abortion legislation based on the new understanding of human conception.

If abortion is a liberty interest under the Fourteenth Amendment, and the unborn are not persons under that Amendment as the Court asserted in *Roe*, why then would state legislative bodies be approving anti-abortion legislation at the same time they approved the passage of the Fourteenth Amendment?[16]

The congressional debates that led to the passage of the Fourteenth Amendment make it abundantly evident that the post-Civil War Congress did not distinguish between personhood and biological humanity for purposes of this Amendment. For example, Representative John A. Bingham of Ohio, a coauthor of the Fourteenth Amendment, declared:

> "[The] Constitution . . . proclaimed that all men in respect of life and liberty and property were equal before the law, and that no person, no human being, no member of the family of man shall . . . be deprived of his life, or his liberty, or his property, but by the law of the land."[17]

Statements from other political leaders at this time support this proposition that the Fourteenth Amendment was in no way intended to endorse the right to abortion.[18]

The case for the constitutional personhood of the unborn child is a compelling one. Yet the Supreme Court's decision in *Roe* ignored the biological realities of the unborn and turned a deaf ear to the proper historical and legal analysis required to decide the dispute before it. More significantly, the Court's decision is a flagrant example of the complete rejection of the natural law and the revealed law of God which had been the foundation of our legal system. This rejection did not happen overnight.

Rejection of the Natural Law

Although the natural law as the source and authenticity for all man-made laws was the prevailing legal philosophy in the English common law and throughout the early days of the American Republic, belief in the natural law began to fade during the nineteenth century. Affecting the perspective on the natural law in philosophical circles was the teaching of German philosopher Georg Wilhelm Friedrich Hegel (1770-1831).

Hegel taught that truth is not absolute but rather originates through a branch of logic known as dialectics. Under this view, truth evolves to a higher plain as mankind evolves and changes. Through dialectics, a value or truth which exists, referred to as a thesis, is challenged by a conflicting value, an antithesis. The resulting conflict between the two values, a process referred to as synthesis, produces a new value or truth. This dialectic process then repeats itself throughout history. Rather than being absolute, truth changes and evolves throughout time.

Another influential philosopher in the nineteenth century was Auguste Comte (1798-1857), sometimes referred to as the founder of positivism. As in dialectics, positivism denies the existence of absolute truth or the natural law. Comte spoke of truth only in what can be actually verified and observed. Comte saw the law evolving in three stages: (1) the *theological stage*, where man attempts to understand everything as having supernatural causes; (2) the *metaphysical stage*, where the concept of a deity is replaced by abstract concepts such as natural rights; and (3) the *positive stage*, where all abstractions about God are discarded and truth is only discoverable through empirical observation of objects and events. Man derives truths out of natural and scientific principles.[19]

The school of legal positivism began to gain influence in the American legal community at the beginning of the twentieth century. This philosophy, which is prominent today in legal circles, rejects the concept of a natural law; law is what the lawmaker, either judge or legislator, says it is without reference to any divine authority.

Through dialectics the law is constantly evolving and changing to meet the needs of the times. Under legal positivism, law is morally neutral, and questions of morality and justice are separated from the basis of law. As one legal positivist states: "It is in no sense a necessary truth that laws reproduce or satisfy certain demands of morality, though in fact they have often done so."[20] This view, according to proponents of legal positivism, permits one to "talk about the law objectively, without casting judgment on its virtue or vice." Further, such an approach to the law allows for the avoidance of "the confusion of law and morals (or value judgments) that may result either in an idealization of the law (as it is) or in a utopian legalism in which that which ought to be is made into law."[21] In short, legal positivism attempts to provide an objective, morally neutral basis for the law.

The most prominent proponent of the school of legal positivism was Supreme Court Justice Oliver Wendell Holmes (1841-1935). Holmes once stated that "truth was the majority vote of that nation that could lick all others."[22] Regarding truth he stated, "I therefore define truth as the system of my limitations, and leave absolute truth for those who are better equipped. With absolute truth I leave absolute ideals of conduct equally on one side."[23] Concerning the natural law Holmes said, "The jurists who believe in natural law seem to me to be in that naive state of mind that accepts what has been familiar and accepted by them and their neighbors as something that must be accepted by all men everywhere."[24] As a positivist, Holmes viewed the law as always evolving and changing to meet the perceived social needs of society. He could say in all sincerity that "the law is always approaching, and never reaching, consistency. It is forever adopting new principles from life at one end, and it always retains old ones from history at the other, which have not yet been absorbed or sloughed off. It will become entirely consistent only when it ceases to grow."[25]

Through the influence of Holmes and other prominent legal scholars, the legal community gradually accepted the idea that law is not an absolute emanating from God, the divine lawmaker. Contrary to the Blackstonian view that all law derives its legitimacy from the natural law, the twentieth-century viewpoint sees law as ever changing through time. University of Virginia law professor G. Edward White states it this way:

> Law is no longer seen as a finite body of universal principles, and judges are no longer seen as persons who merely find and declare those principles. Twentieth-century perspectives on the Court start with two different assumptions. Law is seen as a fluid mix of established principles and changing social values, and judges, in constitutional law and elsewhere, are seen as persons who make law by creating new principles, often in response to changes in social values.[26]

With this as the prevailing twentieth-century viewpoint of the nature of the law, it is not surprising that the Supreme Court rendered its decision in *Roe* v. *Wade*. Having rejected the Judeo-Christian legacy of Blackstone and Locke, modern legal scholars have replaced law with politics. Instead of being proclaimers of the natural law for implementation in the affairs of man, judges are now super-legislators who, at their whim, make changes in the law to meet what they perceive to be the changing needs of society. Instead of discovering those natural laws that already exist, the contemporary judge invents laws that more suitably conform to his own preferences. To the modern-day jurist it is irrelevant that the unborn child is a person under the natural law, the revealed law, or even past statutory and case law. What is now relevant are societal trends and the need to conform to social dictates. Instead of shaping morality, thereby compelling compliance with the laws of nature and nature's God, the courts today enforce conformity to new laws invented to keep up with the contemporary social ethic.

In his dissent in *Roe* v. *Wade*, Justice Byron White summed up the Court's decision this way: "As an exercise of raw judicial power, the Court perhaps has authority to do what it does today; but in my view its judgment is an improvident and extravagant exercise of the power of judicial review that the Constitution extends to this Court."[27]

The denial of personhood to the unborn child is indeed "an exercise of raw judicial power" from a court intent on ignoring clear precedent from history, the natural law, and the revealed law. It is this foundation of personhood which must be re-established if our efforts to rebuild the wall will be successful. Upon establishing this foundation, the national tragedy of abortion will be ended, the right to life will be guaranteed to the unborn, and the "blessings of liberty" for ourselves and our posterity will be secured.

Reversing the Blunder of *Roe* v. *Wade*

The first step towards restoring personhood to the unborn lies in reversing the Court's blunder of *Roe* v. *Wade*. The pro-life movement must accelerate its efforts to achieve this. A reversal of *Roe* can happen in one of three ways:

1. *Constitutional amendment.* Several different versions of a Human Life Amendment have been introduced in

Congress. All such amendments now pending would overturn *Roe* and recognize every human being from the moment of conception to natural death as a person under the Constitution. Yet a successful campaign to amend the Constitution is difficult. The necessary political support must be generated from both houses of Congress to send an amendment to the states for ratification.

Article V of the Constitution, which explains how an amendment may be proposed by Congress and then ratified by the states, says:

> The Congress, whenever two thirds of both Houses shall deem it necessary, shall propose amendments to this Constitution . . . which shall be valid to all intents and purposes, as part of this constitution, when ratified by the legislatures of three fourths of the several States.

For this route to be successfully undertaken, the prolife movement must not only elect a sufficient number of pro-life congressmen and senators but a sufficient number of pro-life state legislators as well. Presently, the pro-life movement is far short of the number of pro-life votes necessary in Congress to pass such an amendment.

2. *Constitutional convention.* While all constitutional amendments have originated in the Congress, Article V allows for another process to be used. This provision states:

> The Congress . . . on the application of the legislatures of two thirds of the several States, shall call a convention for proposing amendments, which . . . shall be valid to all intents and purposes, as part of this Constitution, when ratified . . . by conventions in three fourths thereof.

Twenty of the necessary thirty-four states have called for a constitutional convention to draft an amendment on abortion. As with the prospects of securing an amendment from Congress, it is doubtful that in the near future this process will bring about an amendment to protect the unborn. However, if the number of states calling for a convention comes close to the necessary number, Congress may begin to respond to political pressure and pass a Constitutional amendment.

3. *The Court reversing itself.* The most promising route to reversing *Roe* is through the Supreme Court itself. On at least 120 occasions in the past, the Court has reversed its own rulings.

While the recent events that culminated in the *Webster* decision are promising for an eventual Court reversal, we need to be cautious in our optimism about the direction the Court may head. The Court's reconsideration of *Roe* may fall considerably short of recognizing the personhood and the right to life of the unborn. Furthermore, a complete reversal of *Roe* does not necessarily mean that abortion will be ended. If the Court concludes that abortion is not a constitutional right, then the debate will simply be moved to the fifty state legislative arenas. Some states would undoubtedly outlaw abortion while others would allow it. Some state supreme courts might even discover a right to abortion within their state constitutions.

For the time being, a window of opportunity exists. Decisions by the Court in future abortion cases will clarify the constitutional status of abortion-on-demand. It is now up to the people of God to act upon the opportunity given and present to the Court at the earliest possible time the proper case in which the atrocity of *Roe* v. *Wade* will be discarded and protection of the unborn will once again be a foundational principle recognized in our legal and political system.

Notes

1. Ronald W. Reagan, *Abortion and the Conscience of the Nation* (Nashville: Thomas Nelson Publishers, 1984), 38.

2. C.S. Lewis, *The Abolition of Man* (New York: Macmillan Publishing Co., 1974), 56.

3. Ibid., 28.

4. Blackstone says: "Man, considered as a creature, must necessarily be subject to the laws of his creator, for he is entirely a dependent being. . . . And consequently as man depends absolutely upon his maker for everything, it is necessary that he should in all points conform to his maker's will.

"For as God, when he created matter, and endued it with a principle of mobility, established certain rules for the perpetual direction of that motion; so, when he created man, and endued him with freewill to conduct himself in all parts of life, he laid down certain immutable laws of human nature, whereby that freewill is in some degree regulated and restrained, and gave him also the faculty of reason to discover the purpose of those laws.

"Considering the Creator only as a being of infinite power, he was able unquestionably to have prescribed whatever laws he pleased to his creature, man, however unjust or severe. But as he is also a being of infinite wisdom, he has laid down only such laws as were founded in those relations of justice, that existed in the nature of things antecedent to any positive precept. These are the eternal, immutable laws of good and evil, to which the Creator himself in all his dispensations conforms; and which he has enabled human reason to discover, so far as they are necessary for the conduct of human actions. Such among others are these principles: that we should live honestly, should hurt nobody, and should render to every one its due. . . .

"For [God] has so intimately connected, so inseparably interwoven the laws of eternal justice with the happiness of each individual, that the latter cannot be attained but by observing the former; and, if the former be punctually obeyed, it cannot but induce the latter. In consequence of which mutual connection of justice and human felicity, he has not perplexed the law of nature with a multitude of abstracted rules and precepts, referring merely to the fitness or unfitness of things, as some have vainly surmised; but has graciously reduced the rule of obedience to this one paternal precept, that man should pursue his own happiness. This is the foundation of what we call ethics, or natural law. For the several articles into which it is branched in our systems, amount to no more than demonstrating, that this or that action tends to man's real happiness, and therefore very justly concluding that the performance of it is a part of the law of nature; or, on the other hand, that this or that action is destructive of man's real happiness, and therefore that the law of nature forbids it.

"This law of nature, being co-eval with mankind and dictated by God himself, is of course superior in obligation to any other. It is binding over all the globe, in all countries, and at all times: no human laws are of any validity, if contrary to this; and such of them as are valid derive all their force, and all their authority, mediately or immediately, from this original."

William Blackstone, *Commentaries on the Laws of England* (Birmingham, Ala.: The Legal Classics Library, 1983), 1:39-41.

5. Ibid., 119.

6. Ibid., 125.

7. Ibid., 129.

8. In "A History of American Political Theories," historian C. Edward Merriam states:

> Locke, in particular, was the authority to whom the Patriots paid greatest deference. He was the most famous of seventeenth-century democratic theorists, and his ideas had their due weight with the colonists. Almost every writer seems to have been influenced by him, many quoted his words, and the argument of others shows the unmistakable imprint of his philosophy. The first great speech of Otis was wholly based upon Locke's ideas; Samuel Adams, on the "Rights of the Colonists as Men and as British Subjects," followed the same model. Many of the phrases of the Declaration of Independence may be found in Locke's Treatise; there is hardly any important writer of this time who does not openly refer to Locke, or tacitly follow the lead he had taken. The argument in regard to the limitations upon Parliament was taken from Locke's reflections on the "supreme legislature" and the necessary restrictions upon its authority. No one stated more strongly than did he the basis for the doctrine that "taxation without representation is tyranny." No better epitome of the Revolutionary theory could be found than in John Locke on civil government.

Quoted in *The Christian History of the Constitution of the United States of America*, ed. Verna M. Hall (San Francisco: Foundation for American Christian Education, 1980), 51.

9. In this essay Locke states: "The state of nature has a law of nature to govern it, which obliges every one: And reason, which is that law, teaches all mankind, who will but consult it, that being all equal and independent, no one ought to harm another in his life, health, liberty, or possessions. For men being all the workmanship of one omnipotent, and infinitely wise Maker: All the servants of one sovereign Master, sent into the world by his order, and about his business, they are his property, whose workmanship they are, made to last during his, not one another's pleasure: And being furnished with like faculties, sharing all in one community of nature, there cannot be supposed any such subordination among us, that may authorize us to destroy one another, as if we were made for one another's uses, as the inferior ranks of creatures are for ours. Every one as he is bound to preserve himself, and not to quit his station wilfully, so by the like reason, when his own preservation comes not in competition, ought he, as much as he can, to preserve the rest of mankind, and may not unless it be to do justice on an offender, take away, or impair the life, or what tends to the preservation of the life, the liberty health, limb or goods of another."

John Locke, "Of Civil Government, Book II," quoted in *Christian History*, 58.

10. Lewis, *Abolition of Man*, 59-60.

11. Blackstone, *Commentaries*, 1:42.

12. Of the revealed law Blackstone says: "It is of infinitely more authority than what we generally call the natural law. Because one is the law of nature, expressly declared so to be by God himself; the other is only what, by the assistance of human reason, we imagine to be that law. If we could be as certain of the latter as we are of the former both would have an equal authority; but, till then, they can never be put in any competition together." Ibid., 42.

13. Harold O.J. Brown, *Death Before Birth* (Nashville: Thomas Nelson Publishers, 1977), 118.

14. *Roe* v. *Wade* (1973), 163.

15. Quoted in Gary DeMar, *God and Government: A Biblical and Historical Study* (Atlanta: American Vision Press, 1984), 137-38.

16. Professor Joseph B. Witherspoon of the University of Texas Law School states: "The conjunction of state ratification of these amendments (the Thirteenth, Fourteenth, and Fifteenth) with state adoption or modification (i.e., to make them more restrictive) of anti-abortion statutes designed to protect unborn children constitutes a contemporaneous legislative construction by states of the meaning of the Amendments they ratified. That construction can only be that unborn children are human beings and persons under the Constitution. Any other view of their action would be out of line with the history of this period." Joseph P. Witherspoon, Testimony before the House Subcommittee on Civil and Constitutional Rights of the House Committee on the Judiciary, Ninety-Fourth Congress, Second Session, 1976, cited in *Congressional Record*, 3 March 1976, 5108.

17. Cong. Globe, 40th Cong., 1st Sess. 542 (1867).

18. Representative Joshua R. Giddings clearly stated his conclusion that no class of human beings could be excluded from the persons protected under the Fourteenth Amendment: "Our fathers, recognizing God as the author of human life, proclaimed it a 'self-evident' truth that every human being holds from the Creator an inalienable right to live. . . . If this right be denied, no other can be acknowledged. If there be exceptions to this central, this universal proposition, that all men, without respect to complexion or condition, hold from the Creator the right to live, who shall determine what portion of the community shall be slain? And who may perpetrate the murders?" Cong. Globe, 35th Cong. 1st Sess. App. 65-66 (1858).

The congressional record is full of statements from legislators during this time period who strongly agreed with Senator Sumner's statement, "in the eyes of the Constitution, every human being within its sphere . . . from the President to the slave, is a person." Cong. Globe, 37th Cong. 2d. Sess. 1449 (1862).

There are numerous additional statements from federal legislators during this time period indicating the belief that the personhood protections of the Fourteenth Amendment apply to all human beings. Cong. Globe, 39th Cong., 1st Sess. 77 (1866), Sen. Trumbull: "any legislation or any public sentiment which deprives any human being in the land of those great rights of liberty will be in defiance of the constitution"; id. at 322-23 (1866), Sen. Trumbull: "great object of securing to every human being within the jurisdiction of the Republic equal rights before the law"; id. at 1159 (1866), Rep. Windom: rights to life, liberty, and pursuit of happiness are "rights of human nature," and the most basic "right of human nature [is] the right to exist"; id. at 1151 (1866), Rep. Thayer: "relief of human nature" secured in Thirteenth Amendment; 3 Cong. Rec. 1794 (1875), Senator Allen G. Thurman: may not deny equal protection to "any person" in the jurisdiction, "be he sane or be he insane, be he old or be he young, be he innocent or be he criminal, be he learned or be he ignorant." With such an historical record before it, one does wonder how the Supreme Court in *Roe* could come to the unique conclusion that the humanity of the unborn was not relevant and that legal personhood was not synonymous with "human being."

19. John Eidsmoe, *The Christian Legal Advisor* (Grand Rapids: Baker Book House, 1984), 66.

20. "Beyond Positivism: A Theological Perspective," *The Weightier Matters of the Law: Essays on Law and Religion*, ed. John Witte, Jr. and Frank S. Alexander (Atlanta: Scholars Press, 1988), 253.

21. Ibid., 253.

22. Oliver Wendell Holmes, *The Common Law* (Birmingham, Ala.: The Legal Classics Library, 1982), 310.

23. Ibid., 304-5.

24. Ibid., 312.

25. Ibid.

26. G. Edward White, "Reflections on the Role of the Supreme Court: The Contemporary Debate and 'Lessons' Of History," *Judicature* 162 (1979):163-64.

27. White dissent, *Roe* v. *Wade*, 222.

CHAPTER FOUR

The Four Cornerstones of the Wall

The foundation of the wall of protection, the personhood of the unborn child, must be established. However, as with the wall surrounding the city of Jerusalem in Nehemiah's day, the wall of protection will remain secure from attack and survive the assaults of the enemy only when four cornerstones, four essentials, are placed within the foundation of personhood.

We must emphasize these four essentials, these absolute basics, in order to unite and undergird our efforts to protect unborn human life: the ministry of the resurrection, the ministry of reconciliation, the ministry of reformation, and the ministry of revival.

The Ministry of the Resurrection

There are many valid bases for pro-life activities. For the Christian, however, pro-life efforts should come primarily from a devotion to the One who gave himself for us—Jesus Christ the Lord. Scripture states that the household of God is "built on the foundation of the apostles and prophets, with Christ Jesus himself as the chief cornerstone. In him the whole building is joined together and rises to become a holy temple in the Lord" (Ephesians 2:20-21).

As the "chief cornerstone" Jesus said of himself: "I am the resurrection and the life. He who believes in me will live, even though he dies; and whoever lives and believes in me will never die" (John 11:25-26). Because we are his followers, our efforts should reflect a ministry of the resurrection. We are pro-life because Jesus, our captain, is the resurrection and the life; as his disciples we have no other option but to stand for life. What we represent is the very antithesis of the death ethic of abortion. Everything we believe in, as Christians, can be summed up in the word *life* because Jesus is the life.

Sadly, I have observed questionable motives from some of my allies in the pro-life movement. For many the pro-life movement has become a substitute religion. Though most of these friends mention the Lord as a motivating factor for their efforts, the fruits of their labors indicate that another agenda has priority. Any motive for involvement that is placed before devotion to the Lord of life, no matter how noble or admirable that motive is, constitutes idolatry. As Christians, our reasons for fighting abortion must stem primarily from our commitment to Christ.

Ours is a ministry of the resurrection, because Jesus is the resurrection and the life. Once we understand this and base our energies on this cornerstone, I believe the Lord will begin to move in a mighty way and employ us to end abortion in America. But we must remember that we are soldiers in his army, and we must be willing to place our agendas in subordination to his will.

The Ministry of Reconciliation

God has also called us to a ministry of reconciliation. Second Corinthians 5:17-20 says:

> Therefore, if anyone is in Christ, he is a new creation; the old has gone, the new has come! All this is from God, who reconciled us to himself through Christ and gave us the ministry of reconciliation: that God was reconciling the world to himself in Christ, not counting men's sins against them. And he has committed to us the message of reconciliation. We are therefore Christ's ambassadors, as though God were making his appeal through us. We implore you on Christ's behalf: Be reconciled to God.

The scourge of abortion has divided this nation in a manner not seen since the days of slavery. The deep wounds caused by abortion-on-demand have affected men, women, children, young and old. Even the most intimate relationships God planned for his people have been divided and destroyed by abortion.

Husband and wife. Both parties in a marriage must agree to almost every transaction before it becomes legally binding. Generally speaking, before a married person may purchase a new home, buy a car, place a second mortgage on a home, or go into debt, his or her spouse must agree that the transaction can take place and usually must sign the appropriate legal papers to close the contract. Yet, when the issue is whether to destroy the life of an unborn child conceived out of an act of love, only the wife has a voice in that decision.[1]

As a practicing attorney for more than ten years, I have observed the breakup and dissolution of many marriages through the court system. From my observations I believe abortion is every bit as destructive of the bonds of trust between a husband and wife as is the act of adultery.

Abortion is a destructive force pitting husband against wife. This calls out for a ministry of reconciliation.

Parent and child. Today a teenage daughter must receive parental permission for the most minor medical procedures, such as teeth cleaning or ear piercing. Yet if she wants to kill her unborn child, a procedure that could have serious consequences on her physical and mental health, her parents—the grandparents of the child—have no voice.[2]

I well remember when a client of mine in my law practice asked if he could take me to lunch. This client was a deeply committed Christian and very active in his church. We had developed a good, open relationship so I could tell from the tone of his voice that something was terribly wrong. I anticipated that he had some serious legal matters to discuss.

During most of the lunch my client was unusually quiet until I finally asked him what was on his mind. He then looked at me with tears in his eyes and told me his sixteen-year-old daughter had obtained an abortion the previous week. She had become pregnant through a relationship with a young man in the church youth group and made an appointment with the abortionist through a school counselor. She then confronted her parents with the situation and told them they had two choices. They could support her in the decision so she could obtain the abortion without any further quarrel, or they could resist her decision, in which case she would still obtain the abortion through the help of public assistance. They would then have to deal with a broken relationship with their daughter.

With tears streaming down his face, my client asked, "What kind of country is this that would create such a division between parents and their children?" I realized then that abortion does not impact just the woman who is pregnant; it has repercussions on many other lives as well. Abortion is a destructive force in the parent-child relationship, destroying communication and the bonds of trust. The division between parents and their children in this country calls for a ministry of reconciliation.

Mother and unborn baby. One of the most intimate of all relationships is that between mother and unborn baby. Only a mother truly knows the gloriousness of this bond. We fathers have but a limited understanding of what happens within the wombs of our wives when they are carrying our offspring.

I well remember when my wife was about eight months pregnant, and we were speaking in a Sunday morning service at a Seattle area church. Just before we were introduced the congregation stood and sang a praise chorus with the words, "Let there be glory and honor and praises, glory and honor to Jesus." It was one of those special times in worship when the Spirit of God is very close. As I looked over at my wife I could see her grimacing and holding her abdomen because the baby was becoming quite active during the singing. At first I wondered if the time had come to rush to the hospital, but as Laura quietly told me she was fine I realized something extraordinary was happening. Just as John the Baptist had, in his mother's womb, jumped for joy in the presence of Jesus the Messiah, so our little unborn child, Joshua, was jumping for joy in the presence of the Lord and the Spirit-led worship and praise.

What an incredible God we serve! This same God who created the stars, the planets, and the vast universe is still not too immense to prevent a little unborn child from sensing his presence and worshiping him. A marvelous thing is happening inside a woman during pregnancy. The very God of the universe is at work! Yet the acceptance of abortion-on-demand has turned this beautiful and innermost relationship into a battle zone where, in some metropolitan areas, there are more dead victims than survivors.[3] Abortion is a destructive act which turns mothers and unborn babies into adversaries and places their interests at odds with each other.

In the midst of this destructiveness and division, the people of God are called to a ministry of reconciliation. In all our efforts we should reach out with the message of Christ that in despair there is hope and in the midst of death there is life. We must grasp and understand that God "has committed to us the message of reconciliation. We are therefore Christ's ambassadors, as though God were making his appeal through us."

The Ministry of Reformation

Scripture tells us that as Christians we are citizens of two kingdoms—the kingdom of God and the worldly kingdom under whose jurisdiction we reside. Hebrews 11, which honors those saints whose walk with God was based upon an unshakable faith, talks about our heavenly citizenship:

> All these people were still living by faith when they died. They did not receive the things promised; they only saw them and welcomed them from a distance. And they admitted that they were aliens and strangers on earth. People who say such things show that they are looking for a country of their own. If they had been thinking of the country they had left, they would have had opportunity to return. Instead, they were longing for a better country—a heavenly one. Therefore God is not ashamed to be called their God, for he has prepared a city for them.

As Christians we are citizens of the kingdom of heaven. We are passing through this earth as strangers and aliens, longing for a better country—a heavenly one. But we are reminded in the New Testament that we are also subject "to the governing authorities, for there is no authority except that which God has established. The authorities that exist have been established by God. Consequently, he who rebels against the authority is rebelling against what God has instituted, and those who do so will bring judgment on themselves" (Romans 13:1-2). We are citizens of our earthly country and subject to its laws because the civil government has been ordained by God to keep the order and restrain evil (Romans 13:1-6; Titus 3:1; 1 Peter 2:13-14).

Since civil government is important to God for the preservation of the peace, it should be important to us as his people. We are called to a ministry of reformation that will transform our governmental institutions to bring true justice throughout the land. By striving to uphold divine justice in our society—by being salt and light—we are not only obeying the commands of our Lord but we are pursuing our own happiness. According to Blackstone, the "pursuit of happiness" is akin to obedience to the natural law which is derived from the Creator. Obedience to God's will is the only way to true happiness, and such obedience demands that we seek to implement divine justice in our legal system and in our government.

A couple of summers ago I gained a valuable insight into this truth through my daughter SaraLynn. Our family took a vacation back to our former home in the Seattle area, and we stayed in our old house which had been vacated by our renters. But there were no furnishings in the house, and SaraLynn, age two at the time, had to sleep on blankets and pillows we borrowed from some neighbors. The room she slept in hardly resembled her room in our Virginia home—it had no crib, no rocking chair, no changing table, and no toys. Consequently, she had a hard time sleeping and was cranky because she missed her real home on the East coast. After a few miserable nights and days, some kind neighbors loaned us a crib, a rocker, and some toys. This made a world of difference in our daughter's disposition as her temporary home began to resemble her permanent one.

Sometimes I think many Christians are much like my daughter. They long for their permanent home, heaven, and want to leave all their cares and troubles behind. But while they await their inevitable homecoming with the Lord, they are doing nothing to make this temporary residence in the kingdom of men resemble their permanent home in the kingdom of heaven. By disregarding the affairs of men they are failing to pursue their own happiness. Like SaraLynn they are "cranky," or so heavenly minded they are no earthly good. These brothers and sisters fail to realize that the pursuit of real happiness lies in obedience to the commands of Christ. To strive to see that his "will be done on earth as it is in heaven" is the true pursuit of happiness for the believer.

As believers in Jesus Christ we cannot idly spend the short time given us in this earthly domain ignoring the ills of our temporal kingdom. Through the power of the Holy Spirit we are called to a ministry of reformation which will make a difference in our society. If we refuse this calling, we will be unhappy in our relationship and walk with the Lord. When we are involved in making our temporary society resemble our permanent home we are obeying our Lord and will find peace and contentment despite adverse circumstances.

To be sure, we will never make our earthly realm, which is ruled by sinful men, totally like our heavenly home where true justice reigns. However, our advocacy of Christian values in the public arena is a witness to a lost world and a representation of the eternal kingdom of Christ. To ignore the commands of Scripture that we are to defend the fatherless (Isaiah 1:17) and to speak up for those who cannot speak for themselves (Proverbs 24:11-12) is to deny that we are citizens of a heavenly kingdom and forerunners of that glorious world to come.

The Ministry of Revival

When I first became involved in the pro-life movement I was convinced that education was the key to winning this battle. If only the American public could be educated on the biological facts about conception and life in utero it would understand that the unborn child is indeed a baby. When this education was achieved, abortion-on-demand would end, for what rational human being who understands the facts about the unborn could tolerate the violent slaughter of these children. I believed with all my heart that such an understanding would bring an end to the killing.

I no longer hold this view. With all the medical advances in the last twenty years that allow us to study life in the womb, nobody can argue with any credibility that the unborn child is not a living human being. Even abortion advocates concede as much. And basic ninth grade biology affirms that human life begins at conception. We are winning the debate about the humanity of the unborn, yet abortion continues virtually unrestricted. Today the debate over abortion does not ask the question of when human life begins; it asks, What value do we place on life in the womb? [4]

Perhaps abortion is not the real problem in America but rather a symptom of a greater problem. When Aleksandr Solzhenitsyn pondered the state of civilization in the twentieth century he proclaimed: "If I were called upon to identify briefly the principal trait of the entire twentieth century . . . I would be unable to find anything more precise and pithy than to repeat once again: 'Men have forgotten God.' "

What a powerful thought—"Men have forgotten God." Having forgotten God, we fail to see his image in the unborn child and we accept abortion despite the unquestionable humanity of these little ones. Having forgotten God, we fail to see his image in the handicapped newborn whose quality of life does not measure up to accepted societal norms, and we easily tolerate infanticide. Having forgotten God, we can turn our backs on the elderly, the infirm, and the terminally ill and allow their lives to be taken because they are an inconvenience and a burden. Men have indeed forgotten God!

It will take more than education to end the decadence that exists in America. To end abortion in this country, we need a spiritual awakening that changes the hearts of people.

In 1863, during a bloody civil war, President Abraham Lincoln issued a proclamation of a day of national humiliation, fasting, and prayer. His proclamation reads in part:

> We have been the recipients of the choicest bounties of Heaven; we have been preserved these many years in peace and prosperity; we have grown in numbers, wealth, and power as no other nation has ever grown. But we have forgotten God. We have forgotten the gracious hand which preserved us in peace and multiplied and enriched and strengthened us, and we have vainly imagined, in the deceitfulness of our hearts, that all these blessings were produced by some superior wisdom and virtue of our own. Intoxicated with unbroken success, we have become too self-sufficient to feel the necessity of redeeming and preserving grace, too proud to pray to the God that made us.[5]

Lincoln could very well have been describing America in the 1990s. Men have forgotten God, and it is our responsibility as the people of God to remind our fellow Americans of who God is and what he requires of us. Of all the necessary elements for our cause to be successful, there must be the ministry of revival that will call our nation to repentance and bring forth healing and restoration. And revival starts with true repentance and cleansing of the church of Jesus Christ.

An incident from the book of Joshua is instructive for us. Shortly before he led the nation of Israel against Jericho, Joshua had a unique encounter with the God of heaven:

> Now when Joshua was near Jericho, he looked up and saw a man standing in front of

him with a drawn sword in his hand. Joshua went up to him and asked, "Are you for us or for our enemies?"

"Neither," he replied, "but as commander of the army of the LORD I have now come." Then Joshua fell facedown to the ground in reverence, and asked him, "What message does my Lord have for his servant?"

The commander of the LORD's army replied, "Take off your sandals, for the place where you are standing is holy." And Joshua did so (Joshua 5:13-15).

I find it interesting that when Joshua inquired of the Lord whether he was for Israel or for her enemies in Jericho, the Lord replied, "Neither." This is strange. After all, the children of Israel were God's chosen people, and they were beginning a campaign to possess the promised land. Jericho, on the other hand, was a city under judgment. It was so depraved that, except for Rahab and her family, the children of Israel destroyed "every living thing in it—men and women, young and old, cattle, sheep and donkeys" (6:21). In light of this, why would the Lord tell Joshua that he was neither for the Israelites nor for their enemies?

I believe the answer is straightforward. The question we should ask in our spiritual battles is not, Is God on our side? but Are we on God's side? Even though they were God's special people, the children of Israel were far from sinless. Because of unbelief they were made to wander in the wilderness for forty years before they could go in and possess the promised land. When Moses was on Mt. Sinai receiving the Ten Commandments the Israelites were worshipping a golden calf and blaspheming the Lord. Their complaining about their plight in the wilderness and continuous grumbling to return to Egypt indicated a lack of faith in the God who had delivered them from Pharaoh. In short, Israel was a sinful and rebellious people.

It is easy to understand why the Lord would tell Joshua that he is not on the side of the Israelites. Instead, he instructed Joshua to take off his sandals because he was standing on holy ground. Before the Lord would ever allow Joshua to lead the children of Israel to victory in Jericho, Joshua was first required to consecrate himself before the Lord and clean up his own life.

The parallel of this story with the abortion battle today is clear. Many in the pro-life movement claim that God is on our side. It is not unusual to see a fervent pro-lifer calling down God's judgment on abortionists and those who support abortion rights. Yet, as with Joshua, if the Lord were to walk among us and we asked him, "Are you for us or for our adversaries?" I believe he would respond, "Neither."

I believe there are two sins in America today that will ultimately bring God's wrath upon our nation. One is, of course, the sin of abortion and its destruction of God's handiwork. The other is the sin of the church's indifference to the commands of God. Unless revival comes to cleanse the church, I fear America is headed for judgment. However, the sin of the church is not displayed only in its indifference to the silent screams of the unborn. It is also manifested, in part, in the judgmental and self-righteous attitude many in the pro-life movement exhibit towards those who oppose us. Instead of calling down judgment on these people we should be on our faces before the Lord crying out for mercy and revival in our land. Before we call out for judgment we should remember that when judgment comes it begins "with the family of God" (1 Peter 4:17).

Today, the commander of the army of the Lord is saying to the church, "I have come to deal with the sin in Jericho (abortion), but I have also come to deal with your sin. And before I will permit you to be used to end abortion in America, you must remove your shoes, for you are standing on holy ground. You must repent of all those sins which separate you from me."

For revival to break out in America, the church of Jesus Christ must make sure that we are on God's side. We must renew our relationship with the Lord and renounce anything that would usurp our devotion to Christ. We must also begin to see those who oppose us on this issue not as adversaries but as potential allies to be won into the kingdom of God. Our real enemy in this warfare is not "flesh and blood" but the rulers and principalities of the kingdom of Satan.

During the first century, Saul of Tarsus persecuted the church and even consented to the murder of a Christian. At one time he was the chief enemy of the gospel of Christ. Yet we know how his life was transformed from Saul of Tarsus, an adversary of the gospel, to the apostle Paul, a champion for Christ. We may legitimately ask, "What would the state of Christianity be today if there had not been an apostle Paul?" Yet we should take this question one step further and ask, "What would the state of Christianity be today if there had not been an Ananias who went to this enemy of the faith, laid his hands on him, and prayed that the scales from his eyes be removed?"

As we reach out to those who today support abortion, we will find many Sauls who are potential Pauls. We need to pray for the leaders in the pro-abortion movement that, like Paul, the scales will be removed from their eyes and they will have an experience with the living God that will transform them and their perspective on this issue. In addition, like Ananias, we need to be willing to go to these people and confront them with the claims of Christ. Can you imagine what would happen to abortion-on-demand in this country if revival broke out in the medical community and hundreds of abortionists came to know Christ as their Savior?

I was present this last year at a large pro-life demonstration outside a Boston abortion clinic. As is usually the case, pro-abortion activists showed up to harass those of us who had come to pray and demonstrate. I noticed one young man who was being particularly obnoxious with the insults he shouted to the pro-life demonstrators. Yet there was something within me that took a liking to this young man. Underneath his crude demeanor was potential and dignity that I believe God wants to be used for his glory. After watching this young man for a while, I poured a cup of cold water from our water cooler (it was a hot day) and handed it to him. He was startled, but he took the drink anyway and gave me a peculiar look as if I didn't know to whom I was giving water.

Later in the day I approached him and we began to discuss the issue of abortion. He listened and responded with a much different demeanor than he had been exhibiting previously. As we talked, it was apparent that he agreed with and respected some of the things I was saying. At the end of our conversation he thanked me for taking time to talk and listen. Incidentally, this young man's name is Paul. I don't know if I will ever meet him again, but I am praying for Paul that the scales will be removed from his eyes and he will come to know Christ.

When we approach the abortion issue with humility, prayer, and loving confrontation—in the spirit of Ananias—we will see God work in a mighty way to bring many into his kingdom. And when we repent of our ungodly attitudes toward our neighbors who disagree with us, God will use us to turn these "adversaries" into allies. When this happens we will see revival break out in America.

Building upon the Cornerstones

As our efforts to rebuild the wall of protection for the unborn progress, we must not forget the four cornerstones: the ministries of resurrection, reconciliation, reformation, and revival. Within the foundation of personhood these cornerstones establish the basis for the successful reconstruction of the wall. It is upon this foundation and these corner-stones that the remaining sections of the wall will be built and made secure from the attacks of the enemy. As we now discuss a specific pro-life agenda for the 1990s, we must remember these basics upon which our endeavors are to be based.

Notes

1. In *Planned Parenthood of Missouri* v. *Danforth*, 428 U.S. 52 (1976), the United States Supreme Court invalidated provisions of a Missouri statute requiring the consent of a spouse before an abortion can be obtained. The Court stated, "Since the state cannot regulate or proscribe abortion during the first stage, when the physician and his patient make that decision the state cannot delegate authority to any person, even the spouse, to prevent abortion during that period" (p. 69).

2. In *Planned Parenthood of Missouri* v. *Danforth* the Supreme Court also invalidated the provisions of the Missouri statute which required written consent of a parent or guardian of an unmarried pregnant woman under the age of eighteen. The Court stated: "It is difficult . . . to conclude that providing a parent with absolute veto power to overrule a determination, made by the physician and his minor patient, to terminate the patient's preg-nancy will serve to strengthen the family. . . . Any independent interest the parent may have in the termination of the minor daughter's pregnancy is no more weighty than the right of privacy of the competent minor mature enough to have become pregnant. . . . We emphasize that our holding . . . does not suggest that every minor, regardless of age or maturity, may give effective consent for termination of her pregnancy" (p. 75).

In the subsequent cases of *Bellotti* v. *Baird* (I), 428 U. S. 132 (1976) and *Bellotti* v. *Baird* (II), 443 U.S. 622 (1979), the Supreme Court stated that parental consent laws which allow minors an alternative opportunity for authorization of the abortion by a court are permissible if the minor demonstrates either that she is mature enough to make her own decision, or that the abortion would be in her best interests. Such a "judicial bypass" provision, which must be placed in any parental consent statute, obviously contains a huge loophole for a minor to forego parental involvement in the abortion decision.

Parental consent laws must be distinguished from parental notification laws. The former requires that at least one parent give consent to the abortion before it can be performed. The latter requires only that notice be given to at least one parent that an abortion is about to take place. In *H.L.* v. *Matheson*, 450 U. S. 398 (1981), the Supreme Court upheld a Utah statute which required an abortionist to "notify, if possible, the parents or guardian of the woman upon whom the abortion is to be performed, if she is a minor." The Court stated that the Utah law did not violate any constitutional guarantees, provided that: (a) the girl is "living with and dependent upon her parents"; (b) she is "not emancipated by marriage or otherwise"; and (c) "she has made no claim or showing as to her maturity or as to her relations with her parents" (p. 407). The opinion of the Court further stated:

> Although we have held that a state may not constitutionally legislate a blanket, unreviewable power of parents to veto their daughter's abortion, a statute setting out a mere requirement of parental notice does not violate the constitutional rights of an immature, dependent minor. . . . As applied to immature and dependent minors the statute plainly serves the important considerations of family integrity and protecting adolescents. . . . The medical, emotional and psychological consequences of an abortion are serious and can be lasting; this is particularly so when the patient is immature. . . . The Utah statute is reasonably calculated to protect minors . . . by enhancing the potential for parental consultation concerning a decision that has potentially traumatic and permanent consequences. . . . That the requirement of notice to parents may inhibit some minors from seeking abortions is not a valid basis to void the statute. . . . The Constitution does not compel a state to fine-tune its statutes so as to encourage or facilitate abortion (pp. 409-13).

At the time of this writing the Supreme Court has heard argument on the constitutionality of two parental notification cases from the states of Minnesota and Ohio. The results of these cases are not expected to impact the Court's previous decision regarding parental consent statutes. However, if the statutes from Minnesota and Ohio are upheld, as expected, then a significant breakthrough in the law will have occurred.

In the case of *Hodgson* v. *Minnesota*, Planned Parenthood has challenged a Minnesota law which requires a doctor to give forty-eight hours' notice to the parents of a teenager before the minor can obtain an abortion. The law was challenged in 1981 and was in operation until 1986 when a federal court enjoined its enforcement. The effect of this parental notification in reducing teen abortion and pregnancy rates has been impressive. Statistics from the Minnesota Department of Health show a 27.2 percent decline in the abortion rate and a 20.4 percent decline in the teen pregnancy rate from 1980 through 1986.

In the case of *Ohio* v. *Akron Center for Reproductive Health*, the Court will review a parental notification law which requires a minor to notify one parent twenty-four hours before her abortion and, like the Minnesota law, allows for the teenager to bypass parental notice by going to court and showing that notifying her parents is not in her best interests. The statute was challenged immediately after it was passed in 1986 and never went into effect.

The significance of these two parental notification cases should not be understated. More than one million American teenagers become pregnant each year, and almost half choose to have abortions. The experience of Minnesota in reducing teen pregnancies and abortions through the operation of its parental notification law proves what pro-lifers have been saying for years—teen sexual behavior is modified when parents are involved in the decision-making process.

Clearly, the upholding of these parental notification laws will be a major turning point in the battle to reduce teen abortion and pregnancy. Presently, twenty-six states have laws on their books requiring notice and/or consent from either one or both parents prior to a teenager's abortion. Most of the laws are not enforced, having either been declared unconstitutional by lower courts or presumed to be unconstitutional in light of earlier Supreme Court decisions. A victory for Minnesota and Ohio will clear the way for enforcement of these laws. It will surely mean a decrease in teen abortion and pregnancy.

3. The Alan Guttmacher Institute, the research arm of Planned Parenthood, reports that the following metropolitan areas annually have more abortions than live births:

Atlanta, Georgia
Atlantic City, New Jersey
Charlotte, North Carolina
Columbia, South Carolina
Gainesville, Florida
Harrisburg, Pennsylvania
Madison, Wisconsin
Miami, Florida
Raleigh, North Carolina
Reno, Nevada
San Fransicso-Oakland, California
Seattle-Everett, Washington
Washington, D. C.

4. The biological evidence concerning the humanity of the unborn child is undisputed and is constituted by plain hard facts. The genesis of human life begins when the ovum is fertilized by the sperm. M. Krieger, one of the scientific authorities cited by the Senate Subcommittee on Separation of Powers in its report on the Human Life Bill, says: "In this first pairing [of sperm and ovum], the spermatozoon has contributed its 23 chromosomes, and the oocyte has contributed its 23 chromosomes, thus re-establishing the necessary total of 46 chromosomes. The result is the conception of a unique individual, unlike any that has been born before and unlike any that will ever be born again. (Stephen M. Krason, *Abortion: Politics, Morality and the Constitution* [Washington, D.C.: University Press of America, 1984], 338.)

Of this fertilized ovum West German physician and anatomy professor E. Blechschmidt of the University of Gottingen says:

> Today we know that each developmental stage of the human being is demonstrably a characteristically human one. Already, on the basis of the well-known chromosomes of the human ova, the specificity of a human germ can no longer be doubted. . . . It may be considered today a fundamental law of human octogenesis that not only human specificity but also the individual specificity of each human being remains pre-

served from fertilization to death, and that only the appearance of the individual being changes in the course of its octogenesis (Krason, 348).

The abortion debate is not over the question of when human life begins, because science has proved beyond a reasonable doubt that this point of beginning is conception. The debate is over what value is to be placed upon this human life. Hence, the issue of personhood, as discussed in chapter 3, becomes crucial to this ongoing debate.

5. President Abraham Lincoln, "Presidential Proclamation for a National Day of Fasting, Humiliation and Prayer," 30 April 1863.

A Pro-Life Agenda
for the 1990s

CHAPTER FIVE

Ministries
of
Compassion

In his rebuilding efforts Nehemiah had to establish a solid foundation and secure the cornerstones of the wall before he could construct the remaining sections. The wall had to rest upon a secure foundation if it was to successfully withstand attack. Likewise, in our rebuilding efforts, the different sections of the wall of protection will be secure only if the wall's foundation and cornerstones are firmly in place.

The first section of the wall that must be firmly established is the ministry of compassion offered by the crisis pregnancy centers. An effective pro-life strategy for the 1990s requires that we reach out to women in crisis pregnancies with the love and compassion of Jesus Christ and give them life-affirming alternatives to abortion. Even if we are successful in ending legal abortion during the next few years, we should not deceive ourselves into thinking that abortion will end. Women will still seek illegal abortions, and the abortion industry—an annual multi-million dollar business—will find ways to make abortion accessible. To end abortion in America we must do more than make it illegal. We must reach the hearts and minds of the women in crisis and let them know there is a better way.

Ministry to Women in Crisis
Is Ministry to Our LORD

Let me set a scene for you. It's late on a cold winter evening. You have turned off the television and are going to bed when you hear a knock at the door. Answering it, you are greeted with a shock. At the door stands a teenager who seems young and innocent except for one thing—she is obviously pregnant. With her is a distraught young man who claims to be her fiancé. Her thin dress and his faded jeans do nothing to keep them warm, and they both shiver from the cold.

As you talk you discover that circumstances beyond their control forced them to leave their little farming community. They have arrived in your town with little money and no friends, only to discover that with the holiday crowds there is no place to stay. In desperation they have gone from door to door trying to find someone who will take them in, but everywhere the answer is the same: "Our home is filled with out-of-town guests. We have no room for strangers."

Like your neighbors, you have guests and your home is every bit as filled, but you can't turn this couple out in the cold. Then you remember—the garage! It isn't much, but with a space heater and some blankets they can at least keep warm during the night. You feel a little guilty because rats have been known to frequent your garage on cold nights, and your flea-bitten dog sleeps there. Yet it is the best you can do for them. As you help them settle in for the evening you tell them that in the morning you will assist them in finding a doctor.

When morning arrives, however, you are awakened by the cry of an infant. During the night, their baby has been born. Not wanting to disturb you any further, the young mother has wrapped her baby in the blanket you gave her and placed him inside the old wheelbarrow that had been leaning against the garage wall.

For some, this story is a good reason to support legalized abortion. After all, they argue, who would be happy to see a baby born in such circumstances? There is nothing in this child's future but welfare and crime. Fortunately, this story has a different ending, for all I have done is dress the well-known Christmas story in modern garb.

Jesus Christ knows what it is like to be unwanted. He knows what it is like to be rejected. He identifies with the unborn child and the mother in turmoil over her pregnancy because he too was conceived in what could be described as a "crisis pregnancy." Because of this, ministry to women in crisis pregnancies is ultimately ministry to our Lord who identifies with the defenseless, the spurned, and the unwanted.

About two thousand years ago, a young teenage girl was pregnant out of wedlock. When Joseph, her fiancé, found out, he was intensely troubled—no doubt humiliated and embarrassed. Joseph pondered whether to take the easy way out and send Mary away quietly, but God had another plan. Through this crisis pregnancy the Savior of the world was to be born.

Despite the divine circumstances surrounding this pregnancy, I don't believe it was easy for Mary and Joseph to face their neighbors and friends. Imagine the humiliation they must have faced. She was an unwed pregnant teenager, and her baby was born in a barn and slept on a bed of hay. What better grist for the gossip mills in Nazareth.

Similar circumstances today would raise the clamor for the continuation of legalized abortion. Yet God worked through this crisis pregnancy to bring salvation to the world!

Crisis Pregnancy Centers Are Close
to the Heart of God

Since 1980 the Christian Action Council (CAC) has been committed to providing alternatives to abortion through the work of its affiliated crisis pregnancy centers (CPCs), which now number close to four hundred. The work of these crisis pregnancy centers is close to the heart of God. Those who minister to women in crisis pregnancies bring hope and life to those who are hurting.

The Christian Action Council is not the only organization that has spearheaded efforts in abortion alternatives. Others, such as Birthright, are also involved, and many independent organizations offer services to pregnant women, such as twenty-four hour crisis "hotlines" and maternity homes. In 1986, *USA Today* reported that as many as three thousand agencies exist that offer alternatives to abortion.[1]

In light of the opportunity given to us in the *Webster* decision and the possibility of restricted access to abortion in the future, it is anticipated that the clientele of the CPC ministry will greatly increase in the months and years ahead. These ministries of compassion offer free pregnancy tests; education on abortion through pamphlets, videos, and other educational materials; free maternity clothes and baby accessories; referrals for low-cost medical and legal help; referrals for temporary housing; and on-going friendship and encouragement. While abortion clinics typically demand cash or a major credit card before services will be performed, the CPCs offer all services free.

The CPC ministry is making a difference across the country by saving lives, changing hearts, and introducing people to Jesus Christ. It is estimated that in 1989, CAC-affiliated centers ministered to more than 200,000 women with the vast majority of these choosing to carry their babies to term. The stories of these brave women who, with the support and encouragement of a local CPC, chose life are a testimony to the power of God to work good out of all situations—even a crisis pregnancy.

Against All Odds She Chose Life

"Rita," a beautiful minority woman who was majoring in civil engineering at a prominent university, had an extremely bright future.[2] During the middle of her junior year, however, an unexpected roadblock was thrown into her plans for future success—she became pregnant. She cared about her boyfriend and hoped they would marry some day, but a baby at this point, she felt, would ruin her life.

Rita's friends urged her to abort. Her parents were concerned that she not drop out of school and become another minority mother on public assistance, and they too urged her to obtain an abortion. And her boyfriend told her that if she carried the pregnancy to term, he would refuse to support the child.

With this intense pressure upon her, Rita made an appointment with an abortion clinic only to cancel on the day of her scheduled abortion. She then rescheduled her appointment, and even scheduled two additional appointments at different clinics to make sure that she followed through. It was a good strategy. If she cancelled the first appointment, she had two other scheduled abortions to fall back on. But something within Rita would not let her keep any of her appointments.

Finally, at the urging of a friend, Rita made an appointment at her local crisis pregnancy center. At this point, the only advice she had been given by family and friends was that a baby would ruin her life and she should get an abortion as soon as possible. Rita, however, was desperately looking for someone to give her some hope. She firmly believed that another option had to be available, and she hoped beyond hope that her appointment at the CPC would reveal this to her.

At the CPC Rita found the support and encouragement she needed to carry her baby to term. Her CPC counselor kept in frequent contact with her during her pregnancy and offered a shoulder to cry on during the rough times. The CPC counselor was privileged to be Rita's birth coach during labor and delivery. In the delivery room along with the counselor was Rita's mother, who months before had urged her daughter to get an abortion. When the baby boy was born, Rita's mother looked at the CPC counselor and with tears in her eyes said: "Thank you for all you've done." This new grandmother bonded quickly to her grandson and became a support by providing needed child care while Rita finished school and obtained her first job.

Today, Rita has completed her degree and is working successfully in an engineering job in her city. Life as a single parent can be complicated (the father of the child still refuses to pay support), but it is nonetheless rewarding. Despite adverse circumstances, Rita has learned that God can meet her day-to-day needs. Through the love and care of her CPC counselor and against all odds, Rita chose life. It is a decision she can live with happily.

"Lord, How Could This Be Happening to Me?"

"Robert" is a special baby—alive and happy because supporters cared enough to keep the local CPC open and operating. Robert's mother, "Wendy," was a newly committed Christian when she came to her local CPC to obtain a free pregnancy test. When the test result was positive, fear gripped her. "Lord, how could this be happening to me?" she cried. "I've already repented, Lord. Now I'm pregnant."

Abortion was not a consideration for Wendy, especially after seeing the CPC presentation and talking with her counselor. Wendy loved children and she wanted to keep her baby. Yet the months ahead were difficult.

Her CPC counselor stayed with her throughout the pregnancy. Together they discussed her options and came up with a plan to help her keep the baby. However, after much prayer and tears, Wendy knew that God wanted her to place this baby for adoption.

The thought of never seeing her baby was unbearable, so she asked the Lord for a family who would love her, as well as her baby, and allow her to keep in close contact with them. During Wendy's last month of pregnancy she met a wonderful Christian couple who fell in love with her. They were at the hospital when the baby was born, and since the adoption they have kept a special and close relationship with Wendy.

Today, Wendy is a CPC volunteer counselor. She has learned through her own struggle what it means to rely on the Lord, and she knows the importance of having a committed CPC volunteer at one's side during a crisis pregnancy. God is now using her to bless other young women, and her work and commitment is a blessing to other volunteers at the center.

A Single Parent Learns How to Cope

Baby "Melody" is alive and well today, thanks to a mother who relied on God's conviction in her life and a local crisis pregnancy center that cared. "It was quite a shock," exclaimed "Mary," the baby's grandmother, to learn that her unmarried daughter was carrying a child. Once she recovered, however, Mary strongly supported carrying this baby to term. "I knew from my nurse's training that this was an unborn baby and that the way this life was conceived was immaterial."

"Carrie," Melody's mother, was studying to be a nurse and working as an aide when she discovered she was pregnant. A counselor at the clinic where Carrie went for her pregnancy test asked if she was considering an abortion. "For a minute I thought, could I have an abortion?" Then she visualized "standing in front of the judgment throne," being shown "the daughter you always wanted," and God asking her to justify the abortion. "It would have been selfish of me," she says in retrospect.

Carrie immediately discussed her situation with her parents, who were shocked but supportive. She and her mother went for counseling at a CAC-affiliated CPC, where, with family and CPC support, she was able to work out her plans for raising the child as a single parent.

Carrie temporarily delayed her studies and gave birth with her mother at her side. With the help of her parents as live-in babysitters, she was able to finish nursing school. Now, as a nurse, Carrie works a 7:00 P.M. to 3:00 A.M. shift which allows her to sleep a few hours and then be with her daughter for the day. That schedule is exhausting at times, yet Carrie has no regrets, and she believes that were it not for the CPC she may have made a tragic decision. "Melody has fulfilled all my expectations. I feel sorry for all those women who, on the anniversary days of their abortions, think, 'Would it have been a boy or a girl?' "

"A Lot of Pain and Suffering"

"Debby" had an abortion eight years prior to the birth of her daughter. The birth of this child, however, made her realize that she hadn't recovered from the grief and remorse she felt after her abortion. Although she was happily married at the time of her baby's birth, she needed extensive help and counseling to put her past mistake in the proper perspective.

"I went through a lot of pain and suffering," she says. At the time of her abortion she was in her early twenties, single, living with a roommate, and working on her career. "The father of the child said he would support whatever decision I made," she recalls. "We weren't talking about getting married. At the time I felt I didn't know how I'd raise a child by myself. I decided if I had an abortion it would be the easiest way to get on with my life."

Debby rationalized that having the abortion quickly was best because she believed if she had an early abortion she would not be killing a real child. So she made an appointment and her boyfriend took her to the abortion clinic. Even though she was frightened when she heard the noises and felt the vibrations from the suction machine, she went through with the procedure.

"Afterwards I cried because I felt ugly inside," she remembers. "They said, 'Put it behind you and get on with your life.' " She tried to follow this advice, which worked well until the birth of her daughter. Then remorse took over and she felt "guilty and ashamed" of what she had done.

Post-abortion counseling sessions at Debby's local crisis pregnancy center helped her experience the forgiveness that only Jesus Christ can give. Debby says, "I learned a lot from the Bible and felt that I was really healed." She also learned she was not the only woman experiencing pain after an abortion. To her it was comforting to know that "other people were having regrets for what they had done in the past."

For Debby, the CPC has been invaluable by helping her understand the meaning of forgiveness and how God can put the pieces back together in a life broken by abortion. She wishes someone had counseled her about alternatives to abortion when she was pregnant. "Had I known, I don't know what I would have done. I would have at least known more about making the decision. If I'd known more about adoption, for example, I would have been more open to my alternatives."

"My Parents Will Kill Me"

"Melissa," a nineteen-year-old pastor's daughter, came to her local CPC suspecting she was pregnant. Since she did not want to be identified, she furnished a false name and phone number on the center's information forms. When she learned that the pregnancy test was positive, she determined to obtain an abortion because, as she stated later, if her plight were known "my parents would kill me."

The CPC counselor's attempt to follow up with Melissa after her appointment was unsuccessful due to the false name and phone number. The counselor could do nothing else but pray for God to intervene. Two weeks later, Melissa came back to the CPC still intent on having the abortion but wanting to talk further.

As they talked, Melissa was encouraged to tell her parents about her situation and give them a chance to respond. The counselor, a mother of a daughter herself, told Melissa she might be surprised at their reaction. Reluctantly, Melissa agreed to talk to her parents and temporarily delay any efforts to obtain an abortion.

When Melissa told her mother and father she was pregnant, she received a surprise. As both of them listened, tears came into their eyes and they told her they understood more than she could ever realize. Nineteen years previously they were in the same situation. Because abortion was not an option for them, they chose to be married and raise their baby the best they could. That little baby, of course, was Melissa. As Melissa understood the circumstances surrounding her own conception and birth, she embraced both of her parents with hugs and tears and a determination to give life to the child within her.

Today Melissa is married to the father of their baby daughter and the family is doing well. Both Melissa and her husband have committed their lives to the Lord and are active in their church. Melissa shudders to think what her life would be like had she not listened to her CPC counselor and failed to trust her parents enough to talk with them.

* * * * * * *

The stories recounted here are a small sampling of the success stories happening hundreds of times every day at the crisis pregnancy centers around the country. By receiving loving Christlike support, women in crisis are given encouragement and hope and are responding by choosing life.

One would think that these ministries, which are privately funded and provide all services free of charge, would be well received in the secular world. Yet the abortion industry, in coordination with friends in the media, has attacked the crisis pregnancy centers with vicious accusations making these ministries of compassion controversial in many circles. Just as Nehemiah faced opposition to his reconstruction project, so have the rebuilding efforts of the CPCs come under intense attack.

Crisis Pregnancy Centers under Attack

Dr. Marvin N. Olasky, professor of journalism at the University of Texas at Austin, undertook an extensive study of a highly successful negative public relations campaign to discredit the crisis pregnancy centers. Olasky outlines the details of this effort in his article, "Abortion Rights: Anatomy of a Negative Campaign" (see appendix D), which was based on newspaper articles and telephone interviews with key individuals at Planned Parenthood, the National Abortion Federation (NAF), and the Religious Coalition for Abortion Rights (RCAR).

Olasky talked extensively with Amy Sutnick, public information associate for Planned Parenthood of New York City, who informed him that she began planning the campaign in October 1985, and that by February 1987 she had spent close to one thousand hours on the project.[3]

The efforts of Planned Parenthood and Sutnick focused around accusations that the CPCs are "deceptive"—that they get women to come to them by masquerading as abortion clinics or abortion referral agencies. It is further charged that the CPCs give women misleading and inaccurate information regarding abortion and abortion procedures. According to Sutnick, the two goals of their campaign were "to make women aware of what was going on, and to stop those clinics from deceiving people."[4]

In truth, the majority of the organizations who sponsor crisis pregnancy centers denounce any tactics that are less than forthright and truthful.[5] The Christian Action Council's Statement of Principle for its Crisis Pregnancy Ministry specifically states: "The CPC is committed to integrity in dealing with clients, earning their trust and providing promised information and services. The CPC denounces any form of deception in its corporate advertising or individual conversations with its clients." All CAC-affiliated CPCs must agree with this philosophy before they are allowed to affiliate, and all CPCs are strongly encouraged to advertise in the Yellow Pages under the heading "Abortion Alternatives." Further, it is CAC policy that all telephone inquiries about the availability of abortion or abortion referrals be answered truthfully that those services are not available at the CPC. Other pro-life organizations, such as Birthright, have similar policies. Despite this, proponents of the negative campaign chose to emphasize the questionable tactics of a small minority of abortion alternative centers, claiming that all CPCs use deceptive tactics.[6]

Sutnick's efforts paid off when she convinced a reporter for *USA Today* to write an article about this supposed deception. The article appeared in the July 23, 1986, issue and, according to Olasky, "could hardly have been better from the standpoint of those opposed to pro-life efforts." A brief story was published on the front page of the "Lifestyle" section, followed by a major article on page 4D under the headline, "Anti-abortionists Masquerade as Clinics." One-fourth of the article "was direct quotation and paraphrase from Sutnick, who described her visit to two Manhattan counseling centers, where she was 'overwhelmed by the brainwashing techniques and the lies.' " Interviewed seven months after the story was published, the reporter, Marlene Perrin, said: "The leads were provided by Planned Parenthood. I wouldn't call them an objective source, but a lot of what they sent were newspaper reports, and they had people I could talk to."[7]

Planned Parenthood was joined in these efforts by two pro-abortion organizations, the Religious Coalition for Abortion Rights (RCAR) and the National Abortion Federation (NAF), a trade association for abortion businesses. For their part, RCAR held a press conference in Washington, D.C., on January 22, 1986, which received extensive coverage and led to stories in other publications. At the press conference, William Schulz, president of the Unitarian Universalist Association, called the CPCs "a new and insidious stage" of the pro-life movement. "Like spiders, they lure their victims into their webs and then apply psychological terror."[8]

NAF also attempted to manipulate the media to discredit the CPCs. NAF executive director Barbara Radford stated: "What worked best was to find someone in the local media who was interested, put them on to it, and let them do the work. . . . You don't come right out and ask them if they are [pro-choice]," she said, "but you get a sense that you can work with them."[9]

Planned Parenthood and the NAF also jointly published a document titled, "A Consumer's Alert to Deception, Harassment and Medical Malpractice." A section of this document reads:

> In their zeal to stop women from having abortions, anti-abortion activists have set up "counseling centers" in hundreds of communities around the country. Far from true counseling, these centers are designed to misinform and intimidate women—some will go to any lengths necessary to dissuade women from ending their pregnancies.

Increasingly, women complain about their unwitting encounters with anti-abortion centers. Women describe being harassed, intimidated, and given blatantly false information. They complain that confidential information they provided was used against them. In some cases, they describe instances of medical malpractice which threatened their lives.

Planned Parenthood has gone one step further in its fervor to discredit the work of the CPCs. In 1989 full-page ads which slandered CPC efforts were placed in *Time* magazine and other national publications. The ad carried the headline, "Would you lie to a pregnant teenager?" and claimed the following:

So-called "pro-lifers" have launched a campaign of violence and intimidation against women and health professionals.

But their lowest tactic is deception.

Across the country, thousands of "crisis pregnancy centers" offering "free pregnancy tests" have opened with the sole purpose of luring desperate women to a session of lies about abortion.

These outfits aren't staffed by medical professionals. The pregnancy test they offer is an over-the-counter kit available at any drugstore. The results are often withheld. And "counseling" means being left alone in a darkened room to watch a barrage of horrifying and misleading slides and films.

But the deception may not stop there. According to police, a center in California tried to lure a pregnant 14-year-old away from home, even supplying her parents with a letter saying she had been awarded an overseas scholarship. By the time her parents had discovered the ruse, it was too late for an abortion.

Other woman have been promised material support during their pregnancies: a referral to the local welfare office.

Meanwhile, women are being denied access to birth control that can avert an unintended pregnancy—and information about the actual medical risks of pregnancy before full maturity.

Law enforcement and public health officials have denounced these tactics as false and misleading. At Planned Parenthood, we discuss alternatives in a responsible way. But extremists who lie are endangering people in crisis. And that shows no regard for anyone's life.[10]

This negative publicity generated by Planned Parenthood and its cohorts has had an effect on the operation of some CPCs. One CAC affiliate in northern California has had complaints filed against it to state health regulatory agencies five times, only to be exonerated by the state five times. In Seattle the CAC affiliate has received a continuing bombardment of negative press and harassment from pro-abortion picketers, including a brick thrown through a window with a threatening note attached. The student newspaper at the University of Virginia has harrassed the Crisis Pregnancy Center in Charlottesville with negative articles, editorials, and periodic letters to the editor from members of the campus chapter of the National Organization of Women (NOW). Other CPCs around the country report periodic negative press, usually generated by a local chapter of NOW or Planned Parenthood.

Despite active opposition, the work of the crisis pregnancy centers has not been deterred. CPCs around the country continue to report a growing number of clients, with the vast majority of them choosing life for their babies. In light of this, the strong opposition from the abortion industry and the pro-abortion movement is understandable. The abortion industry has a financial stake in the abortion issue, and every woman who chooses life represents a lost profit for an abortionist.

The pro-abortion movement has built its influence and prestige upon the false premise that abortion is a constitutional right, and this belief has become dogma in the ideological tenets of feminism, humanism, and certain segments of the liberal establishment. To call into question this sectarian dogma, which has planted its roots deep into American culture, challenges the legitimacy of the work and influence of those who have promoted abortion and the multi-million dollar industry behind them. Is it any wonder that the CPCs have come under such intensive assault for what they are accomplishing?

The Work Must Continue until the Wall Is Rebuilt

Despite fervent antagonism from pro-abortion proponents, the ministry of the CPCs continues through the committed work of volunteers who, like Nehemiah, will not be deterred from the task God has called them to accomplish. Nehemiah faced intense opposition to his rebuilding efforts, but he was not hindered from his calling. The same is true for all those who dare to challenge the dominant institutions that promote abortion as an acceptable solution to a social problem.

Those who work at the crisis pregnancy centers will come under keen attack and opposition, but through their efforts lives are saved and relationships are restored. Such results run counter to the abortion industry and the destruction it promotes throughout the land. The pro-life movement must resolve to continue the vital work of the CPCs in the 1990s if we are to be successful in our efforts to rebuild the wall of protection.

Furthermore, the establishment of additional crisis pregnancy centers throughout America must be a priority on the pro-life agenda for the coming decade. Every major metropolitan area should have a network of CPCs. If your community does not have such a network in place, perhaps God is calling you to establish the first CPC in your area. For more information on how to successfully start a CPC, write to the Christian Action Council at 101 West Broad Street, Suite 500, Falls Church, Virginia, 22046.

Notes

1. "Anti-Abortionists Masquerade as Clinics," *USA Today*, 23 July 1986, 4D.

2. All stories reported in this chapter are true and accurate accounts of CPC clients who have consented to having their stories told. However, all names have been changed to protect the privacy of the individuals involved.

3. Marvin N. Olasky, "Abortion Rights: Anatomy of a Negative Campaign," *Public Relations Review*, Autumn 1987, 15.

4. Ibid.

5. In preparing his article Olasky interviewed numerous parties involved with crisis pregnancy centers, including CPC directors, and concluded: "The majority of counseling centers offer free pregnancy tests to draw clients, as many pro-choice groups and abortion businesses do, but they tell callers that they do not perform abortions. Centers affiliated with Birthright, the Christian Action Council, and other organizations are encouraged to emphasize, in the words of one director, 'the Christian duty of telling the truth.' Interviews show that in order to obey one commandment against killing (with the implication that Christians should attempt to save the lives of others), most pro-life volunteers are not willing to disobey the commandment about bearing false witness." (Olasky, "Abortion Rights," 14-15.)

6. Ibid., 15.

7. Ibid., 17.

8. Ibid., 16.

9. Ibid.

10. Planned Parenthood advertisement, *Time*, 6 March 1989.

CHAPTER SIX

A
Political Strategy
for the 1990s

The second section of the wall to be reconstructed is a well-organized political strategy calculated to restore the right to life in the laws of our land. In our rebuilding efforts we must elect pro-life officials at all levels of government who will enact protective legislation for the unborn.

For many Christians involvement in the political process is repugnant. Indeed, politics can be a dirty game of name-calling and mudslinging. Because of this, many Christians believe our sole purpose is to evangelize the unsaved; political involvement, if undertaken at all, must take a back seat to the true mission of the church.

Yet throughout history, whenever the church of Jesus Christ has failed to obey the commands of God it has become complacent towards evil and has unwittingly become its ally. To ignore our societal responsibilities and the ills of our government will grant free reign to the forces of evil in the institutions of America. We cannot let this happen. We must live out the truths of Scripture in a culture which disregards and mocks the claims of Christ. We must challenge the powers of darkness in every realm, including the political arena.

As citizens of this republic we share the responsibility for the present moral state of our nation. In addition, as Christians we are responsible to God and to the laws of his kingdom. This responsibility requires that we seek to implement divine justice throughout the land. The law of God—the natural law—is the basis for establishing justice among our citizens. Through the divine prescriptions for justice found in Scripture, the guilty are punished and the innocent are protected and delivered from their oppressors. The prophet Zechariah says:

> "This is what the LORD Almighty says: 'Administer true justice; show mercy and compassion to one another. Do not oppress the widow or the fatherless, the alien or the poor. In your hearts do not think evil of each other' " (Zechariah 7:9-10).

We cannot ignore the teaching of Jesus that his church must stand for righteousness and be the salt and light of our nation. The establishment of justice requires that we work within the political arena to end abortion-on-demand. While personal sins must be corrected with personal repentance, corporate and national sins, such as the law which permits abortion-on-demand, must be changed through the lawmaking process. This change will occur only through the combination of a strategically planned political agenda and the committed grass roots political efforts of the pro-life movement.

The Political Battle Ahead

The enactment of laws to protect the unborn requires that we elect pro-life majorities in the state legislatures and in the Congress. The pro-life movement currently has a slight majority in the U.S. House of Representatives but is in the minority in the Senate. With President Bush in office there is sufficient political clout at the federal level, for the time being, to stop pro-abortion initiatives. However, there is not sufficient support to advance the pro-life cause and pass a constitutional amendment that will overturn *Roe* and grant personhood to the unborn.[1]

At the state level, pro-life support varies. Presently, thirty-five states prohibit public funding of abortions and five others have been enjoined by state courts from enforcing similar bans.[2] This does not necessarily mean that these states will enact other restrictions on abortion. A state legislature may be persuaded that it is unwise to fund abortions with tax dollars but might not agree that abortion should be otherwise restricted. However, these states should be considered prime battlegrounds for legislative initiatives to restrict and possibly prohibit abortions during the next decade. Of these states, fifteen have anti-abortion laws on the books which have not been repealed since the issuance of *Roe*.[3] These laws would become immediately enforceable should *Roe* be reversed.

This present assessment indicates that while the pro-life movement has significant support in many state legislatures and in Congress, we fall far short of the political clout needed to end abortion in America. Electing pro-life majorities in both houses of Congress and in every state legislature during the 1990s must have priority if we are to succeed.

Since the *Webster* decision, the pro-abortion movement has organized with a vengeance and they have been effective. Three highly publicized elections during November 1989 were promoted by the pro-abortion movement as indicators of public sentiment on abortion. In each election—the gubernatorial race in Virginia, the race for mayor of New York City, and the gubernatorial race in New Jersey—the candidate who supported abortion won, although the elections in Virginia and New York City were extremely close. While I believe the results of these elections are inconclusive as to what Americans believe about abortion, the pro-abortion movement has used these perceived "victories" to claim momentum and to declare that the majority of Americans are "pro-choice" on abortion. The national media, for the most part, has promoted this perception. For the pro-life movement to ultimately prevail, we must counter the other side's public relations claims that they represent the majority opinion in America.

Is "Pro-choice" the Majority?

Abortion proponents claim with great pride that they represent the majority opinion in America, and these pronouncements have intensified since the issuance of the *Webster* decision. A recent post-*Webster* memorandum from Kate Michelman, executive director for the National Abortion Rights Action League (NARAL), is typical of these claims of majority status. In this memo Michelman states that immediately following the *Webster* decision:

> [NARAL] organized with a determination as fierce as any we have ever felt. In key elections across the nation, we set out to send the most powerful message possible to the politicians: "IF YOU'RE OUT OF TOUCH WITH THE PRO-CHOICE MAJORITY, YOU'RE OUT OF OFFICE."

> We organized neighborhood walks door to door, ran newspaper ads exposing anti-choice positions, and operated targeted phone banks to identify pro-choice voters and urge them to vote. In Virginia alone, for example, NARAL's independent expenditure campaign spent nearly $400,000 in a carefully researched and targeted campaign to help defeat anti-choice candidate Marshall Coleman.

Just before the election, we helped win a resounding victory when Florida Governor Robert Martinez—who had called a post-*Webster* special session of the state legislature to try to restrict abortion in Florida—saw every one of his proposals go down to humiliating defeat.

And on Election Day, the message rang out just as loudly and clearly—a wake-up call for George Bush and any other politician who thinks they can ignore the majority of the American voters.[4]

Michelman's claims of majority status for the pro-abortion view is a common one heard from other organizations that promote abortion. These abortion advocates assert that public opinion polls indicate that a majority of Americans are pro-choice and support abortion-on-demand. Yet a careful analysis of the numerous public opinion polls available shows just the opposite. The American public strongly opposes abortion-on-demand and supports substantial restrictions on the practice of abortion.

The *Boston Globe* published an insightful poll in March 1989 under the front-page headline, "Most In U.S. Favor Ban on Majority of Abortions, Poll Finds."[5] In reporting its findings, the newspaper cited a 1987 survey from the Alan Guttmacher Institute (the research arm of Planned Parenthood) which acknowledged that three-quarters of American women obtaining an abortion did so because they felt that having a baby would interfere with their career, school, or other responsibilities. Of this group, according to the Guttmacher findings, about two-thirds said they could not afford to have a child, and half said they did not want to be a single parent, citing problems in the relationship with the father. The *Globe* summarizes its poll data by saying:

When pregnancy poses financial or emotional strain, or when the woman is alone or a teenager—the reasons given by most women seeking abortions—an overwhelming majority of Americans believes abortion should be illegal.[6]

Of those questioned, 25 percent stated that they oppose abortion in all circumstances while 53 percent said they oppose abortion except in certain limited circumstances. In other words, 78 percent of those polled oppose abortion-on-demand.

Among those who said abortion should be allowed in certain circumstances, 82 percent said it should be illegal to obtain an abortion because a woman "feels it's the wrong time in her life to have a child"; 75 percent opposed abortion simply because "a woman . . . cannot afford to have a child"; 83 percent said abortion should be illegal in a case where the "father is unwilling to help raise a child"; 64 percent said abortion should not be allowed simply because "pregnancy would cause too much emotional strain"; 93 percent opposed abortion for sex selection purposes; 89 percent opposed abortion "as a means of birth control"; and 81 percent opposed abortion simply because the father is absent from the home.

The limited circumstances where the majority polled by the *Boston Globe* said abortion should be allowed were in cases where pregnancy results from rape (86 percent) or incest (83 percent), or in cases where there is likely to be a genetic deformity of the baby (65 percent). Yet these circumstances account for less than 3 percent of all abortions annually.[7] In other words, according to this poll, the vast majority of Americans (78 percent) oppose 97 percent of the abortions performed in this country.

Another national poll published by the *Los Angeles Times* on March 19, 1989, came to similar conclusions. A strong majority of the adults polled opposed abortion "when a married woman does not want any more children" (54 percent); "as a form of birth control" (80 percent); or "no matter what reason" (57 percent). In reporting these findings the newspaper stated:

Among those interviewed, 61% said they believe abortion to be "morally wrong." Just 22% said it is "morally right." Even women who have had an abortion are divided on the moral question, with 37% considering it to be "wrong," 39% "right" and 24% "not sure." Indeed, a large majority—57%—think "abortion is murder.". . . It even is considered "murder" by a third of the women who have had an abortion and a fourth of the people who generally favor it.[8]

An interesting poll which verifies that Americans oppose unrestricted abortion comes from none other than NARAL. In a telephone survey in December 1987, NARAL discovered that only 39 percent of the public believe abortion should be unrestricted and "allowed under any circumstances to any woman who wants one."[9] In other words, according to NARAL's own polling, 61 percent of the American public supports restrictions on abortion.

The findings of this NARAL poll were similar to the findings of a poll conducted by *USA Today* in early January 1990. This poll found that 37 percent of adults nationwide believe abortion should always be a decision left to a woman and her doctor. The remaining 63 percent believe the law should be changed to allow significant restrictions on abortion.[10]

The findings of these polls are verified by numerous additional polls taken around the time of the *Webster* decision. Those samplings show strong public opinion against abortion-on-demand and solid support for restrictions on abortion.

In light of this, it is difficult to understand the claims of NARAL and its pro-abortion allies that support for unrestricted abortion-on-demand constitutes the majority opinion in America. To the contrary, the pro-life movement should take heart in knowing that the American public is uncomfortable with abortion and there is room to maneuver in the political arena to advance the pro-life cause. Although Americans are uncomfortable with a total ban on abortion, they show strong support for legislation that will greatly reduce the number of abortions performed. (For a detailed look at the results of these polls and their implications for various legislative endeavors, see Appendix E, "Public Opinion and Abortion Restrictions.")

Framing the Issue

There are clear trends in the public opinion of this nation from which to derive a winning political strategy for a pro-life candidate. To be successful, pro-life candidates must understand public opinion on abortion and then properly frame the discussion of the abortion issue around those themes where they and the public agree.

For example, it is clear that Americans are uncomfortable with abortion-on-demand and they oppose it. Only in the cases of rape, incest, and fetal deformity does it appear that the public presently supports abortion. Yet these "hard" cases account for a very small number of abortions annually. The pro-life candidate must not allow a pro-abortion opponent to frame the issue by these "hard" cases. If this happens, the pro-life candidate runs the risk of being painted as one who lacks compassion and is insensitive to women. Rather, the pro-life candidate must seize the initiative and emphasize that any candidate who supports *Roe* v. *Wade* supports abortion at any time during a woman's pregnancy for any reason, which amounts to support for abortion for birth control and convenience. This is drastically out of step with mainstream public thinking. By properly framing the discussion, the pro-life candidate has aligned himself with the majority opinion in America. The pro-abortion candidate, on the other hand, will be put on the defensive and have to respond as to which circumstances he believes abortion should be allowed under the law.

The polls reveal that the public strongly supports restrictions that will dramatically reduce the number of abortions each year. Measures that require parental consent or parental notification before a minor may obtain an abortion are endorsed by all segments of American society. A majority of men and women support requirements for waiting periods before an abortion may be obtained and for notice to the father of the child. And the public is particularly strong in opposing abortion for birth control or sex selection.

In short, the American public does not take kindly to abortion for trivial reasons. As the *Boston Globe* poll noted, Americans strongly oppose the main reasons that women in America seek abortions. Pro-life candidates should emphasize this and force their opponents to clarify whether or not they oppose legislative initiatives that restrict abortion for such reasons.

The 1989 race for governor of Virginia gives an excellent example of a pro-life candidate who failed to properly frame the public discussion of the issue and lost an extremely close election. Republican Marshall Coleman was publicly committed to the pro-life position while his opponent, Democrat Douglas Wilder, passionately supported abortion. Coleman was advised to avoid the abortion issue at all costs. He therefore employed a passive approach, trying for as long as he could not to mention abortion in public.

Douglas Wilder, on the other hand, made support for abortion a central theme of his campaign, attacking Coleman relentlessly in campaign ads and speeches. Morton Blackwell, Virginia Republican National Committeeman and a committed activist for Marshall Coleman, describes the Coleman strategy and response:

> The Coleman campaign allowed Wilder to spend what I estimate was more than $2.5 million on unanswered attack advertising on the abortion issue.

Of course, Wilder's advertising stressed the question of abortions for rape and incest victims, an aspect of the issue on which polls showed the pro-abortion position to be a big majority. But the Coleman campaign never held Wilder accountable for his positions on those abortion-related issues on which majority opinion is against the extreme pro-abortion activists. Among them:

- Sex selection abortions
- Fetal viability testing
- Parental consent
- Abortion as birth control[11]

Coleman's inaction gave Wilder free rein to spend millions of dollars exploiting the abortion issue to his advantage. For many voters the abortion issue was not a decisive one, yet Coleman's failure to respond to the political attacks led them to believe Wilder's charges that Coleman was an extremist. Coleman could have easily deflected those attacks had he demanded that Wilder publicly state his position on sex-selection abortions and other cases where public opinion is decidedly in the pro-life camp.

Marshall Coleman ultimately lost the race by less than 7,000 votes out of the 1.7 million cast. It was the closest gubernatorial race in Virginia's history, and the Wilder campaign and the media were quick to boast that Coleman lost because of his stand on abortion. But it was not Coleman's position on abortion which cost him the race; it was his failure to properly frame the discussion of the issue. By allowing his opponent to discuss the issue on his terms, Coleman failed to capitalize on the strong voter sentiment against abortion-on-demand. Instead, he appeared as a candidate fearful of the issue and hesitant to respond to the Wilder attacks. Many voters reluctantly concluded that the attacks bore truth, and they voted for Wilder. As Blackwell puts it: "Coleman vs. Wilder is a great lesson in campaign dynamics. It was not a referendum on abortion. In a referendum, both sides are publicly discussed."[12]

Coleman made another crucial mistake in failing to properly discuss the issue—he offended many pro-life voters who were a key element of his political coalition. The pro-life voter is intensely committed to ending abortion and is more likely than the pro-choice voter to base his vote solely on this issue. It is essential that the pro-life candidate not waffle or backtrack on his opposition to abortion or else he runs the risk that many of these voters will stay home on election day out of frustration.

One has to wonder whether Coleman would have inspired at least an additional 7,000 Christians who did not vote to turn out and vote for him had he strongly defended the right to life of the unborn. Had he done so, I believe he would now be the governor of Virginia.

A Legislative Strategy for the 1990s

Electing pro-life majorities in the state legislatures and in the United States Congress is the first item on the pro-life movement's political agenda in the 1990s. However, once these majorities are obtained (and there are majorities in many state legislatures right now) it is crucial that there be a unified front within the pro-life movement which will insure the passage of laws to end abortion.

Historically, the pro-life movement has been divided on political strategy and has fought within its own ranks. The results of this infighting have been disastrous, insuring the defeat of many pro-life initiatives. As Jesus said, "a house divided against itself cannot stand." The tragic fact of this division is that it has not been based on differences in philosophy but rather on disagreements in strategy.

A crucial disagreement is over what exceptions to abortion should be allowed in legislative proposals. A consistent pro-life philosophy holds that the only valid exception to abortion is the rare case when the life of the mother would be endangered if the pregnancy were carried to term.[13] Exceptions in the "hard" cases of rape, incest, and fetal deformity have universally been rejected as not compatible with the sanctity-of-life ethic.[14]

As the decade of the nineties begins, we have to concede that while the American public is opposed to abortion-on-demand (that is, abortion for convenience or birth control) it does support abortion in the cases of rape, incest, and fetal deformity. This puts the pro-life legislator in a bit of a quandary. Does he support legislation that has public support but allows for these exceptions, or does he insist on a bill that is "pure" before he will support it? The same dilemma exists for the pro-life voter who is working diligently to see protective legislation passed for the unborn. In many legislatures, those laws will not pass unless they contain the "hard" case exceptions.

Opposing legal abortion in these cases makes pro-lifers appear uncaring and cruel, even though there are countless testimonies of these tragedies turning into triumph for the mother and child. On the other hand, supporting these exceptions makes pro-lifers inconsistent. If we believe there are some cases where abortion is justified, why not include other exceptions as well? The dilemma becomes more complex when we factor in the reality that legislation barring abortion except in the hard cases would end the vast majority of abortions.

I was recently at a meeting of national pro-life leaders where one participant said the pro-life movement must demand unconditional surrender like the U.S. government did at the end of World War II—that is, we must not support exceptions to abortion in any legislation. While I agree that our ultimate goal is to completely end abortion in America, we, as a political movement, have not yet marched into Berlin. Rather, the *Webster* decision only landed us on Normandy Beach. We have many battles to fight before we arrive at our intended destination.

As we advance towards Berlin (and eventual unconditional surrender), we will face some setbacks. We may be required in some state legislatures to temporarily accept "hard" case exceptions in order to save the vast majority of unborn babies who are now subject to abortion for any reason. Such laws, if passed in every state, would end 97 percent of all abortions in America and make significant progress towards our goal of an abortion-free America by 2001. Compromising on legislation in order to limit most abortions is not the same as compromising on principle. However, refusing to back legislation because it is not "pure" enough means the continuing slaughter of unborn babies at any time during a woman's pregnancy, for any reason.

Using *temporary* tactics to save as many babies from abortion as quickly as possible does not mean we are unconcerned about all babies subject to abortion. We must eventually convince the American public and our legislators that even babies conceived from an act of rape or incest, or those who are physically handicapped, have the God-given inalienable right to life. This task will require an intensified commitment from the pro-life movement to educate the American public. And it will require God's people to apply the Nehemiah Principles as we continue in this struggle for the sanctity of human life.

A Legislative Agenda for the 1990s

In order for the pro-life movement to be politically successful in the 1990s, we must attack abortion at both the state and federal levels. We must continue to pursue with vigor the passage of a federal Human Life Constitutional Amendment which will reverse *Roe* v. *Wade* and grant personhood to the unborn. The constitutional recognition of the personhood of the unborn will ultimately guarantee an end to abortion in America. We must not forget that this is our ultimate goal in rebuilding the wall of protection for innocent human life.

In addition, a successful federal legislative strategy requires that we protect the pro-life advances made in the last decade, such as the federal prohibition of tax funding of abortion in the Hyde Amendment. Likewise, the legislative achievements of the 1980s which prohibit federal funding of "population control" organizations that promote abortion must survive.[15]

The pro-life movement does not yet have sufficient support in the U.S. Congress to pass a Constitutional Amendment, and pro-abortion forces have maintained a consistent attack on laws that prohibit abortion funding in hopes of eroding the pro-life legislative gains of the eighties. Therefore, a successful political strategy for the 1990s requires that we give priority to the election of pro-life congressmen and senators. If we allow the pro-life support in Congress to further erode, we may tragically see the gains from the previous ten years reversed. And such a scenario means, among other things, the reinstitution of federal funding of abortion. Further, if we are serious about our commitment to the personhood of the unborn, we must elect serious-minded representatives who are committed to seeing protection for the unborn placed within the text of our Constitution.

Effective pro-life political activity at the state level is now possible for the first time since 1973 because of the *Webster* decision. The pro-life movement may now politically maneuver in state legislatures to protect unborn children. Legislation that prohibits abortion, except in the rare cases where the mother's life is endangered, should be passed immediately in all state legislatures where this is politically feasible. While it is an open question as to whether a state may prohibit abortion outright in this manner, such legislation would set the stage for a Supreme Court review of the fundamental premises of *Roe* which were left intact after *Webster.*[16] While such state laws may not be immediately enforceable, they would hasten the day when *Roe* is eventually discarded.

In states where it is not yet politically achievable to ban abortion, legislative initiatives must be calculated to accomplish two purposes.

First, all legislative undertakings must challenge the fundamental premise of *Roe* which says that the constitutional right to privacy recognized by the Supreme Court is broad enough to allow for abortion. If a sufficient number of states pass legislation of this nature, a case that will challenge *Roe* directly will eventually make its way to the Supreme Court and give the Court a vehicle for reversal. The eventual reversal of *Roe* v. *Wade* and the granting of constitutional personhood to the unborn is the chief political objective for the pro-life movement in the 1990s. All legislative endeavors must be undertaken with this ultimate goal in mind.

Second, state legislation must be as restrictive of abortion as is politically attainable to immediately protect as many babies from abortion as possible. The specifics of such legislation will differ depending upon the political dynamics of each state. To hasten the day when *Roe* v. *Wade* is reversed, however, every statute passed should open the door wider for future restrictions until abortion is eventually prohibited. Such a step-by-step process will insure the eventual direct challenge of *Roe*.

With these two points in mind, the following legislative initiatives should be pursued at the state level to restrict abortion and set the stage for an eventual Supreme Court reversal of *Roe* v. *Wade*. (Sample statutes of some of the suggested legislation are included in the appendices of this book.)

1. Legislation Banning Abortion for Birth Control

As the polls indicate, the American public strongly opposes the use of abortion as birth control. Yet abortion is being used today for just this purpose. Legislation that would ban abortion for birth control (defining "birth control" as any reason for abortion except in the cases of rape, incest, and fetal deformity) would end most abortions.

Indeed, in March 1990 the Idaho state legislature passed a statute banning abortion for birth control reasons. Feminists around the country were furious and called for a boycott of Idaho potatoes. Yet, this piece of legislation successfully brought to light the true agenda of the pro-abortion movement. They are not content to have abortion available for only the "hard" cases. They want abortion-on-demand—that is, abortion at any time and for any reason. Unfortunately, Governor Cecil Andrus vetoed the bill after the legislative session concluded, ending for the time being the possibility of this law going to the Supreme Court and challenging *Roe* v. *Wade*. However, similar legislation is bound to pass elsewhere in the next few years.

Pursuit of this legislation does not mean that the abortion of children conceived from rape or incest or the abortion of children who have genetic deformities is acceptable. Such legislation only recognizes present political realities and endeavors to save as many children from abortion as is possible under those realities. The pro-life movement has a major job ahead of it to educate the public on the sanctity-of-life ethic to which we adhere. The care for mothers who are victims of rape and incest and the care and concern for handicapped infants should be a major focus of our educational efforts in the 1990s.

2. Legislation Banning Abortion for Sex Selection

The polls indicate that there is a strong public reaction against abortion to select the gender of the child. Following the *Webster* decision, the Pennsylvania legislature acted upon this public sentiment and enacted a law which bans sex selection abortions. While not affecting a large number of abortions performed each year, this legislation does challenge the abortion-on-demand mentality of *Roe*. In addition, such laws help to raise the consciousness of many who are undecided on abortion. These people can be challenged to ask themselves why they consider abortion for gender selection to be abhorrent when they believe that abortion for other trivial reasons is not.

Legislation banning sex selection abortions can also be couched in terms of anti-sex discrimination laws. Even some feminists who otherwise support abortion have voiced opposition to sex selection abortions because those abortions generally are intended to destroy little girls. Senator Humphrey's efforts, as described in chapter 1, give one example of how to frame sex selection abortions as sex discrimination against women.

3. Legislation Requiring Informed Consent

Before obtaining an abortion, every woman should be fully advised about the abortion procedure, the potential physical and emotional consequences of the abortion, the physical appearance of the child within her, and the availability of alternatives to abortion in her community. There are thousands of testimonies from women—stories of anguish and regret—which indicate they never would have had an abortion had they been given full information about the child within them and about available alternatives.

In the state of Washington there has been a recent unsuccessful attempt to place on the ballot an informed consent statute titled the "Woman's Right to Know Initiative." It is unfortunate that this measure did not make the ballot because it has some commendable elements. The statute requires that an abortionist, before performing an abortion, inform the woman of the approximate age of the unborn child, give a general anatomical description of the child using distinct photographs of an unborn child at a similar stage of development, describe the risks of the particular abortion procedure to be used, and present the available alternatives to abortion "such as child birth and adoption and information concerning public and private agencies registered with the state that will assist in those alternatives."

4. Legislation Requiring Parental Consent and/or Notification

As mentioned previously, laws requiring parental consent or notification before an abortion may be performed are effective in reducing the number of teen pregnancies and abortions. If teens are required to consult with their parents over decisions affecting their sexuality, then teen behavior changes. The passage of these laws makes good common sense as they protect teens from destructive behavior and preserve the family unit.

Unemancipated minors cannot consent to minor medical treatment or even obtain their own records without parental approval. Since the law has traditionally recognized the custodial role of parents in protecting their minor children in medical decisions, such legislative enactments must be pursued. It does not make sense to require parental consent before a minor may have her ears pierced but not require it if the minor wants to kill her unborn baby.

5. Legislation Banning Abortion after the Unborn Child Is Viable

According to public opinion polls, support for abortion drops dramatically, even in the hard cases, once the child is viable (able to live outside the mother's womb). Even in *Roe* v. *Wade* the Court conceded that the states have a "compelling interest" to protect unborn life at this stage. Under *Webster* this "compelling interest" no longer begins at the point of viability but exists "throughout pregnancy." While it is still an open question whether or not this new standard allows a state to totally prohibit abortion, at a minimum the *Webster* standard means states can prohibit abortion after the point of viability.

At issue in *Webster* were provisions of the Missouri statute that required tests for viability for an unborn child believed to be twenty weeks gestational age. Those requirements were upheld. Any legislation that restricts abortion after viability should require such tests and stipulate that they be performed by a physician other than the proposed abortionist.

6. Legislation Requiring Spousal Consent

The law has traditionally required that both parties to a marriage agree before any legal transactiotakes place that affects either of them individually. The same standard should apply to decisions that affect the life of a married couple's unborn child.

In its previous decision of *Planned Parenthood* v. *Danforth* the Supreme Court held that spousal consent provisions were unconstitutional since the Court considered husbands as outside third parties in the abortion decision. Spousal consent legislation will give the Court an opportunity to correct this grievous error.

7. Legislation Prohibiting Public Funding and Assistance for Abortion

Presently, thirty-five states prohibit funding of abortion through their public assistance programs. Missouri's ban is the most comprehensive as it prohibits public funds to be used "for the purpose of performing or assisting an abortion" and makes it unlawful "for any public employee within the scope of his or her employment to perform or assist an abortion not necessary to save the life of the mother." The Missouri law also makes it "unlawful for a doctor, nurse, or other health-care personnel, a social worker, a counselor, or persons of similar occupation who is a public employee within the scope of his or her employment to encourage or counsel a woman to have an abortion not necessary to save her life." Finally, this statute makes it "unlawful for any public facility to be used for the purpose of performing or assisting an abortion not necessary to save the life of the mother or for the purpose of encouraging or counseling a woman to have an abortion not necessary to save her life."

Since this Missouri statute was upheld by the Supreme Court in *Webster*, statutes that severely restrict abortion funding can pass constitutional scrutiny. State legislatures should be lobbied vigorously to pass similar legislation.

8. Legislation Requiring Malpractice Coverage and Setting Certain Standards for Abortion Clinics

In 1989, the Tennessee state legislature passed a law requiring that all abortion clinics obtain at least $2 million in malpractice coverage. As a practical matter, most abortion clinics are unable to obtain that amount of coverage and, under such a law, would go out of business. Indeed, most of the abortion clinics in Tennessee reported that as of the operable date of the law, July 1, 1989, they were unable to obtain the needed insurance coverage.[17]

In addition to insurance requirements, abortion facilities should be required to have on their premises certain equipment and staff, including a general and a gynecological surgeon, an anesthesiologist, a blood bank, a laboratory, and custodial care for incapacitated patients. Contrary to what the abortion industry wants the public to believe, abortion is a dangerous medical procedure that can result in serious life-threatening complications. Statutes of the kind suggested can be framed as safety and health care legislation and, if passed, would make it difficult for many clinics to continue operating.

9. Legislation Requiring Waiting Periods before an Abortion May Be Obtained

The decision to have an abortion is an emotional one usually made under extreme pressure and in a state of panic. The requirement of a waiting period, usually forty-eight hours, from the time a woman schedules an abortion until she undergoes the procedure should be placed into law to enable the woman to thoroughly consider other options. The statute should require the abortionist to give to the woman during the waiting period a list of agencies registered with the state, public and private, that provide alternatives to abortion.

10. Legislation Requiring Abortion Counselors to Be Licensed and Prohibiting Financial Kickbacks for Abortion Referrals

A woman in a crisis pregnancy is vulnerable, and she has the right to expect that the counselors at an abortion clinic are trained to provide accurate information in an unbiased manner. Abortion counselors should be licensed by the state and required to take state-accredited courses in fetal development, gynecological physiology, and counseling. The law requires licensure for real estate agents, lawyers, doctors, chiropractors, insurance agents, psychologists, and others. Counselors at abortion clinics should be similarly licensed.

In addition, these laws should prohibit individuals who provide abortion counseling from receiving a kickback or fee from abortionists for each patient referred. This practice predisposes counselors to guide the choice of the woman towards abortion, and it amounts to nothing short of exploitation of women in crisis. Statutory prohibitions should include suspension of licenses for both the abortionist and counselor involved.

11. Legislation Amending State Privacy Laws and Equal Rights Amendments to Make Them Abortion Neutral

Some states have right-to-privacy provisions in their constitutions, and some state high courts have ruled that these provisions allow for a right to abortion under the state constitution.[18] Likewise, attorneys who support abortion rights have argued that an Equal Rights Amendment in any state constitution insures the right to abortion under the state law, irrespective of how the federal constitution is interpreted.

These state constitutional provisions must be amended to insure that abortion does not become a right under the different state constitutions. While the Supreme Court may indeed overrule *Roe* v. *Wade*, that victory would ring hollow if the high courts of the fifty states declare that abortion is a right under state constitutional law.

Personal Involvement

For the pro-life cause to be successful in the political arena, each and every Christian must become personally involved. Many Christians who are not now active should seriously consider running for public office. Even local school board races will now be affected by the abortion issue under the *Webster* decision. Christians must not let abortion advocates claim these public positions.

The relatively obscure office of precinct committee-person is one almost every Christian could hold if sought. Each legislative district is divided into precincts. Both major political parties have committee-people elected in each precinct. In many precincts these offices remain vacant because nobody has sought to fill them. Usually the filing fee is small (as low as one dollar in some states) and there are rarely contested elections for these positions. Yet once elected, the precinct committeeman has much influence over party decisions.

Precinct committee-people are the grass roots activists who form the infrastructure of the party system and work each precinct on behalf of political candidates. They also have influence in party caucuses which set the party plat-forms and, to a great extent, set the rules under which the party candidates are chosen. If pro-life Christians were to control these precinct positions around the country, we would be able to wield significant influence on the party deliberations.

I also challenge Christians to run for legislative offices at both the state and national level. These positions will be influential on the abortion issue during the next decade. We must have them filled with godly men and women who will protect the unborn from abortion.

Personal involvement is not limited to running for political office. Christians must also effectively write and lobby their legislators for changes in the law. Writing to elected officials and other government authorities can make a difference. Since the format, content, and style of the letters are important, here are some helpful tips for writing to a public official:

- Don't write too often. Once a month is plenty.

- Use your personal stationery. Be sure to include your return address, since congressional members generally respond only to people in their own districts.

- Address your correspondence correctly.

For Senators:

The Honorable _____
Senate Office Building
Washington, D.C. 20510

Dear Senator _____,

For Representatives:

The Honorable _____
House Office Building
Washington, D.C. 20515

Dear Congressman/
Congresswoman_____,

- Be brief and to the point. Use your own words, never a form or mass duplicated letter. Write intelligently so legislators know that you know what you're talking about.

- Don't insult them. Don't say things like, "I'm pro-life and I vote."

- Keep your letter to one page whenever possible.

- Address only one topic or one piece of legislation. Remember that your letters will be given to the congressional staff person responsible for that issue.

- Use facts and logical reasoning. Emotional rhetoric and statements that can't be supported are counterproductive. Don't threaten or make demands. Legislators know the power of your vote.

- Explain how this legislation or new program will impact the legislator's district or state. Be as specific as possible.

- Cite your awareness of his or her past voting record.

- Refer to the bill by name as well as by number. For example: H.R. 2369, the Reauthorization Bill for Title X of the Public Health Service Act. This ensures that your letter will get to the right assistant.

- Ask him or her to vote in a specific way. Be specific but courteous: "Can I count on you to support H.R. 555?"

For your letter writing to be effective you must learn how the ultimate decision-maker gets the information he or she uses to decide. Is there a key staff aide who handles certain issues? If so, that's the person you want to reach. Does a particular newspaper or television reporter seem to influence the decision-maker? Write a letter to the editor or see about getting that reporter to cover your story.

You always need to know exactly what you want to say to the people you are contacting. And you must make sure that your message is a simple and repetitive one. You need not give a lawmaker a college education on the topic, but you should give a few key facts that will convince your elected official to view things from your perspective.

Summary

If Christians become personally involved in the political process, pro-life legislation will be passed during the next decade that will ultimately ban abortion. That accomplishment will not come about, however, until the people of

God take seriously the command to be the salt and light of our society. Once Christians are convicted to act and become part of a well-planned political strategy, we will see an abortion-free America by 2001.

Notes

1. During the autumn of 1989, following the *Webster* decision, President Bush vetoed four bills passed by Congress which attempted to liberalize federal policy regarding funding of abortion. He vetoed congressional attempts to add rape and incest exceptions to the Hyde Amendment, a rider annually attached to the appropriations bill for the Department of Health and Human Services which bans the use of federal tax dollars for abortion except to save the mother's life. In addition, he twice vetoed congressional moves to allow the District of Columbia to fund abortion from its budget. Finally, Mr. Bush vetoed a congressional move to restore $15 million to the United Nations Fund for Population Activities (UNFPA) which helps fund the brutal coercive abortion policy from the People's Republic of China.

These vetoes, which were not overridden by Congress, indicate that the current situation on Capitol Hill is a stalemate. The pro-life movement has sufficient support to stop pro-abortion initiatives from passing but lacks the strength to take the offensive and get pro-life legislation adopted.

2. Most of the states which severely restrict abortion funding allow for such funding in the rare cases where the mother's life would be endangered if the pregnancy were carried to term. These states are: Alabama, Arizona, Arkansas, Colorado, Delaware, Florida, Georgia, Idaho, Illinois, Iowa, Kansas, Kentucky, Louisiana, Maine, Michigan, Mississippi, Missouri, Montana, Nebraska, Nevada, New Hampshire, New Mexico, North Dakota, Ohio, Oklahoma, Pennsylvania, Rhode Island, South Carolina, South Dakota, Tennessee, Texas, Utah, Virginia, Wisconsin, and Wyoming. In addition, due to recent congressional action, the District of Columbia does not fund abortions.

3. These states are: Alabama, Arkansas, Arizona, Connecticut, Delaware, Idaho, Illinois, Louisiana, Michigan, Mississippi, New Hampshire, Oklahoma, South Dakota, West Virginia, and Wisconsin.

4. NARAL memo from Kate Michelman to NARAL supporters, on file with the Christian Action Council office.

5. "Most in U.S. Favor Ban on Majority of Abortions, Poll Finds," *The Boston Globe*, 31 March 1989, 1, 12-13.

6. Ibid.

7. See J.C. Wilkie, *Abortion: Questions and Answers* (Cincinnati: Hayes Publishing, 1985), 143-52.

8. *The Los Angeles Times*, 19 March 1989, 26.

9. Analytical Report Prepared for the National Abortion Rights Action League, 18 January 1988, Hickman-Maslin Research.

10. "Poll: Abortion Key For Voters," *USA Today*, 2 January 1990, 1A, 2A.

11. Morton Blackwell, "Don't Let Proponents Define Abortion Issue," *Human Events*, 2 December 1989, 10-11.

12. Ibid.

13. Some in the pro-life movement do not believe abortion should be allowed, even in the rare cases where a mother's life would be endangered if she carried the baby to term. Generally, these cases come about when there is an ectopic pregnancy or where the mother has contracted uterine cancer. In such situations, these pro-life advocates correctly assert that a consistent sanctity-of-human-life position requires that no life be valued over another. These friends do, however, allow for medical intervention to save the life of the mother in such cases if all reasonable steps are also taken to save the life of the baby. In practical application these cases generally result in the loss of the life of the child since, usually, the child is not sufficiently developed to survive outside the womb.

14. The cases where abortion is desired because the pregnancy has resulted from an act of rape or incest or because the child has been determined to suffer a genetic deformity are what I refer to as the "hard" cases. A consistent sanctity-of-human-life ethic requires that these lives be valued despite the circumstances surrounding conception and despite the physical attributes of the child in the womb.

15. During the Reagan administration, Congress passed legislation which denied funds to the United Nations Fund for Population

Activities (UNFPA) after revelations were made regarding brutal forced abortions in the People's Republic of China. The UNFPA provides funds, in part, for China's population control program which uses coercive abortion as a means to enforce its "one family-one child" policy. (See note 1 for a further discussion regarding congressional attempts to repeal this legislation.)

The Reagan Administration also instigated its "Mexico City Policy" which denies federal assistance to "family planning" organizations such as Planned Parenthood which promote abortion as a means of birth control and contraception in third-world countries. There have been recent congressional attempts to overturn this policy as well.

16. In *Webster* the Supreme Court stated that the states now have a "compelling" interest to protect unborn human life "throughout pregnancy." One might argue that this means that states can now prohibit abortion completely. However, since *Roe* v. *Wade* was not completely reversed in *Webster* there still remains a recognized constitutional liberty to abortion. Thus, apparently the "compelling" interest of the states to protect unborn babies now conflicts with a woman's liberty to abort. This conflict will eventually have to be resolved in subsequent decisions from the Court. Until then it is probably safe to conclude that as long as *Roe* v. *Wade* remains there will be some kind of legal protection for abortion rights.

17. A pro-life organization, The American Rights Coalition, in a news release dated 23 August 1989, reports: "All of Tennessee's abortion clinics, with the possible exception of Planned Parenthood, have reported back to the State Licensing Board that they cannot obtain the required $2 million in malpractice coverage as set for the new law."

18. The Supreme Court of Florida ruled on 5 October 1989 that the right-to-privacy provisions of the state constitution requires that Florida's parental consent statute be struck down. The court stated that the state privacy provision guarantees the right to abortion in Florida. Likewise, a California Court of Appeals has thrown out the California parental consent law stating that the privacy provisions of the California constitution protect the abortion decision.

CHAPTER SEVEN

Activism
for the 1990s

The third section of the wall will be built through strategically designed activism that testifies to the values of the kingdom of God. Abortion will cease only when it is made a scandal in every neighborhood in this nation. In order to remind our fellow citizens of the killing that occurs daily within our communities, we must maintain consistent demonstrations and protests outside abortion clinics. The battle for human life is being waged in every part of the nation, and those activists who are taking the pro-life message to the streets are the front-line soldiers in this struggle.

This conflict is for the hearts and minds of the nation. The forces warring against each other are diametrically opposed. The sanctity-of-life ethic, which is based on a biblical world view, says that every human being, regardless of race, condition of dependency, physical handicap, ethnic origin, or gender, is made in the image of God and has value.

The quality-of-life ethic is based on the opposing secular humanist world view. Under this philosophy there is no place for God. The value of every human being is relative and is based upon personal attributes such as certain physical or mental abilities. Society determines which attributes grant value to each individual. If a person does not measure up to those societal standards, then the life of that individual is disposable.

In 1973 a number of prominent men and women produced and signed a document entitled *The Humanist Manifesto II*. This document accurately sums up the world view which is now warring against Christian values and the sanctity-of-human-life ethic. It says in part:

> We find insufficient evidence for belief in the existence of a supernatural; it is either meaningless or irrelevant to the question of the survival and fulfillment of the human race. As non-theists, we begin with humans not God, nature not deity. . . . We can discover no divine purpose or providence for the human species. While there is much that we do not know, humans are responsible for what we are or will become. No deity will save us; we must save ourselves.[1]

To those who adhere to this philosophy, moral values are not absolute. Christian values regarding sexuality and abortion are outdated relics of an old puritanical order. The *Manifesto* continues:

> We affirm that moral values derive their source from human experience. Ethics is autonomous and situational needing no theological or ideological sanction. . . . In the area of sexuality, we believe that intolerant attitudes, often cultivated by orthodox religions and puritanical cultures, unduly repress sexual conduct. The right to birth control, abortion, and divorce should be recognized. . . . [Freedom] also includes a recognition

of an individual's right to die with dignity, euthanasia, and the right to suicide.[2]

The battle lines are drawn and the stakes are high. Strategic activism by pro-lifers is essential in keeping the abortion issue in the minds of the public. A failure to proclaim the truth of the Bible and to cry out against oppression and injustice will insure the defeat of Christian values in the public arena. Such a defeat will also insure that the judgment of God will be pronounced against our civilization for its mockery of the Creator.

A similar battle raged in Ezekiel's day. The Lord spoke clearly to this prophet about the depravity in his nation. A war was raging between God's righteous standards and the twisted values of a society that devalued human life. The nation of Israel had corrupt leaders who robbed the widows and "kill[ed] people to make unjust gain" (Ezekiel 22:27). The religious leaders refused to speak out in protest; instead they turned their backs on the oppression in the land and "whitewashed" the evil deeds Ezekiel spoke against (v. 28). The situation was so bad that the Lord says to Ezekiel:

> "I looked for a man among them who would build up the wall and stand before me in the gap on behalf of the land so I would not have to destroy it, but I found none. So I will pour out my wrath on them and consume them with my fiery anger, bringing down on their own heads all they have done, declares the Sovereign LORD" (22:30-31).

I believe the situation in America is similar. Oppression is rampant throughout the land through the destruction of innocent unborn life. Yet many religious leaders "whitewash" the situation with either intentional avoidance of the issue or outright support for abortion. As in Ezekiel's day, the battle for innocent human life requires that the people of God "stand in the gap" before the Lord in order to avert judgment upon our civilization. Through continual pro-life activism we can "stand in the gap" and witness to the truths of the gospel. Such activism requires that in every community across the nation, local institutions that promote abortion be confronted—beginning with hospitals.

Pastors' Protest against Abortion: Challenging the Abortion Practices of Hospitals

One of the great tragedies of modern-day American culture is the acceptance of abortion by the medical community which once condemned it through the Hippocratic Oath. Hospitals throughout the country routinely perform abortions. Many of these institutions were originally formed as Christian hospitals. Today their names are just a remnant of an abandoned faith. While at one time they were institutions of healing, they now are participants in the deliberate killing of the unborn.

Even prior to the *Webster* decision, which upheld the right of the state of Missouri to prohibit abortions in its public hospitals, the law was clear that no hospital need be involved in abortion.[3] Yet the American Hospital Association reported in 1984 that over fourteen hundred hospitals nationwide participate in abortion services.

Abortion clinics usually perform abortions in the early stages of pregnancy, but hospitals perform most late-term abortions. While abortion clinics frequently have a shabby, sleazy image, the abortions performed at hospitals are the bloodiest. Because of the advanced gestational ages of the babies, late-term abortions inflict the most pain on the unborn.

The abortion techniques used for these late-term abortions include the dilatation and evacuation (D & E) where the unborn child is dismembered and removed piece by piece. Also used is the saline abortion where a high concentration of saline solution is injected into the mother's uterus, poisoning the child who suffers a lengthy, agonizing death.

Since 1985 the Christian Action Council has sponsored Pastors' Protest against Abortion, an annual event scheduled for the Saturday immediately before the opening session of the Supreme Court in October. At this demonstration, local pastors lead concerned citizens in lawful protest outside hospitals that continue to practice abortion. This event has grown substantially since its inception, and in 1989 approximately 45,000 gathered on this day in 125 cities across the United States and Canada to protest the abortion policies of hospitals. Since these protests began, many hospitals have changed their abortion policies with some refusing to perform abortions altogether.

Pastors' Protest is unique in that it is headed by the spiritual leaders of the community, the ones best equipped to provide the prophetic voice needed to call our nation and its institutions back to God. A shining example of such a person is Dietrich Bonhoeffer, a Lutheran pastor and seminary professor who exhorted the church in Nazi Germany to speak up in defense of the Jews. Bonhoeffer was imprisoned for his protest, and while in prison he continued to exhort the church through his writings. In his last book, *Ethics*, published posthumously, he speaks up on behalf of the unborn, arguing that to deny the unborn child life is to deny the God who created that life.

Pastors' Protest against Abortion is held in the spirit of Bonhoeffer and grants Christians an opportunity to "stand in the gap" and speak out against the atrocity of abortion. For the pro-life message to be successful in the 1990s we must put pressure upon hospitals that perform abortions and urge them to become once again the institutions of healing they were meant to be.

The Ethic of Fulfillment: Confronting the Abortionist

To "stand in the gap" on behalf of our nation means that we must confront the abortionist at the clinic, an action we can refer to as an "ethic of fulfillment." Christ's teaching was radically different from that of the Pharisees. He taught an ethic of fulfillment while they taught an ethic of avoidance. An ethic of avoidance means that one must do his best to keep clean and not break any law. An ethic of fulfillment, however, asserts that it is not enough to simply avoid doing evil. One must also be concerned with doing good. If we see an injustice and do nothing, then we are guilty.

Picketing outside an abortion clinic is one way to confront the abortionist and to speak up against the killing occurring at the clinic. A consistent witness and presence in front of clinics will challenge the abortionist and inform the community of what is going on. There are, however, a number of tips to follow when organizing a successful picket outside a clinic.

Do your homework. To have an effective picket you must get people to attend, which means aggressively publicizing the event. This is hard work, but it is essential. Activists often find preparation work tedious and would rather be on the front lines, but a good picket requires good attendance.

To publicize the picket, place announcements in church bulletins and newsletters. Then follow up by sending individuals who have been involved in the past a postcard announcing the date and the time. Finally, set up a phone tree to call individuals about a week to three days before the picket. While you can't make people come, you can make sure they don't forget.

If it is possible before the picket, meet with the abortionist or a person on his staff in a neutral setting to explain your views. Strangely enough, most of these medical personnel will admit that abortion is the taking of a life. Explain to them why we can't tolerate the killing of innocent human life and, if the opportunity presents itself, share the gospel. Most importantly, pray for the abortionist and for his salvation. (Remember the ministry of Ananias to Saul of Tarsus.)

Call the police department ahead of time and ask if a permit is needed for the protest. If not, courteously inform them of your plans so they might monitor the event if they wish.

Prepare the picketers. Picketers should be trained before they picket. An open workshop is a good idea, but don't be surprised or disappointed if the attendance is low. Inform the picketers of general rules, which should include the following:

1. No more than two people should be designated as "picket leaders." These people are the only parties who should be allowed to speak to the police, abortion facility personnel, and the media. If any other picketer is approached by any of these people, he should direct them to the designated "picket leader."

2. All picketers should be instructed to obey the "picket leaders" and to maintain a legal and peaceful presence in front of the facility.

3. Do not block driveways or sidewalks or impede traffic in any way. Picketers should keep moving and remain orderly.

4. Do not bunch up on the sidewalk. Signs are much easier to read and the group looks larger if picketers are spread out.

5. Do not get into shouting matches with those who support abortion rights. If someone wishes to yell at you, simply tell them that you would be happy to discuss the issue with them in a civilized manner or say nothing at all.

6. Try to remain in a prayerful attitude. Pray for the mothers, the abortionists and their staff, the pro-choice demonstrators, and the women who have been victimized by abortion.

7. Be careful not to litter or lay personal belongings such as picket signs on the property of the facility.

8. Two or three monitors should survey the picketers to make sure everything is done properly and orderly. The monitors should ask people carrying inappropriate signs to put them away. It is best not to have a "picket leader" in charge of this, as he or she will need to be free to talk with the police or media.

Distribute literature. Make literature available to the public as you picket. All literature should be handed out individually (with a smile) and not just left in a pile for people to take. The literature should be positive, stating the problem in a manner that will make the average reader interested.

Inform the media. Send out news releases at least two weeks in advance of any major picketing event. Attempt to put something unusual in the release to get the attention of the media. For example, one Christian Action Council chapter announced in a news release that one helium balloon for each baby aborted at the clinic would be released at the time of the picket. This brought the media out to cover the event.

Respond to requests to stop. If you are requested to stop picketing by owners of the complex, ask what laws you are violating. If the police ask you to stop picketing, ask what laws you are violating and whether you will be arrested if you do not stop. If you are told you will be arrested, ask what changes you would have to make in order to continue your right to picket in accordance with the law. If you are ordered to stop picketing by the police, have the verbal order witnessed by at least one other person. It is not necessary to be arrested to test the constitutionality of the police request. If necessary, end the picket and obtain legal advice before continuing. Always get the name and badge number of the police officer with whom you are dealing. Remember that police officers are people too, so the best results will arise when you are cooperative, friendly, and respectful. If you disagree with or question a police officer, do so in a respectful manner.

Carry signs. Signs are a vital element to any protest. It is always a good idea for the organizers to bring as many signs as possible. Make the slogans brief so that the signs can be read at a glance. In general, the signs should be positive and should not condemn. Here are some sign slogans supplied by the Alameda County (California) Christian Action Council.

- Abortion isn't the answer

- Doctors should heal, not kill

- Can you imagine Jesus performing an abortion? Why not?

- Choose life for your baby

- Adoption, not abortion

- Equal rights for unborn children

- A person's a person no matter how small

- Jesus loves the little children

- Abortion: Your child can live without it!

Sidewalk Counseling

Every picket outside an abortion clinic should be accompanied by good sidewalk counseling for those women attempting to enter the abortion clinic. The counselor approaches a woman and tries to engage her or her friend in conversation, ultimately to talk the woman out of having an abortion and to direct her to available alternatives.

Sidewalk counseling is similar to evangelism in that there is no best way to do it. Everyone must develop his or her own style. In general, you want to communicate the idea that no matter what the current problem, abortion is not the solution, and there are people who can help through this difficult time.

Have a handout listing local services available to help, such as adoption agencies and crisis pregnancy centers.

Some helpful suggestions. Jeannie Hill, an R.N. and author of a manual on sidewalk counseling, gives the following suggestions for every sidewalk counselor:[4]

• The clinic area is not the ideal place to persuade and convince. The first approach should be on an emotional level with an offer to help this person who is troubled. Try to put off any "heavy" discussion of the evils of abortion until you are convinced that she is not going away from this place for comprehensive counseling.

• Remember the urgency of the situation. This is the baby's very last chance to live out his or her life.

• Meet the patient as far away from the clinic as you can, on the sidewalk or at her car if she parks on the street. Station your counselors at key points where patients ordinarily gain access to the clinic, either on foot or by car. Don't stroll too far from these points.

• Maintain a comfortable distance from the patient and put her at ease with a calm and cheerful posture.

• When you approach a patient, smile, maintain eye contact, and tell her your first name. Offer your business card. These little cards are rarely refused, probably because they typically show only a name, mailing address, and phone number. You may want to write a little message on the back.

• Tell her a little bit about yourself and why you want to help girls who are troubled. Offer brochures. If she accepts the literature but still wants to enter the clinic, boldly tell her that it may be taken from her by the clinic personnel because they don't want her reading the truth.

• Always assume that the girl is going in for an abortion. If she tells you that she is only there for pills, a check-up, counseling, etc., just say, "That's okay, will you talk with me anyway?" Again, offer her the literature as you begin to speak.

• Ask the woman if you may talk with her for just a minute. Be honest with her and mention that you are there to counsel with girls since Planned Parenthood often fails to provide the whole truth to them.

• Be authoritative and kind.

• In reference to the baby, avoid the word *it*; instead, refer to the child as *he* or *she*.

• Try to ignore the escorts and keep your focus on the patient.

• The first question is an important one. You might say, "I know that you don't want to be pregnant at this time or you would not be here, but can you tell me what is making it difficult for you to carry this baby for just a while longer?" Then you can respond to the particular difficulty which she has just mentioned and offer to help carry this burden as she carries her child. Be sympathetic and understand that the problem may seem catastrophic to her.

• Ask her if there is someone who loves her, who would support her in a decision to have this baby. If there isn't, tell her you would like to be that friend.

• Ask her support person if he or she really cares about her. Or ask, "Do you love her?" Appeal to the friend's concern for the girl's best interests. (This may make them both think, maybe for the first time, "What are we doing here?")

• Encourage her friend to be involved in the conversation. We have found that sometimes the friend is basically against abortion but is just doing the patient a favor by coming with her.

• If it's a boyfriend, appeal to his masculinity. Tell him that she needs someone who is strong.

• Present the positive literature first . . . the pictures of a developing baby. These are generally nonthreatening. Pictures of aborted babies, if used at the beginning of the conversation, may well cause anger and impede any further discussion. If she is unresponsive and unaffected by fetal facts and offers of help, then show her what happens to her child during the abortion, with literature showing the reality of what the procedure does to her baby.

• Ask the patient how far along she thinks she is and ask if she's aware that at nine weeks "he" already has a bladder, or that "she" already has a uterus of "her" own. Facts presented through pictures and medical textbooks are a help.

• Ask her if she would put off going into the clinic for just a few hours or until tomorrow. Tell her that they will always gladly take her money if she reschedules the appointment.

• Your immediate goal is to get this patient away from the clinic. Ask her to go with you to a coffee shop and just talk about things over a cup of coffee or a Coke. Offer her alternatives. If you feel uncomfortable counseling the patient yourself, offer to lead her to your closest pro-life pregnancy center.

• At the restaurant, start with small talk to create a relaxing atmosphere. Again, tell her a little about yourself and how you became involved in helping girls with problem pregnancies. This will allow you to ease the conversation back to the problem at hand, her pregnancy.

• Now is the time to keep the focus of the conversation on the woman and her baby. Keep reminding the girl that although she may not be ready for the baby, he or she is ready for her. It's too late to think about whether or not to have a child; she already has one. (The girl has a problem, but the baby has a bigger one.) You can help her, if she will help the baby.

• You can offer to let the girl see her baby, and/or to hear his heartbeat, if you have made arrangements with a pro-life ob/gyn doctor in your community.

• If you feel that the girl is not close to changing her mind, suggest more professional counseling, and offer to either show her the way to the pro-life center, or make the appointment for her.

• As a last resort, if the patient seems determined to go through with the abortion, you can remind her that if her baby did not exist the abortion would be unnecessary. Therefore, her only choices are to carry her child or hire a killer.

• Your counseling may have to take place at the clinic. You can periodically suggest that it really would be nice if you could talk some place where it's more comfortable. Tell her that the clinic is probably used to a lot of rescheduling and that ignoring the appointment is no big deal.

• Tell the patient about the social services available to her such as:

1. Medicaid: Complete prenatal care, with delivery in the hospital, which will be pro-rated based on ability to pay;

2. Homes for unwed mothers;

3. Shepherding homes (a family who would care for the girl in their own home);

4. Adoption agencies. Other welfare assistance such as WIC (Women, Infants, and Children), WIN (Women in Need), AFDC (Aid to Families with Dependent Children).

• Ask the patient for her phone number and address so that you may follow up your counseling with support. Call her once or twice the first week to offer help and see how she's doing. Keep in close contact with your new friend. (Girls who don't have follow-up care feel abandoned and have been known to return to the abortionist.) Some will accept your help of referral and get on with their lives, choosing no further communication with you.

Dealing with escorts. Sometimes it is difficult to talk to a woman about to enter an abortion clinic because some clinics use "escorts" to accompany women past the picket lines. Don't become discouraged if this happens. Remember to bathe your efforts in prayer before you begin and then trust God that somehow your message will be received—even by the women who are shielded by the clinic escorts.

It is usually best to ignore the escorts and concentrate on the client. Do not be surprised if the escorts try to distract you and even blaspheme the name of the Lord to keep you from talking with the woman. *Ignore them.* Let the woman see for herself the difference in your attitude.

What about Rescue Operations?

In 1988 thousands of pro-lifers began a strategy called "rescue operations" outside abortion clinics. Using this strategy, pro-lifers prevent access to an abortion clinic by blocking its entrances. The term *rescue* is derived from Proverbs 24:11-12:

> Rescue those being led away to death;
> hold back those staggering toward
> slaughter.

If you say, "But we knew nothing about this,"
    does not he who weighs the heart perceive
        it?
Does not he who guards your life know it?
    Will he not repay each person according
        to what he has done?

Proponents of "rescue operations" argue that this passage commands us to rescue the innocent by blockading the entrances to abortion clinics. Failure to do so, they argue, is to obey man rather than God. The hoped for result is that the abortion clinic will not be able to service clients for that day, and babies will be saved. To date, thousands of pro-life activists have been arrested for trespass during "rescue operations."

When this strategy was first proposed, I felt a deep inner conflict. On the one hand was my intense desire to end the slaughter of babies at abortion clinics and my frustration that the traditional activism of picketing and sidewalk counseling was not doing enough. On the other hand, I have a profound and abiding respect for the civil law. As a Christian I have a high duty to obey the law because God ordained civil government for his glory and for our good (Romans 13; Titus 3:1; 1 Timothy 2:1-2). Added to these internal struggles was a sincere doubt about the overall effectiveness of "rescue operations."

Without doubting the courage and convictions of those involved, I have concluded, after much prayer and study of God's Word, that "rescue operations" cannot be justified scripturally or strategically. I do not in any way intend to demean the integrity or the motives of my brothers and sisters who participate in "rescue operations." I have nothing but love and respect for all pro-life activists willing to take such risks. In addition, I denounce in the strongest possible terms the confirmed incidents of police brutality toward those who have nonviolently placed their bodies on the line to save unborn babies. If demonstrators for any other cause were treated as severely as some pro-life rescuers, the national media would create a major scandal. Sadly, the media has raised no such scandal on behalf of pro-lifers.

In assessing the scriptural justification for "rescue operations," we should first note that while we are under a duty as Christian citizens to obey the civil law, that duty is not absolute. A Christian must not comply with any law that requires disobedience to God's commands. We must obey God rather than man (Acts 5:29). When the civil law requires a Christian to disobey the commands of Scripture, that provision of the law is invalid and must be rejected. The natural law of God, as revealed in Scripture, takes precedence over any law of man. If a Christian is commanded to do evil, he must disobey. Scripture is full of examples of saints, such as Daniel, Peter, and Paul, who refused to obey civil authorities precisely because to do so would be to participate in evil.

While abortion is contrary to God's law, neither *Roe* v. *Wade* nor any other law requires any person to obtain an abortion or to participate in the act of abortion. Therefore, a Christian is not required to break the law through acts of civil disobedience to avoid participating in evil. This key factor distinguishes the abortion issue in our society from those acts of civil disobedience recorded in the Bible. Daniel was commanded to forsake his prayer life—to obey would be to disobey God. Shadrach, Meshach, and Abednego were commanded to bow down to an idol—to obey would be to violate a commandment of God. Peter was told not to preach in the name of Jesus—to obey would be to turn his back on his calling from God. The Hebrew midwives were commanded to kill Hebrew baby boys—to obey would be to commit murder.

In the abortion issue, no Christian is placed in the position where he or she is commanded by civil authorities to disobey a commandment of God, a point Rousas John Rushdoony emphasizes:

No Scriptural justification is offered by these demonstrators. The closest thing to a text to justify them is Acts 5:29, the answer of Peter and the other apostles, "We ought to obey God rather than men." What does this mean, however? There is no civil government anywhere which does not disobey God at some points, and, for that matter, there are no perfect churches either. The best of churches fall short of perfect obedience. Are we then justified in obeying only when we believe God's Word is faithfully observed? Then are those around us or under us entitled to rebel against our authority whenever they feel we fall short of or neglect God's Word? Nothing in Scripture gives warrant to that. David's respect for Saul, despite Saul's sin, gives us another model. . . . Where freedom of God's Word in the church, its schools, its families and members is denied, then we must obey God, not the state. We do not disobey to save our money nor even our lives but where God's Word and its proclamation is at stake.[5]

What then of the passage from Proverbs 24:11-12 cited to justify these "rescue operations"? Are Christians commanded to rescue innocent unborn babies from abortion? I respond with an emphatic *yes*! However, the question is not, "Should a Christian rescue the unborn from abortion?" Rather, the question to ask is, "*How* should a Christian rescue the unborn from abortion?" Well-planned picketing with good sidewalk counseling rescues babies from abortion. The work of crisis pregnancy centers rescues babies from abortion. Legislative restrictions on abortion rescue the unborn. There is much to be accomplished through these rescue efforts and believers should be involved in all of them. However, I do not believe the illegal activity of blocking entrances to abortion clinics is a rescue strategy justified by Scripture.

We should also take counsel from the examples of

Daniel, Shadrach, Meshach, and Abednego who, before disobeying the edict to drink the king's wine and eat his meat, proposed the constructive alternative of eating vegetables and drinking water for ten days (Daniel 1). Would Daniel and his friends have violated the king's command had their alternative not been accepted? Their actions throughout the book of Daniel unquestionably show their resolve to disobey civil authority if its commands required disobedience to God. However, they first sought an alternative before choosing to violate the commands of civil authorities.

Like Daniel and his friends, we should seek constructive alternatives before choosing to break the civil law. Activities such as sidewalk counseling and legal picketing are resourceful options to the blockade of abortion clinics and, I believe, are more effective in rescuing unborn babies. Many women have been turned away from an abortionist when lovingly confronted by caring people outside the clinic. There is no substitute for a well-organized picket accompanied by well-trained sidewalk counselors. We should emphasize these efforts and vigorously pursue all similar alternatives.

Finally, I must question the strategic wisdom in using blockade to stop abortion. Has the time, energy, and money poured into these "rescue operations" produced the desired results? I know of no abortion clinic that has permanently closed down as a result of blockades. Proponents of blockades claim that babies have been saved, and for that I rejoice. However, if we added up all the money spent in "rescue operations" for travel costs and hotels, court fines, legal fees, and days missed from work, it would total hundreds of thousands of dollars. Would not more babies have been saved if this money had been given to crisis pregnancy centers which struggle day to day for their very existence? Certainly that much money would have a dramatic impact on the legislative scene if used to elect pro-life legislators who would seek to ban abortion under the law. Had these monies been used differently within the pro-life cause, I believe many more babies would have been saved.

Ethics of Choice Chorus

John Rankin, a Christian Action Council leader in Massachusetts, has implemented a unique strategy as an alternative to "rescue operations." Rankin calls his demonstration, "The Ethics of Choice Chorus." According to Rankin, true "choice is a gift of God, meant to serve the prior gift of life."[6] We must confront the woman who is ready to enter the abortion clinic in a manner that will empower her to choose life. Generally, this will not happen through blockade but through a well-organized picket using strategically written signs which ask key questions of the women considering abortions.

The suggested questions for the signs were chosen from Rankin's years of direct communication with pro-abortion advocates and with his personal experience of seeing hundreds of pro-choice college students open their hearts toward a pro-life position. The logic behind the use of these questions is uncomplicated. Jesus often used this tactic to draw correct answers from his hostile interrogators. In addition, the use of questions serves our purposes much better than the familiar but time-worn pro-life slogans. Slogans are easy to disregard but well-thought-out questions are harder to resist. According to Rankin, "the placing of a good question in someone's mind and heart is most effective, for as they possess the question, they are more empowered to possess the answer."[7] Rankin suggests that the following questions be used to raise the issue of life to a woman about to enter an abortion clinic.

- Is this really *your own decision?* You and your baby are loved—we're here to help.

- Aren't *you* glad *you* weren't aborted?

- Why do you feel *no choice* but abortion?

- How does abortion add to *your own dignity?*

- Might you *regret* this abortion someday?

- Can anything good be said about *abortion?*

- Does *good choice* nurture life or destroy life?

- Why does the human fetus *fight* to stay alive?

- If *feminism* = human care, why destroy the unborn human?

- Is not all *law* based on a prior *definition* of human life?

- Can you *imagine Jesus* performing an abortion? Why not?

In the "Ethics of Choice Chorus" the signs are placed where clients of the clinic will most likely see and read them. Sidewalk counselors are stationed in strategic areas where they can come in contact with women about to enter the clinic. Other participants in the picket are stationed outside the entrances to the clinic prayerfully singing songs of praise to the Lord. The singing is important for this is a "chorus" and the music serves as a witness to the love of God. As Rankin states:

> The placing of a song in a woman's heart, as she goes in for an abortion, without any physical blockade, is by far the most effective means to bring about a change of attitude. If such songs can reach back into the more innocent memories of her childhood, then she will be brought closer to identifying with her maternal nature, and the plight of her unborn child. A tract can be discarded (offer them anyway for those times when they are actually read), a blockade can be resisted and hated, but a song in the heart has much greater staying power.[8]

I was invited to participate in the first "Ethics of Choice Chorus" John Rankin organized in Boston during the summer of 1989, just prior to the issuance of the *Webster* decision. (I briefly mentioned a small part of this experience in chapter 4.) The results were impressive not only from the standpoint of saving babies from abortion but also from the witness given to the pro-abortion demonstrators who had come to harass us.

As we sang our choruses on that hot summer day, the abortion proponents began to chant louder and louder intending to drown out the singing. When I decided to share some of our drinking water with Paul—the young pro-abortion demonstrator I described in chapter 4—several other pro-life demonstrators began to share water with those who had come to oppose us.

About an hour later we began to infiltrate the ranks of the pro-abortion demonstrators and to talk about abortion. For about forty-five minutes several groups of two or three people from both sides formed and began communicating in a civil manner. The pro-abortion crowd ceased their obnoxious chanting and placed their pro-abortion signs on the ground as the discussions continued.

I talked to one woman in her early twenties who said she was a firm believer in "choice." Yet as we talked, it was clear that she was uneasy with abortion and even agreed with many of the things I said. My conversation with her was cut short, however, because the pro-abortion leaders, once they saw what was happening, instructed their people not to talk with us. "These people are playing with your minds," they said.

As we parted, I said to this young lady, "You're a thoughtful and intelligent young woman. I thoroughly expect to see you joining me on my side of the picket line one day." She was left speechless.

This first "Ethics of Choice Chorus" lasted about five hours and the sidewalk counselors reported that at least four women were turned away from the clinic. Lives were saved and Christlike communication with people who oppose us had taken place.

The "Ethics of Choice Chorus" is an effective alternative to "rescue operations." John Rankin reports that demonstrations every Saturday outside this Boston clinic have significantly reduced the clinic's clientele. Furthermore, the "Ethics of Choice Chorus" has the potential to increase the number of Christians involved in activism. Many Christians have been convicted about abortion but do not have the fervent commitment or the freedom from other responsibilities necessary to continually be arrested. Yet, when given a viable alternative to blockade, these same Christians willingly become activists, speaking out against abortion in their communities. Entire families can become actively involved, and the presence of families "will more accurately represent who we are, and has tremendous pedagogic power for our children through example and involvement."[9]

Sanctity of Human Life Sunday

An activist agenda for the pro-life movement must include a challenge to the Christian community to become involved in ending abortion. Historically the church has observed special seasons and days, such as Reformation Day, Worldwide Communion Sunday, Missions Sunday, and Stewardship Sunday, to underscore the importance of certain teachings in the life of the church. One important teaching that has been neglected is the sanctity of human life. Few pastors and churches today preach on the dignity of each human being and on the need for Christians to actively oppose abortion.

Since 1985 the Christian Action Council has sponsored Sanctity of Human Life Sunday, a strategic event to teach Christians about their obligation to protect innocent human life. Held annually on the Sunday closest to January 22nd, the anniversary date of *Roe* v. *Wade*, Sanctity of Human Life

Sunday can be a major pro-life event in the Christian community. On this day thousands of congregations across the nation affirm together that our God is the sovereign Author of life; we celebrate the dignity and worth he bestows on his people. On this day thousands of intercessory prayers are offered for our nation and for an end to abortion.

Both President Ronald Reagan and President George Bush, at the request of the Christian Action Council, acknowledged the significance of this event by issuing Presidential Proclamations designating this Sunday as Sanctity of Human Life Day. In President Reagan's proclamation of 1988, the personhood of the unborn was boldly proclaimed:

> I, Ronald Reagan . . . do hereby proclaim and declare the unalienable personhood of every American, from the moment of conception until natural death, and I do proclaim, ordain, and declare that I will take care that the Constitution and laws of the United States are faithfully executed for the protection of America's unborn children. Upon this act, sincerely believed to be an act of justice, warranted by the Constitution, I invoke the considerate judgment of mankind and the gracious favor of Almighty God. I also proclaim Sunday, January 17, 1988, as National Sanctity of Human Life Day. I call upon the citizens of this blessed land to gather on that day in their homes and places of worship to give thanks for the gift of life they enjoy and to reaffirm their commitment to the dignity of every human being and the sanctity of every human life.

President Bush also issued a call for an end to abortion in his proclamation of National Sanctity of Human Life Day for January 21, 1990:

> The prevalence of abortion in America today is a tragedy not only in terms of human lives lost, but

also in terms of the values we hold dear as a Nation. We pray for a recognition that the principle of life's sanctity should guide public policy on this question and others, just as moral principles should guide our individual lives. . . . Let us then on this day speak for those who cannot speak and join with other Americans in reaffirming the sanctity of life.

Why should Christians participate in Sanctity of Human Life Sunday? Since Scripture affirms that judgment begins with the family of God (1 Peter 4:17), it is proper to challenge the church of Jesus Christ to take seriously the scriptural commands to defend the fatherless. Before we can speak to the world of the great evil of abortion, we must first make sure our own house is in order. Before we remove the speck of sawdust from another's eye, we must remove the plank from our own. Simply put, the church must be convicted about its failure to speak up for innocent human life before the pro-life message will effectively reach the rest of the nation. I hope this is what participation in Sanctity of Human Life Sunday will achieve.

To facilitate worship on this day the Christian Action Council produces four-color bulletin inserts, a worship manual, sermon outlines, and brochures which help educate the congregation about abortion. This Sunday is also an appropriate time to invite speakers from a local crisis pregnancy center or other pro-life organization to describe the ministry God has given them. Many local Christian Action Councils and crisis pregnancy centers have organized city-wide prayer services uniting believers from different denominations in prayer for an end to abortion. Sanctity of Human Life Sunday has become a vehicle to convict and challenge Christians to action. It should be a priority for every pro-life activist who wants the church to make a difference on this issue.

Overcoming the Causes of Abortion: Suggested Local Projects

Abortion becomes acceptable within communities for many reasons. To be effective at the local level, pro-life activists must identify these reasons, or causes of abortion, and then develop efforts to overcome them. As Nehemiah undoubtedly discovered, the wall in Jerusalem was rebuilt only through direct and careful planning. Likewise, only through insightful design will abortion be eradicated from our communities.

Various Christian Action Council chapters have identified the following causes for abortion and the suggested responses to overcome them:

- *Cause*: Few pastors preach against abortion and hence few people in the community are sure that it is wrong.

- *Response*: Organize a breakfast or luncheon and invite pastors *and their wives* to hear a challenging pro-life speaker. (Pastor's wives have confirmed to me again and again that often the key to getting on a pastor's busy schedule is to first challenge the pastor's wife.) Make sure that each pastor receives good literature which speaks clearly to the abortion issue and the Christian's responsibility to become involved.

- *Cause*: Christian lay people are not exposed to the facts about abortion or what their obligations are to stop it.

- *Response*: Train speakers with a presentation on abortion and schedule them in churches during Sunday school, evening services, and so on. Promote Sanctity of Human Life Sunday in the churches of your community.

- *Cause*: The newspaper is biased in support of abortion both in its news reporting and in its editorial comments.

- *Response*: Arrange for a meeting with the editorial board of the paper to make a pro-life presentation. Organize a letter writing campaign to the editor whenever biased pieces are printed. Publish a newsletter to get the other side of the news distributed to friends and churches.

- *Cause*: The abortion facility in your community goes unchallenged.

- *Response*: Arrange a protest outside the facility. Include press releases to attract the media. Arrange for regular protests and sidewalk counseling outside the facility on the days when abortions are performed.

- *Cause*: No social service agency is providing an effective ministry to provide alternatives to abortion.

- *Response*: Promote and encourage the formation of a crisis pregnancy center.

- *Cause*: Key elected officials support abortion and speak on behalf of the pro-abortion movement.

- *Response*: Publish the officials' voting records or statements on abortion. Set up a voter registration drive among the churches. Seek a meeting with the officials to discuss your concerns with them.

- *Cause*: There are no abortion facilities in town but there are several doctors who perform abortions in their offices.

- *Response*: Arrange to picket the offices of the physicians. Have local pastors sign a letter to the physicians requesting a meeting to discuss their practices.

- *Cause*: Your community is complacent towards abortion, and local citizens ignore the problem.

- *Response*: Organize an annual March for Life on or about January 22nd of each year. Make this a major media event. Take out an educational advertisement in the local paper. Arrange for a pro-life leader in the community to be interviewed by both the written and electronic media to publicize the event. In addition, schedule a day just prior to the march to distribute literature to homes in your community.

This list of causes for abortion is far from exhaustive. As you plan responses in your community, undoubtedly you will identify other reasons abortion is allowed to continue. The key is to meet each cause with a properly planned response that will challenge the abortion ethic and keep the issue alive in the minds of your neighbors and friends.

Standing Firm for Life

An activist agenda that will effectively confront abortion in America must be bathed in prayer and empowered by the Spirit-led determination of God's people to do what is right and stand firm for life. We must "stand in the gap" on behalf of this nation and call our people to righteousness. Through protests, demonstrations, prayer vigils, and other activities that challenge the legitimacy of the abortion industry, we can make abortion a scandal in our communities and in our nation. When this occurs we will begin to see our fellow citizens join us to end the tragedy of abortion in our land.

Notes

1. *Humanist Manifestos I & II* (Buffalo, N.Y.: Prometheus Books, 1982), 16.

2. Ibid., 17, 18, 19.

3. The leading case, *Poelker* v. *Doe*, 432 U.S. 519 (1977), considered this question. The city of St. Louis operated two municipal hospitals and established a policy which prohibited the performance of abortions in city hospitals, except where there was a threat of "grave physiological injury or death to the mother." In reversing a decision of the Eighth Circuit Court of Appeals, the Supreme Court upheld the city's policy stating that there was no

violation of the Constitution by St. Louis "in electing, as a policy choice, to provide publicly financed hospital services for childbirth without providing corresponding services for non-therapeutic abortions" (p. 521).

4. Jeannie Hill, *Sidewalk Counseling Workbook* (Wheat Ridge, Colo.: Sidewalk Counselors for Life, 1986), 21-24.

5. Rousas John Rushdoony, "Revolution or Regeneration," *Chalcedon Report*, January 1989, 14.

6. John Rankin, "The Ethics Of Choice Chorus: Non-Blockade Direct Action at Abortion Facilities," (Gloucester, Mass.: New England Christian Action Council, 1989), 3.

7. Ibid., 24-25.

8. Ibid., 33.

9. Ibid., 33-34.

CHAPTER EIGHT

Fighting the Planned Parenthood Plague

The fourth section of the wall will be rebuilt through a strategically designed effort to combat the influence of Planned Parenthood,[1] the nation's foremost provider of abortion services. As the erosion of *Roe* v. *Wade* continues, many independent abortion providers will be legislated out of business. Regulations that require abortionists to carry malpractice insurance and clinics to meet certain health standards may make it impossible for a local abortionist to continue his trade. This, however, will not be the case for Planned Parenthood, which receives millions of tax dollars each year and millions of dollars from corporate foundations and other private sources. As we proceed into the nineties, Planned Parenthood with its abortion advocacy programs will increasingly become the chief adversary of the pro-life movement.

Planned Parenthood is the best-known "family planning" agency in the world. Headquartered at London,

England, the International Planned Parenthood Federation (IPPF) is involved in more than a hundred countries. The Planned Parenthood Federation of America (PPFA) is the American affiliate.

The PPFA has about two hundred affiliates and operates about seven hundred clinics. Affiliation allows the local organization to use the Planned Parenthood name and logo and participate in PPFA financial programs. The local affiliates pay dues to the PPFA, and the PPFA pays dues to the IPPF. All parts of Planned Parenthood are connected by a common mission.

Margaret Sanger

Most Americans consider Planned Parenthood a benevolent organization which, as its primary focus, gives "family planning" information and counsel to married couples. Few know the roots of this organization, which was founded by Margaret Sanger.

Sanger was active in the eugenics movement (the "science" that seeks to improve races through controlled breeding) during the first part of the twentieth century. She sought to protect the freedom and power of "superior" human beings who, she believed, should rule over the impure masses.[2] Sanger sought to control the reproduction of poor people and immigrants, especially nonwhite immigrants. She called them "reckless breeders" who knew how to do nothing but produce children, and claimed that they were "unceasingly spawning a class of human beings who never should have been born."[3]

Sanger believed that providing charity to the poor only perpetuated poverty. If the poor were not given any assistance, she reasoned, they would die out and the problem would be solved. If the poor were allowed to breed unchecked, she warned, they would eventually produce enough of their own kind to rise up and topple proper society. The world would face "biological destruction" caused by "the gradual but certain attack upon the stocks of intelligence and racial health by the sinister forces of the hordes of irresponsibles and imbeciles."[4]

An opponent of marriage, Sanger supported a casual and voluntary connection between sexual partners. In her own words, "the marriage bed is the most degenerating influence in the social order."[5] She believed that married couples should be required to get a permit before having a child, and that each permit would be valid for only one birth. Individuals who were declared to be of an inferior genetic code would be sterilized. "The purpose," she wrote, "shall be to provide for a better distribution of babies, to assist couples who wish to prevent overproduction of offspring and thus to reduce the burdens of charity and taxation for public relief, and to protect society against the propagation and increase of the unfit."[6]

In this age of broad social concern for minorities and the disadvantaged, one might expect that Planned Parenthood would back away from Margaret Sanger's radical positions. This, however, is not the case. Actress Katharine Hepburn, an avid supporter of abortion rights, wrote a fundraising letter promoting Planned Parenthood's abortion advocacy and noted that "Planned Parenthood is not losing sight of Margaret Sanger's original goal."[7]

Another fundraising letter signed by Faye Wattleton, Planned Parenthood's president, hailed Sanger as "an American pioneer in the truest and noblest self-sacrificing sense. . . . Sanger's memory is honored throughout the world by men and women who understand her monumental achievements for humanity."[8] Ironically, Wattleton grew up in an evangelical home. Her mother was a fundamentalist minister in the Church of God, and her family traveled together on missionary tours. Wattleton today is a member of Marble Collegiate Church in New York, which is pastored by Norman Vincent Peale.

Sanger founded Planned Parenthood in the early 1900s as the American Birth Control League. The racial policies of Nazi Germany in the thirties and forties soured the American public on the concept of eugenics, and the name was changed to Planned Parenthood in 1942. Throughout the fifties Planned Parenthood was generally viewed as a private organization which supported birth control and sterilization. The subject of abortion was avoided at this time, although the organization's president, Alan Guttmacher, supported the liberalization of abortion laws.

The Abortion Connection

Planned Parenthood's budget and influence grew during the sixties and seventies. In the early seventies the organization began to receive federal support through the nation's family planning program, Title X. This program was initially funded by Congress to provide family planning resources and contraceptives to the poor. The use of those funds for programs of abortion advocacy is specifically prohibited under the law. However, receiving these monies frees Planned Parenthood to spend funds from other resources on abortion advocacy.

Just before it began receiving federal support, Planned Parenthood's political agenda to repeal anti-abortion laws surfaced. Planned Parenthood opened its first abortion clinic in New York in the midsixties in the same month that abortion was legalized in that state. Today, Planned Parenthood operates at least sixty abortion clinics, the largest chain of such clinics in the world, and terminates the lives of almost one hundred thousand unborn children every year. In promoting abortion, Planned Parenthood has been involved in almost every Supreme Court case dealing with the liberalization of abortion laws.

Planned Parenthood is by far the most vocal proponent of abortion rights and birth control for teens. They have published countless ads, brochures, and documents that make their position clear. Faye Wattleton says:

> We committed ourselves to restoring access to abortion to the poor and to preserving it as a matter of choice to individuals throughout the economic spectrum. . . . When you support Planned Parenthood you support a campaign to work against the enactment of laws that restrict the availability of abortions.[9]

Beginning in 1989 Planned Parenthood placed a series of full-page ads in many major newspapers and magazines, including *The Washington Post*, *The New York Times*, *Time*, and *Newsweek.* Designed to convince the public that abortion should remain legal, the ads have succeeded in getting Planned Parenthood's message heard and in mobilizing support for lobbying efforts. The ads attack pro-lifers, depicting them as middle-aged men who find women detestable and want to oppress them by denying them their rights. One ad, mentioned previously in chapter 5, portrays the crisis pregnancy centers as deceitful organizations which exploit vulnerable young women in crisis pregnancies.

One full-page ad in *The New York Times* was headlined, "Nine Reasons Why Abortions Are Legal." Another full-page ad, running in the same newspaper one day later, described "Five Ways to Prevent Abortion (And One Way That Won't)." Each ad was filled with Planned Parenthood propaganda about the need to keep abortion legal.

Although Planned Parenthood has nonprofit status from the IRS (that is, none of its income is taxable) its annual income makes it a multimillion dollar abortion business. Planned Parenthood clinics performed approximately 104,000 abortions in 1988 and made an equal number of abortion referrals.[10] At an average cost of $215 for a first-trimester abortion, this translates into estimated revenue of $22.3 million from abortions—all of it tax-free!

Planned Parenthood, Teens, and Parents

Planned Parenthood has been criticized that its programs promote teen sexual activity. To quiet these criticisms, Planned Parenthood attempts to represent itself as a voice for abstinence and self-control. One pamphlet, "Teen Sex? It's Okay to Say: No Way!" says it is not true that "everybody's doing it. It may be true that nearly half of today's young people have had intercourse. It's just as true that *more than half have not.*" However, such statements serve Planned Parenthood purposes. Though their own surveys show that only 20 to 28 percent of teens have had intercourse (many only once), exaggerated estimations of teen sexual activity provide arguments for continued federal support, and give the impression that Planned Parenthood opposes premarital sex.

In reality Planned Parenthood is committed to offering minors birth control and abortion services without the knowledge or guidance of their parents. A Planned Parenthood brochure for teenagers titled "The Perils of Puberty" states: "There are certain things you do not want to talk about to your parents. There are certain things they don't want to talk about to you. . . . The only thing you owe anyone is courtesy. . . . You don't owe anyone 'love'." Another Planned Parenthood ad headlined, "Since Your Parents Are Afraid to Talk to You and Your School's Hands Are Probably Tied, Here's Some Hard Facts" states: "*Myth*: I can't get birth control, I'm under 18. *Fact*: Wrong. If your parents are stupid enough to deny you access to birth control and you are under 18, you can get it on your own without parental consent. Call Planned Parenthood right now."

Does Planned Parenthood mean what they say when they tell teenagers that it's okay to say no to premarital sex? In a publication titled, "Is It Okay for PPFA to Say 'No Way'?" Susan Newcomer, director of education for Planned Parenthood Federation of America until 1989, argues that it may not be in the best interest of teens or Planned Parenthood to tell teens that it's okay to say no. Newcomer argues that chastity training "seems to set up moral conflicts" in children. However, she says it may be necessary to include some discussion of chastity if there is no other way to get Planned Parenthood into the schools.[11] Newcomer is concerned that if children are told to say no to sex they might stay away from Planned Parenthood when they want to get involved sexually. She writes: "Planned Parenthood has always presented abstaining from sex as one contraceptive option. We must remember, though, that it is *only* one of the many, and informed choice is critical."[12]

In a radio debate with Doug Scott, director of public policy for the Christian Action Council, Newcomer defended her beliefs: "Sometimes the decision [to include chastity training] is more an implicit assumption about the value of abstinence for young people. The age at which intercourse is thought to be acceptable varies widely, though I have met few people who wholeheartedly think twelve- or thirteen-year-olds are ready."

Scott argued that the statement was ridiculous and that young people should be taught abstinence.

Newcomer: "That is your value judgment."

Scott: "No, it's not my value judgment. That's what's best for teens. There are certain basics that are not a question of values but a question of what is good for teens. It is not good for teens to be involved with drugs. It is not good for teens to be involved with alcohol. It is not good for teens to be involved in sexual activity. It is just not good for them—psychologically, physically, emotionally—there is no positive aspect."

Newcomer: "I can't say I can be as categorical about sexual behavior as I am about the use of cigarettes and illicit substances."[13]

Defunding Planned Parenthood

Major corporations are increasingly giving large financial donations to Planned Parenthood, which has given high priority to soliciting these gifts. Their efforts have been greatly rewarded. When we support these corporations, we enable them to contribute to Planned Parenthood from their excess profits. The Christian Action Council publishes an up-to-date list of corporate sponsors of Planned Parenthood and urges all concerned citizens to write letters of protest to the corporate executives in charge of the decision to fund Planned Parenthood. (You may obtain a copy of this list by writing the Christian Action Council, 101 West Broad Street, Suite 500, Falls Church, VA 22046. Please enclose a self-addressed stamped envelope with your request.)

Corporations usually donate their money through a foundation, and corporate leaders, when pressed, often justify their donations by saying they are not being used for abortion but for Planned Parenthood's educational programs. Some corporate executives claim that the foundations are independent from the main company even though the foundation's funds come directly from corporate profits. Others admit that they support Planned Parenthood because they adhere to its philosophy.

Corporate leaders should be made to understand that Planned Parenthood is a controversial organization, and no funds should go to them. Any money given to Planned Parenthood for any purpose frees up other monies for abortion advocacy. Put simply, it is bad business to donate to an organization such as Planned Parenthood whose programs are pro-abortion and anti-family. If companies support Planned Parenthood, they support abortion—it's as simple as that. Conversely, to work against the funding of Planned Parenthood is to work against abortion, a worthy task for any pro-life organization to undertake.

If you are willing to take on the challenge of defunding Planned Parenthood, first familiarize yourself with the list of corporate sponsors. Then organize a letter-writing campaign to voice displeasure with a corporation's support of Planned Parenthood. The letters should state that you will refuse to give your business to any company that supports Planned Parenthood. Inform the company that you will purchase a competitor's product as long as the company continues its support. Finally, tell the company why you oppose Planned Parenthood. Take time to educate the corporate executive who may be totally unaware of Planned Parenthood's agenda.

Letter-writing campaigns work. In March 1990, executives from AT&T, a corporation that had generously supported Planned Parenthood, informed the Christian Action Council that their support would end. AT&T acknowledged that it made its decision after receiving numerous letters and phone calls from concerned consumers.

Doug Scott of the Christian Action Council was recently contacted by a salesman for a major U.S. company that donates to Planned Parenthood. The salesman said he was tired of having people refuse to buy his product because of his company's support of Planned Parenthood. The salesman had been in the dark about his company's policy and said he was going to complain about it to his superior.

Employees of companies that support Planned Parenthood are becoming increasingly nervous when they ascertain that a large segment of the public disapproves of those contributions. A slowdown in sales means a loss of business and a loss of jobs. The thought of layoffs is not pleasant to any hard-working employee who cares about his career. Thus, many corporate leaders have decided to stop funding Planned Parenthood due to pressure brought by the public and the employees of the company.

Planned Parenthood not only obtains large corporate grants, it also receives considerable government funding. However, local efforts to end funding of Planned Parenthood can pay off if pursued with diligence. After years of effort, the Christian Action Council chapter in North Carolina was successful in 1988 in stopping taxpayer funds in Mecklenburg county from going to Planned Parenthood.

Mecklenburg county had been funding Planned Parenthood for many years. Led by local Christian Action Council leader Barrett Mosbacker, a group calling itself "The Ad Hoc Committee to Oppose Public Funding of Planned Parenthood" lobbied aggressively behind the scenes and rallied support for their cause. Mosbacker was criticized by the media, led by *The Charlotte Observer.* This is not surprising considering that the newspaper's publisher received the "Margaret Sanger Award" from Planned Parenthood in 1985. The publisher even vowed to "personally make up the difference in the budget" if the county commission refused to fund Planned Parenthood.

When the vote was taken, two county commissioners who had supported Planned Parenthood in the past changed sides, giving the pro-life side a 4-3 victory. In response, Planned Parenthood took out a full-page advertisement in the *Observer* attacking, by name, the four commissioners who had opposed funding.

Guidelines for Defunding Planned Parenthood

From the experience in Mecklenburg county, Barrett Mosbacker and the CAC developed the following guidelines as a long-term strategy for defunding Planned Parenthood in the local community. This strategy will need to be adapted to each local situation, but through hard work and the use of as many of the guidelines as possible, the Mecklenburg county success story can be repeated.

1. Begin to gather data on the level of teenage pregnancy in your area. Be sure to keep this data separate from pregnancies of married teenagers and teenagers who are 18 years of age or older. Gather information on the effectiveness of sex education and family planning programs in reducing teenage pregnancy rates. Such informa-

tion is readily available from major Christian and conservative organizations across the country. It is important that all information gathered be factual, in its proper context, and properly footnoted whether presented orally or in writing.

2. Prepare factual and concise flyers and/or short reports for distribution to local government officials, the media, and others interested in the issue.

3. Set up breakfast and lunch meetings with key members of the media, local government officials, and other community leaders to discuss the problem of teenage pregnancy and Planned Parenthood in particular. Personal contact is an effective method of communicating your point of view. As you build personal relationships your credibility and your effectiveness will increase.

4. Remember that the media is not your enemy. Develop cordial, professional relationships with key media figures whenever possible, and be prepared to provide them with factual information when they request it or as you deem appropriate.

5. Identify and recruit as many professionals as possible (lawyers, doctors, nurses, teachers, business executives, clergy) to work with you. They can provide valuable insight, add credibility to your efforts, and are excellent spokespersons.

6. Form a committee to develop a plan of action and delegate responsibilities. The plan of action should be clear and concise. Everyone should know exactly what is expected of them and, when possible, on what date it will be expected. It may be best not to identify the committee with a pro-life group as this will automatically bias the

press coverage and the perceptions of elected officials.

7. Do not resort to unnecessary and inflammatory rhetoric. For example, do not refer to Planned Parenthood as "sex-perts" or to school-based clinics as "sex clinics." Such language only serves to detract from your credibility and does nothing to enhance your arguments. Moreover, such language is unprofessional and connotes "fanaticism" in the minds of the media and the general public.

8. Gather factual information on the level of public spending in support of Planned Parenthood over the same period. Was there an increase in expenditures for Planned Parenthood as well as pregnancy rates? This will be the case in most areas. Use this information to demonstrate that Planned Parenthood cannot prove that their programs have been effective.

9. Get a written legal opinion from the state attorney general regarding the impact of state parental notification/consent laws. It is important to document, in those states with such laws, that Planned Parenthood is providing abortion and/or contraceptive services to minors without parental notification or consent. Parents, school board members, the media, and local government officials need this information. Because each state is different, a written opinion from the state attorney general should be obtained. You may have to go through a member of state legislature to get such an opinion.

10. Submit in advance a list of qualified individuals to those who will be appointing members of various committees and task forces established to study teenage pregnancy and intervention strate-

gies. Preferably, the list should be comprised of professionals. Because such committees are almost always a part of the implementation strategy employed by Planned Parenthood supporters, it is important to be prepared in advance to submit qualified nominees for such committees.

11. Identify those who are supporting Planned Parenthood and the groups or agencies with which they are affiliated. Pay close attention to the arguments they are using to justify support of Planned Parenthood, and be prepared in advance to respond to their arguments with carefully reasoned responses and documented facts.

12. Do not use outdated information about Planned Parenthood. Gather current material and information, preferably from the local Planned Parenthood affiliate. Avoid quoting material from sources that are obviously Christian or pro-life. Unfortunately, the media and the public consider information provided from such sources as suspect because it comes from "biased" organizations. It is best to reference material from government agencies, respected journals, and from Planned Parenthood itself. Discussions concerning Margaret Sanger should be limited or eliminated.

13. Be prepared to offer alternatives to funding of Planned Parenthood. This is critical as it is difficult for elected officials to vote against a proposed "solution" to a real problem unless they have an alternative they can support. One alternative could include revising the sex education curriculum.

14. Compile a comprehensive list of all services available throughout the community which provide counseling, family planning, and health care

services to adolescents. It is not necessary that the list include only those agencies with which you are in agreement. The point is to prove that services exist and to provide the total cost of providing each service. Generally, such a list reveals that substantial sums of money are already being spent on a wide range of services available to adolescents. In such cases, funding of Planned Parenthood is an expensive and unnecessary duplication of services.

15. Monitor the budget process. A good time to make a concerted effort to defund Planned Parenthood is when elected officials are looking for ways to cut the budget. If Planned Parenthood becomes a controversial and time-consuming item in the budget, elected officials are more likely to cut their funding.

Why Pick On Planned Parenthood?

Our legitimate concern is Planned Parenthood's philosophy of "family planning" which includes advocacy of abortion and unrestricted access to contraceptives for teens without parental knowledge or consent. The fact that Planned Parenthood is the nation's number one abortion provider is enough to call into question its legitimacy.

As restrictions on abortion are adopted by state legislatures during the next few years, the chief antagonist to the pro-life movement will be Planned Parenthood. Perhaps it is accurate to say that Planned Parenthood will become "public enemy number one" to the pro-life community in the very near future. A comprehensive pro-life agenda which will end abortion in America must challenge the ethic of Planned Parenthood and its aggressive public advocacy of abortion-on-demand.

For many this challenge may seem insurmountable.

This is the same attitude the Israelites had about Goliath. However, like David, we must not be afraid to challenge this giant which has infiltrated our culture with its philosophy and ethic. Instead, we must rely on strength from above to accomplish the task of defeating the giant and restoring Christian values in the public arena. As we undertake spiritual warfare against this promoter of abortion, we should commit to pray for Faye Wattleton, president of Planned Parenthood, that her eyes would be opened to the destruction her organization has done in the lives of many and that she personally will return to the Christian faith in which she was raised.

The rebuilding of this particular section of the wall may be the most difficult part of the task which is before us. Yet, by the grace of God, this monumental challenge can be met through the devotion and determined work of his people.

Notes

1. There have been several books recently published which discuss in detail the philosophy of Planned Parenthood. I believe the most comprehensive publication is *Inside Planned Parenthood* by Douglas R. Scott, director of public policy for the Christian Action Council. Copies may be purchased from the Christian Action Council, 101 West Broad Street, Suite 500, Falls Church, VA 22046. I have relied heavily on this book as resource material for this chapter.

2. Elasah Drogrin, *Margaret Sanger: Father of Modern Society* (Coarsegold, Calif.: CUL Publications, 1979, 1980), 15.

3. Margaret Sanger, *Pivot of Civilization* (New York: Brentano's, 1922), 146, 189.

4. Ibid., 186.

5. David Kennedy, *Birth Control in America: The Career of Margaret Sanger* (New Haven and London: Yale University Press, 1970), 23.

Catch the Vision

As we enter the decade of the nineties, the people of God have been given a unique opportunity. The destiny of our nation may well be determined within the next few years, and the church of Jesus Christ can, if it so chooses, lead this country down the road to revival, restoration, and healing. Yet such a journey will not be easy and many road-blocks will be placed in our way. Like Nehemiah, however, we can be confident that despite temporary setbacks, the wall of protection shall be rebuilt through the Spirit-directed work of God's people.

Nehemiah was not the only man of God who faced discouragement and obstructions to his efforts. Neither was he the only one to battle evil in his society. Near the end of the seventh century B.C., the prophet Habakkuk voiced his dismay about the evil running rampant in Judah. Habakkuk's lament over the evil in his land could well be our own. God's response to Habakkuk should comfort us today as we battle the evil of abortion and attempt to rebuild the wall of protection for the unborn.

Habakkuk, A Frustrated Prophet

Habakkuk first observes that the leaders in Judah are oppressing the poor, and he asks God why he allows the wicked to prosper:

> How long, O LORD, must I call for help,
>   but you do not listen?
> Or cry out to you, "Violence!"
>   but you do not save?
> Why do you make me look at injustice?
>   Why do you tolerate wrong?
> Destruction and violence are before me;
>   there is strife, and conflict abounds.
> Therefore the law is paralyzed,
>   and justice never prevails.
> The wicked hem in the righteous,
>   so that justice is perverted.
>
> (Habakkuk 1:2-4)

The Lord is quick to respond, but in a manner Habakkuk did not expect:

> "Look at the nations and watch—
>   and be utterly amazed.
> For I am going to do something in your days
>   that you would not believe,
>   even if you were told.
> I am raising up the Babylonians,
>   that ruthless and impetuous people,
> who sweep across the whole earth
>   to seize dwelling places not their own."
>
> (Habakkuk 1:5-6)

Habakkuk was upset when he heard that God's judgment would come upon Judah through the conquering Babylonian empire. And who could blame him? Can you imagine how we would feel today if the Lord answered our prayers for our nation by saying he was raising up the Soviet Union to invade America and destroy it as judgment for our sins? Habakkuk's response was understandable, and he registers a second grievance before the Lord:

> O LORD, are you not from everlasting?
>   My God, my Holy One, we will not die.
> O LORD, you have appointed them to
>   execute judgment;
>   O Rock, you have ordained them to
>   punish.
> Your eyes are too pure to look on evil;
>   you cannot tolerate wrong.
> Why then do you tolerate the treacherous?
>   Why are you silent while the wicked
>   swallow up those more righteous than
>   themselves?
> You have made men like fish in the sea,
>   like sea creatures that have no ruler.
> The wicked foe pulls all of them up with
>   hooks,
>   he catches them in his net,
> he gathers them up in his dragnet;
>   and so he rejoices and is glad.
> Therefore he sacrifices to his net
>   and burns incense to his dragnet,
> for by his net he lives in luxury
>   and enjoys the choicest food.
> Is he to keep on emptying his net,
>   destroying nations without mercy?
>   (Habakkuk 1:12-17)

So far we see a picture of a frustrated prophet. Habakkuk observes evil in his land and cries out to the Lord. When the Lord responds, the answer is not what

Habakkuk wanted to hear. I believe Christians in twentieth-century America can identify with Habakkuk in our frustrations over the evil of abortion. Perhaps if Habakkuk were a modern-day American, his complaint to the Lord would sound something like this:

> "Lord, why do you allow wicked men to continue to kill unborn babies? And why do you allow them to prosper for such acts? When will you bring about an end to this slaughter? Lord, Planned Parenthood receives honor in the eyes of our countrymen, yet this organization promotes the destruction of your little ones. Your people who do your work in crisis pregnancy centers receive scorn and ridicule from the media and disdain from government officials. Politicians are rewarded for their votes to kill the innocent while those who stand for life are mocked. How long, O Lord, must we call for an end to the bloodshed before you will listen? How many times must we cry out to you, 'Violence!' but you do not save?"

The Lord's Response

Habakkuk's complaining before the Lord does not go unanswered. The Lord's reply, I believe, is relevant to those of us who long to see an end to the violence of abortion in our land.

> Then the LORD replied:
> "Write down the revelation
>   and make it plain on tablets
>   so that a herald may run with it.
> For the revelation awaits an appointed time;
>   it speaks of the end
>   and will not prove false.
> Though it linger, wait for it;
>   it will certainly come and will not delay."
>   (Habakkuk 2:2-3)

The Lord continues by assuring Habakkuk that Babylon will be dealt with in God's good timing, "for the earth will be filled with the knowledge of the glory of the LORD, as the waters cover the sea" (v. 14). To Babylon the Lord says:

> "You will be filled with shame instead of
>   glory.
>   Now it is your turn! Drink and be
>   exposed!
> The cup from the LORD's right hand is
>   coming around to you,
>   and disgrace will cover your glory.
> The violence you have done to Lebanon will
>   overwhelm you,
>   and your destruction of animals will terrify
>   you.
> For you have shed man's blood;
>   you have destroyed lands and cities and
>   everyone in them" (2:16-17).

The Lord's response to Habakkuk's frustrations is a powerful message to the pro-life movement today. Can we catch the divinely inspired vision God has for his people? Can we see the big picture that God will eventually triumph over evil, even the evil of abortion? Though at times it appears that God's justice is silent, do we have the faith to believe that we can be his divinely appointed vessels to eliminate abortion from our land?

God's answer to Habakkuk contains three points that will instruct us in our efforts to rebuild the wall of protection. In setting forth our plans and strategies to end abortion, we should note how the Lord advised Habakkuk to implement the promised revelation.

First, write down the blueprint for action. God instructed Habakkuk to "write down the revelation." That guidance makes good sense in our planning for pro-life activism in the nineties. Our strategy for rebuilding the wall must be written down as a permanent record to pass on to our successors. As the Lord said to Habakkuk, the revelation should be written down "so that a herald may run with it."

We may not live to see the divinely inspired vision God has given us for an abortion-free America come to fruition. Like Moses, we may never enter the "promised land," only view it from afar. Therefore, all our pro-life efforts must be preceded by prayer and a strategically planned blueprint for action. Making a written record of those plans is crucial if they are to be passed on for future enactment.

Second, be specific in your game plan. The Lord instructed Habakkuk to write down the vision and "make it plain on tablets." To be victorious we must plan specific details for implementation. During wartime, the general of the army plans the precise moves of his troops in order to have the strategic advantage. It is no different in the battle over abortion. By enlisting in this campaign one is committed to fighting a war for the very soul of this country. To be successful we must have a specific game plan made plain for all its adherents to follow.

Third, trust in God's perfect timing for the ultimate victory. The Lord gives comfort to us in his message to Habakkuk when he says,

> "For the revelation awaits an appointed time;
>   it speaks of the end
>   and will not prove false.
> Though it linger, wait for it;
>   it will certainly come and will not delay."

God's timing is different from ours, which is riddled with impatience and often lacks God's perspective. We must understand that the sovereignty of God guarantees that abortion will end. We must be patient and trust him for the ultimate results of our labors. A great hero of the faith, William Wilberforce, understood this in his more than fifty-year battle to end slavery in England. Not until the end of his life did Wilberforce see the institution of slavery dissolve as a result of his prayerful and Spirit-led efforts. Yet he trusted the results of his endeavors to God whose timing is perfect.

We may not live to see the end of abortion in our country, yet God's timing is perfect and his promises are true. Habakkuk finally understood this truth as he boldly proclaimed at the end of his book:

> Though the fig tree does not bud
>   and there are no grapes on the vines,
> though the olive crop fails
>   and the fields produce no food,
> though there are no sheep in the pen
>   and no cattle in the stalls,
> yet I will rejoice in the LORD,
>   I will be joyful in God my Savior.
>   (Habakkuk 3:17-18)

To achieve an abortion-free America by 2001 we must catch the vision that God is triumphant and will ultimately destroy this evil in our land. And we must commit ourselves to his service, proclaiming the sanctity of all human life regardless of gender, race, handicap, or condition of dependency.

Through a commitment to the Lordship of Jesus Christ and a firm resolve to obey him, we can be effective during the decade of the nineties in abolishing abortion. Nehemiah understood that without a complete consecration of his labors to the Lord, he would not succeed in rebuilding the wall in Jerusalem. Habakkuk understood that we may not see the end results of our work, but God is sovereign and will be triumphant. To end abortion in America the people of God must, like Nehemiah and Habakkuk, dedicate themselves to the cause of Christ and then move out in faith, knowing that even though we may not see the fruits of our labors we are on the winning side.

We can be confident of ultimate victory because we are representatives of a new world yet to come where the Lord of Life will reign supreme. As we work for the day when the evil of abortion is ended, we should take inspiration from the psalmist David, the forerunner of King Jesus:

Commit your way to the LORD;
   trust in him and he will do this:
He will make your righteousness shine like
      the dawn,
   the justice of your cause like the noonday sun.

(Psalm 37:5-6)

I am still confident of this:
   I will see the goodness of the LORD
   in the land of the living.
Wait for the LORD;
   be strong and take heart
   and wait for the LORD.

(Psalm 27:13-14)

Justice for innocent human life made in the image of God shall come to pass! As followers of Christ we can be used in a powerful way at this crucial time in our country's history. Let us resolve within ourselves to respond to this challenge and to rescue the innocent being led to slaughter every day at abortion clinics in America. With the help of God, and through a passionate commitment to his kingdom, we shall prevail.

APPENDIX A

Roe v. *Wade*

(Edited)

**MR. JUSTICE BLACKMUN
delivered the opinion of the Court . . .**

We forthwith acknowledge our awareness of the sensitive and emotional nature of the abortion controversy, of the vigorous opposing views, even among physicians, and of the deep and seemingly absolute convictions that the subject inspires. One's philosophy, one's experiences, one's exposure to the raw edges of human existence, one's religious training, one's attitudes toward life and family and their values, and the moral standards one establishes and seeks to observe, are all likely to influence and to color one's thinking and conclusions about abortion.

In addition, population growth, pollution, poverty, and racial overtones tend to complicate and not to simplify the problem.

Our task, of course, is to resolve the issue by constitutional measurement, free of emotion and of predilection. We seek earnestly to do this, and, because we do, we have inquired into, and in this opinion place some emphasis upon, medical and medical-legal history and what that history reveals about man's attitudes toward the abortion procedure over the centuries. . . .

The Texas statutes that concern us here . . . make it a crime to "procure an abortion," as therein defined, or to attempt one, except with respect to "an abortion procured or attempted by medical advice for the purpose of saving the life of the mother." Similar statutes are in existence in a majority of the States. . . .

The principal thrust of appellant's attack on the Texas statutes is that they improperly invade a right, said to be possessed by the pregnant woman, to choose to terminate her pregnancy. Appellant would discover this right in the concept of personal "liberty" embodied in the Fourteenth Amendment's Due Process Clause; or in personal, marital, familial, and sexual privacy said to be protected by the Bill of Rights or its penumbras, see *Griswold* v. *Connecticut*, 381 U. S. 479 (1965); *Eisenstadt* v. *Baird*, 405 U. S. 438 (1972); id., at 460 (WHITE, J., concurring in result); or among those rights reserved to the people by the Ninth Amendment, *Griswold* v. *Connecticut*, 381 U. S., at 486 (Goldberg, J., concurring). . . .

The Constitution does not explicitly mention any right of privacy. . . . [T]he Court has recognized that a right of personal privacy, or a guarantee of certain areas or zones of privacy, does exist under the constitution. In varying contexts, the Court or individual Justices have, indeed, found at least the roots of that right in the First Amendment . . . in the penumbras of the Bill of Rights . . . in the Ninth Amendment . . . or in the concept of liberty guaranteed by the first section of the Fourteenth Amendment. . . . These decisions make it clear that only personal rights that can be deemed "fundamental" or "implicit in the concept of ordered liberty" . . . are included in this guarantee of personal privacy. They also make it clear that the right has some extension to activities relating to marriage. . . .

This right of privacy, whether it be founded in the Fourteenth Amendment's concept of personal liberty and restrictions upon state action, as we feel it is, or, as the District Court determined, in the Ninth Amendment's reservation of rights to the people, is broad enough to encompass a woman's decision whether or not to terminate her pregnancy. The detriment that the State would impose upon the pregnant woman by denying this choice altogether is apparent. Specific and direct harm medically diagnosable even in early pregnancy may be involved. Maternity, or additional off-spring, may force upon the woman a distressful life and future. Psychological harm may be imminent. Mental and physical health may be taxed by child care. There is also the distress, for all concerned, associated with the unwanted child, and there is the problem of bringing a child into a family already unable, psychologically and otherwise, to care for it. In other cases, as in this one, the additional difficulties and continuing stigma of unwed motherhood may be involved. All these are factors the woman and her responsible physician necessarily will consider in consultation.

On the basis of elements such as these, appellant and some *amici* argue that the woman's right is absolute and that she is entitled to terminate her pregnancy at whatever time, in whatever way, and for whatever reason she alone chooses. With this we do not agree. . . . The Court's decisions recognizing a right of privacy also acknowledge that some state regulation in areas protected by that right is appropriate. As noted above, a State may properly assert important interests in safe-guarding health, in maintaining medical standards, and in protecting potential life. At some point in pregnancy, these respective interests become sufficiently compelling to sustain regulation of the factors that govern the abortion decision. The privacy right involved, therefore, cannot be said to be absolute. In fact, it is not clear to us that the claim asserted by some *amici* that one has an unlimited right to do with one's body as one pleases bears a close relationship to the right of privacy previously articulated in the Court's decisions. The Court has refused to recognize an unlimited right of this kind in the past. . . .

We, therefore, conclude that the right of personal privacy includes the abortion decision, but that this right is not unqualified and must be considered against important state interests in regulation. . . .

Where certain "fundamental rights" are involved, the Court has held that regulation limiting these rights may be justified only by a "compelling state interest" . . . and that legislative enactments must be narrowly drawn to express only the legitimate state interests at stake. . . .

A. The appellee and certain *amici* argue that the fetus is a "person" within the language and meaning of the Fourteenth Amendment. In support of this, they outline at length and in detail the well-known facts of fetal development. If this suggestion of personhood is established, the appellant's case, of course, collapses, for the fetus' right to life would then be guaranteed specifically by the Amendment. The appellant conceded as much on reargument. On the other hand, the appellee conceded on reargument that no case could be cited that holds that a fetus is a person within the meaning of the Fourteenth Amendment.

The Constitution does not define "person" in so many words. Section 1 of the Fourteenth Amendment contains three references to "person." The first, in defining "citizens," speaks of "persons born or naturalized in the United States." The word also appears both in the Due Process Clause and in the Equal Protection Clause. "Person" is used in other places in the Constitution: in the listing of qualifications for

Representatives and Senators, Art. I, §2, cl. 2, and §3, cl. 3; in the Apportionment Clause, Art. I, §2, cl. 3; in the Migration and Importation provision, Art. I, §9, cl. 1; in the Emolument Clause, Art. I, §9, cl. 8; in the Electors provisions, Art. II, §1, cl. 5; in the Extradition provisions, Art. IV, §2, cl. 2, and the superseded Fugitive Slave Clause 3; and in the Fifth, Twelfth, and Twenty-second Amendments, as well as in §§2 and 3 of the Fourteenth Amendment. But in nearly all these instances, the use of the word is such that it has application only postnatally. None indicates, with any assurance, that it has any possible prenatal application.

All this, together with our observation, *supra*, that throughout the major portion of the 19th century prevailing legal abortion practices were far freer than they are today, persuades us that the word "person," as used in the Fourteenth Amendment, does not include the unborn. . . .

This conclusion, however, does not of itself fully answer the contentions raised by Texas, and we pass on to other considerations.

B. The pregnant woman cannot be isolated in her privacy. She carries an embryo and, later, a fetus, if one accepts the medical definitions of the developing young in the human uterus. See Dorland's Illustrated Medical Dictionary 478-479, 547 (24th ed. 1965). The situation therefore is inherently different from marital intimacy, or bedroom possession of obscene material, or marriage, or procreation, or education, with which *Eisenstadt* and *Griswold, Stanley, Loving, Skinner*, and *Pierce* and *Meyer* were respectively concerned. As we have intimated above, it is reasonable and appropriate for a State to decide that at some point in time another interest, that of health of the mother or that of potential human life, becomes significantly involved. The woman's privacy is no longer sole and any right of privacy she possesses must be measured accordingly.

Texas urges that, apart from the Fourteenth Amendment, life begins at conception and is present throughout pregnancy, and that, therefore the State has a compelling interest in protecting that life from and after conception. We need not resolve the difficult question of when life begins. When those trained in the respective disciplines of medicine, philosophy, and theology are unable to arrive at any consensus, the judiciary, at this point in the development of man's knowledge, is not in a position to speculate as to the answer.

It should be sufficient to note briefly the wide divergence of thinking on this most sensitive and difficult question. There has always been strong support for the view that life does not begin until live birth. This was the belief of the Stoics. It appears to be the predominant, though not the unanimous, attitude of the Jewish faith. It may be taken to represent also the position of a large segment of the Protestant community, insofar as that can be ascertained. . . . As we have noted, the common law found greater significance in quickening. Physicians and their scientific colleagues have regarded that event with less interest and have tended to focus either upon conception, upon live birth, or upon the interim at which the fetus becomes "viable," that is, potentially able to live outside the mother's womb, albeit with artificial aid. Viability is usually placed at about seven months (28 weeks) but may occur earlier, even at 24 weeks. . . .

In areas other than criminal abortion, the law has been reluctant to endorse any theory that life, as we recognize it, begins before live birth or to accord legal rights to the unborn except in narrowly defined situations and except when the rights are contingent upon live birth. For example, the traditional rule of tort law denied recovery for prenatal injuries even though the child was born alive. That rule has been changed in almost every jurisdiction. In most States, recovery is said to be permitted only if the fetus was viable, or at least quick, when the injuries were sustained, though few courts have squarely so held. In a recent development, generally opposed by the commentators, some States permit the parents of a stillborn child to maintain an action for wrongful death because of prenatal injuries. Such an action, however, would appear to be one to vindicate the parents' interest and is thus consistent with the view that the fetus, at most, represents only the potentiality of life. Similarly, unborn children have been recognized as acquiring rights or interests by way of inheritance or other devolution of property, and have been represented by guardians *ad litem.* Perfection of the interests involved, again, has generally been contingent upon live birth. In short, the unborn have never been recognized in the law as persons in the whole sense.

In view of all this, we do not agree that, by adopting one theory of life, Texas may override the rights of the pregnant woman that are at stake. We repeat, however, that the State does have an important and legitimate interest in preserving and protecting the health of the pregnant woman, whether she be a resident of the State or a nonresident who seeks medical consultation and treatment there, and that it has still *another* important and legitimate interest in protecting the potentiality of human life. These interests are separate and distinct. Each grows in substantiality as the woman approaches term and, at a point during pregnancy, each becomes "compelling."

With respect to the State's important and legitimate interest in the health of the mother, the "compelling" point, in the light of present medical knowledge, is at approximately the end of the first trimester. This is so because of the now-established medical fact, referred to above . . . that until the end of the first trimester mortality in abortion may be less than mortality in normal childbirth. It follows that, from and after this point, a State may regulate the abortion procedure to the extent that the regulation reasonably relates to the preservation and protection of maternal health. Examples of permissible state regulation in this area are requirements as to the qualifications of the person who is to perform the abortion; as to the licensure of that person; as to the facility in which the procedure is to be performed, that is, whether is must be a hospital or may be a clinic or some other place of less-than-hospital status; as to the licensing of the facility; and the like.

This means, on the other hand, that, for the period of pregnancy prior to this "compelling" point, the attending physician, in consultation with his patient, is free to determine, without regulation by the State, that, in his medical judgment, the patient's pregnancy should be terminated. If that decision is reached, the judgment may be effectuated by an abortion free of interference by the State.

With respect to the State's important and legitimate interest in potential life, the "compelling" point is at viability. This is so because the fetus then presumably has the capability of meaningful life outside the mother's womb. State regulation protective of fetal life after viability thus has both logical and biological justifications. If the State is interested in protecting fetal life after viability, it may go so far as to proscribe abortion during that period, except when it is necessary to preserve the life or health of the mother.

Measured against these standards, Art. 1196 of the Texas Penal Code, in restricting legal abortions to those "procured or attempted by medical advice for the purpose of saving the life of the mother," sweeps too broadly. The statute makes no distinction between abortions performed early in pregnancy and those performed later, and it limits to a single reason, "saving" the mother's life, the legal justification for the procedure. The statute, therefore, cannot survive the constitutional attack made upon it here. . . .

To summarize and to repeat:

1. A state criminal abortion statute of the current Texas type, that excepts from criminality only a *life-saving* procedure on behalf of the mother, without regard to pregnancy

stage and without recognition of the other interests involved, is violative of the Due Process Clause of the Fourteenth Amendment.

(a) For the stage prior to approximately the end of the first trimester, the abortion decision and its effectuation must be left to the medical judgment of the pregnant woman's attending physician.

(b) For the stage subsequent to approximately the end of the first trimester, the State, in promoting its interest in the health of the mother, may, if it chooses, regulate the abortion procedure in ways that are reasonably related to maternal health.

(c) For the stage subsequent to viability, the State in promoting its interest in the potentiality of human life may, if it chooses, regulate, and even proscribe, abortion except where it is necessary, in appropriate medical judgment, for the preservation of the life or health of the mother.

2. The State may define the term "physician," as it has been employed in the preceding paragraphs of this Part XI of this opinion, to mean only a physician currently licensed by the State, and may proscribe any abortion by a person who is not a physician as so defined. . . .

This holding, we feel, is consistent with the relative weights of the respective interests involved, with the lessons and examples of medical and legal history, with the lenity of the common law, and with the demands of the profound problems of the present day. The decision leaves the State free to place increasing restrictions on abortion as the period of pregnancy lengthens, so long as those restrictions are tailored to the recognized state interests. The decision vindicates the right of the physician to administer medical treatment according to his professional judgment up to the points where important state interests provide compelling justifications for intervention. Up to those points, the abortion decision in all its aspects is inherently, and primarily, a medical decision, and basic responsibility for it must rest with the physician. If an individual practitioner abuses the privilege of exercising proper medical judgment, the usual remedies, judicial and intra-professional, are available. . . .

It is so ordered.

**MR. JUSTICE REHNQUIST,
dissenting. . . .**

I have difficulty in concluding, as the Court does, that the right of "privacy" is involved in this case. Texas, by the statute here challenged, bars the performance of a medical abortion by a licensed physician on a plaintiff such as Roe. A transaction resulting in an operation such as this is not "private" in the ordinary usage of that word. Nor is the "privacy" that the Court finds here even a distant relative of the freedom from searches and seizures protected by the Fourth Amendment to the Constitution, which the Court has referred to as embodying a right to privacy. . . .

If the Court means by the term "privacy" no more than that the claim of a person to be free from unwanted state regulation of consensual transactions may be a form of "liberty" protected by the Fourteenth Amendment, there is no doubt that similar claims have been upheld in our earlier decisions on the basis of that liberty. I agree . . . that the "liberty," against deprivation of which without due process the Fourteenth Amendment protects, embraces more than the rights found in the Bill of Rights. But that liberty is not guaranteed absolutely against deprivation, only against deprivation without due process of law. The test traditionally applied in the area of social and economic legislation is whether or not a law such as that challenged has a rational relation to a valid state objective. . . . The Due Process Clause of the Fourteenth Amendment undoubtedly does place a limit, albeit a broad one, on legislative power to enact laws such as this. If the Texas statute were to prohibit an abortion even where the mother's life is in jeopardy, I have little doubt that such a statute would lack a rational relation to a valid state objective under the test stated in *Williamson, supra.* But the Court's sweeping invalidation of any restrictions on abortion during the first trimester is impossible to justify under that standard, and the conscious weighing of competing factors that the Court's opinion apparently substitutes for the established test is far more appropriate to a legislative judgment than to a judicial one.

The Court eschews the history of the Fourteenth Amendment in its reliance on the "compelling state interest" test. . . . But the Court adds a new wrinkle to this test by transposing it from the legal considerations associated with the Equal Protection Clause of the Fourteenth Amendment to this case arising under the Due Process Clause of the Fourteenth Amendment. Unless I misapprehend the consequences of this transplanting of the "compelling state interest test," the Court's opinion will accomplish the seemingly impossible feat of leaving this area of the law more confused than it found it. . . .

The fact that a majority of the States reflecting, after all, the majority sentiment in those States, have had restrictions on abortions for at least a century is a strong indication, it seems to me, that the asserted right to an abortion is not "so rooted in the traditions and conscience of our people as to be ranked as fundamental. . . ." Even today, when society's views on abortion are changing, the very existence of the debate is evidence that the "right" to an abortion is not so universally accepted as the appellant would have us believe.

To reach its result, the Court necessarily has had to find within the scope of the Fourteenth Amendment a right that was apparently completely unknown to the drafters of the Amendment. As early as 1821, the first state law dealing directly with abortion was enacted by the Connecticut Legislature. . . . By the time of the adoption of the

Fourteenth Amendment in 1868, there were at least 36 laws enacted by state or territorial legislatures limiting abortion [Alabama, Arizona, Arkansas, California, Colorado, Connecticut, Florida, Georgia, Kingdom of Hawaii, Idaho, Illinois, Indiana, Iowa, Kansas, Louisiana, Maine, Maryland, Massachusetts, Michigan, Minnesota, Mississippi, Missouri, Montana, Nevada, New Hampshire, New Jersey, New York, Ohio, Oregon, Pennsylvania, Texas, Vermont, Virginia, Washington, West Virginia, and Wisconsin]. While many States have amended or updated their laws, 21 of the laws on the books in 1868 remain in effect today [Arizona (1865), Connecticut (1860), Florida (1868), Idaho (1863), Indiana (1838), Iowa (1843), Maine (1840), Massachusetts (1845), Michigan (1846), Minnesota (1851), Missouri (1835), Montana (1864), Nevada (1861), New Hampshire (1848), New Jersey (1849), Ohio (1841), Pennsylvania (1860), Texas (1859), Vermont (1867), West Virginia (1863), and Wisconsin (1858)]. Indeed, the Texas statute struck down today was, as the majority notes, first enacted in 1857 and "has remained substantially unchanged to the present time. . . ."

There apparently was no question concerning the validity of this provision or of any of the other state statutes when the Fourteenth Amendment was adopted. The only conclusion possible from this history is that the drafters did not intend to have the Fourteenth Amendment withdraw from the States the power to legislate with respect to this matter. . . .

For all of the foregoing reasons, I respectfully dissent. . . .

MR. JUSTICE WHITE, with whom MR. JUSTICE REHNQUIST joins, dissenting.

At the heart of the controversy in these cases are those recurring pregnancies that pose no danger whatsoever to the life or health of the mother but are, nevertheless, unwanted for any one or more of a variety of reasons—convenience, family planning, economics, dislike of children, the embarrassment of illegitimacy, etc. The common claim before us is that for any one of such reasons, or for no reason at all, and without asserting or claiming any threat to life or health, any woman is entitled to an abortion at her request if she is able to find a medical advisor willing to undertake the procedure.

The Court for the most part sustains this position: during the period prior to the time the fetus becomes viable, the Constitution of the United States values the convenience, whim, or caprice of the putative mother more than the life or potential life of the fetus; the Constitution, therefore, guarantees the right to an abortion as against any state law or policy seeking to protect the fetus from an abortion not prompted by more compelling reasons of the mother.

With all due respect, I dissent. I find nothing in the language or history of the Constitution to support the Court's judgment. The Court simply fashions and announces a new constitutional right for pregnant mothers and, with scarcely any reason or authority for its action, invests that right with sufficient substance to override most existing state abortion statutes. The upshot is that the people and the legislatures of the 50 States are constitutionally disentitled to weigh the relative importance of the continued existence and development of the fetus, on the one hand, against a spectrum of possible impacts on the mother, on the other hand. As an exercise of raw judicial power, the Court perhaps has authority to do what it does today; but in my view its judgment is an improvident and extravagant exercise of the power of judicial review that the Constitution extends to this Court.

The Court apparently values the convenience of the pregnant mother more than the continued existence and development of the life or potential life that she carries.

Whether or not I might agree with that marshaling of values, I can in no event join the Court's judgment because I find no constitutional warrant for imposing such an order of priorities on the people and legislatures of the States. In a sensitive area such as this, involving as it does issues over which reasonable men may easily and heatedly differ, I cannot accept the Court's exercise of its clear power of choice by interposing a constitutional barrier to state efforts to protect human life and by investing mothers and doctors with the constitutionally protected right to exterminate it. This issue, for the most part, should be left with the people and to the political processes the people have devised to govern their affairs.

It is my view, therefore, that the Texas statute is not constitutionally infirm because it denies abortions to those who seek their life or health. Nor is this plaintiff, who claims no threat to her mental or physical health, entitled to assert the possible rights of those women whose pregnancy assertedly implicates their health. . . .

APPENDIX B

Webster v. *Reproductive Health Services*

(Edited)

**CHIEF JUSTICE REHNQUIST
announced the judgment of the Court. . . .**

This appeal concerns the constitutionality of a Missouri statute regulating the performance of abortions. . . .

The Act consisted of 20 provisions, 5 of which are now before the Court. The first provisions, or preamble, contains "findings" by the state legislature that "[t]he life of each human being begins at conception," and that "unborn children have protectable interests in life, health, and well-being." The Act further requires that all Missouri laws be interpreted to provide unborn children with the same rights enjoyed by other persons, subject to the Federal Constitution and this Court's precedents. Among its other provisions, the Act requires that, prior to performing an abortion on any woman whom a physician has reason to believe is 20 or more weeks pregnant, the physician ascertain whether the fetus is viable by performing "such medical examinations and tests as are necessary to make a finding of the gestational age, weight, and lung maturity of the unborn child." The Act also prohibits the use of public funds, employees, or facilities for the purpose of "encouraging or counseling" a woman to have an abortion not necessary to save her life. . . .

The Act's preamble, as noted, sets forth "findings" by the Missouri legislature that "[t]he life of each human being begins at conception," and that "[u]nborn children have protectable interests in life, health, and well-being." The Act then mandates that state laws be interpreted to provide unborn children with "all the rights, privileges, and immunities available to other persons, citizens, and residents of this state," subject to the Constitution and this Court's precedents. In invalidating the preamble, the Court of Appeals relied on this Court's dictum that " 'a State may not adopt one theory of when life begins to justify its regulation of abortions.' " It rejected Missouri's claim that the preamble was "abortion-neutral," and "merely determine[d] when life begins in a nonabortion context, a traditional state prerogative." . . .

In our view, the Court of Appeals misconceived the meaning of the *Akron* dictum, which was only that a State could not "justify" an abortion regulation otherwise invalid under *Roe* v. *Wade* on the ground that it embodied the State's view about when life begins. Certainly the preamble does not by its terms regulate abortion or any other aspect of appellees' medical practice. The Court has emphasized that *Roe* v. *Wade* "implies no limitation on the authority of a State to make a value judgment favoring childbirth over abortion." The preamble can be read simply to express that sort of value judgment.

We think the extent to which the preamble's language

might be used to interpret other state statutes or regulations is something that only the courts of Missouri can definitively decide. State law has offered protections to unborn children in tort and probate law, and §1.205.2 can be interpreted to do no more than that. . . .

Section 188.210 provides that "[i]t shall be unlawful for any public employee within the scope of his employment to perform or assist an abortion, not necessary to save the life of the mother," while §188.215 makes it "unlawful for any public facility to be used for the purpose of performing or assisting an abortion not necessary to save the life of the mother.". . . The Court of Appeals held that these provisions contravened this Court's abortion decisions. We take the contrary view. . . .

[T]he State's decision here to use public facilities and staff to encourage childbirth over abortion "places no governmental obstacle in the path of a woman who chooses to terminate her pregnancy." Just as Congress' refusal to fund abortions . . . left "an indigent woman with at least the same range of choice in deciding whether to obtain a medically necessary abortion as she would have had if Congress had chosen to subsidize no health care costs at all," Missouri's refusal to allow public employees to perform abortions in public hospitals leaves a pregnant woman with the same choices as if the State had chosen not to operate any public hospitals at all. The challenged provisions only restrict a woman's ability to obtain an abortion to the extent that she chooses to use a physician affiliated with a public hospital. . . . Having held that the State's refusal to fund abortions does not violate *Roe* v. *Wade*, it strains logic to reach a contrary result for the use of public facilities and employees. If the State may "make a value judgment by the allocation of public funds," surely it may do so through the allocation of other public resources, such as hospitals and medical staff. . . .

Nothing in the Constitution requires States to enter or

remain in the business of performing abortions. Nor, as appellees suggest, do private physicians and their patients have some kind of constitutional right of access to public facilities for the performance of abortions. . . .

Section 188.029 of the Missouri Act provides:

"Before a physician performs an abortion on a woman he has reason to believe is carrying an unborn child of twenty or more weeks gestational age, the physician shall first determine if the unborn child is viable by using and exercising that degree of care, skill, and proficiency commonly exercised by the ordinarily skillful, careful, and prudent physician engaged in similar practice under the same or similar conditions. In making this determination of viability, the physician shall perform or cause to be performed such medical examinations and tests as are necessary to make a finding of the gestational age, weight, and lung maturity of the unborn child and shall enter such findings and determination of viability in the medical record of the mother." . . .

The viability-testing provision of the Missouri Act is concerned with promoting the State's interest in potential human life rather than in maternal health. Section 188.029 creates what is essentially a presumption of viability at 20 weeks, which the physician must rebut with tests indicating that the fetus is not viable prior to performing an abortion. It also directs the physician's determination as to viability by specifying consideration, if feasible, of gestational age, fetal weight, and lung capacity. . . .

In *Roe* v. *Wade*, the Court recognized that the State has "important and legitimate" interests in protecting maternal health and in the potentiality of human life. 410 U. S., at 162. During the second trimester, the State "may, if it chooses, regulate the abortion procedure in ways that are reasonably related to maternal health." *Id.*, at 164. After viability, when the State's interest in potential human life was held to become compelling, the State "may, if it chooses, regulate, and even proscribe, abortion except where it is necessary, in appropriate medical judgment, for the preservation of the life or health of the mother." . . . *Id.*, at 165.

To the extent that §188.029 regulates the method for determining viability, it undoubtedly does superimpose state regulation on the medical determination of whether a particular fetus is viable. The Court of Appeals and the District Court thought it unconstitutional for this reason. To the extent that the viability tests increase the cost of what are in fact second-trimester abortions, their validity may also be questioned under *Akron*, 462 U. S., at 434-435, where the Court held that a requirement that second trimester abortions must be performed in hospitals was invalid because it substantially increased the expense of those procedures.

We think that the doubt cast upon the Missouri statute by these cases is not so much a flaw in the statute as it is a reflection of the fact that the rigid trimester analysis of the course of a pregnancy enunciated in *Roe* has resulted in subsequent cases . . . making constitutional law in this area a virtual Procrustean bed. Statutes specifying elements of informed consent to be provided abortion patients, for example, were invalidated if they were thought to "structur[e] . . . the dialogue between the woman and her physician." *Thornburgh* v. *American College of Obstetricians and Gynecologists*, 476 U. S. 747, 763 (1986). As the dissenters in *Thornburgh* pointed out, such a statute would have been sustained under any traditional standard of judicial review. . . .

[T]he rigid *Roe* framework is hardly consistent with the notion of a Constitution cast in general terms, as ours is, and usually speaking in general principles, as our does. The key elements of the *Roe* framework—trimesters and viability—are not found in the text of the Constitution or in any place else one would expect to find a constitutional principle. Since the bounds of the inquiry are essentially indeterminate, the result has been a web of legal rules that have become increasingly intricate, resembling a code of regulations rather than a body of constitutional doctrine. . . . As JUSTICE WHITE has put it, the trimester framework has left this Court to serve as the country's "*ex officio* medical board with powers to approve or disapprove medical and operative practices and standards throughout the United States." *Planned Parenthood of Central Missouri* v. *Danforth*, 428 U. S. . . .

In the second place, we do not see why the State's interest in protecting potential human life should come into existence only at the point of viability, and that there should therefore be a rigid line allowing state regulation after viability but prohibiting it before viability. The dissenters in *Thornburgh*, writing in the context of the *Roe* trimester analysis, would have recognized this fact by positing against the "fundamental right" recognized in *Roe* the State's "compelling interest" in protecting potential human life throughout pregnancy. "[T]he State's interest, if compelling after viability, is equally compelling before viability." *Thornburgh*, 476 U. S., at 795 (WHITE, J., dissenting); see *id.*, at 828 (O'CONNOR, J., dissenting) ("State has compelling interests in ensuring maternal health and in protecting potential human life, and these interests exist 'throughout pregnancy' ") (citation omitted).

The tests that §188.029 requires the physician to perform are designed to determine viability. The State here has chosen viability as the point at which its interest in potential human life must be safeguarded. . . . It is true that the tests in question increase the expense of abortion, and regulate the discretion of the physician in determining the viability of the fetus. Since the tests will undoubtedly show in many cases that the fetus is not viable, the tests will have been performed for what were in fact second-trimester abortions. But we are satisfied that the requirement of these tests permissibly furthers the State's interest in protecting potential human life, and we therefore believe §188.029 to be constitutional. . . .

The Missouri testing requirement here is reasonably designed to ensure that abortions are not performed where the fetus is viable—an end which all concede is legitimate—and that is sufficient to sustain its constitutionality. . . .

Both appellants and the United States as *Amicus Curiae* have urged that we overrule our decision in *Roe* v. *Wade*. . . . The facts of the present case, however, differ from those at issue in *Roe*. Here, Missouri has determined that viability is the point at which its interest in potential human life must be safeguarded. In *Roe*, on the other hand, the Texas statute criminalized the performance of *all* abortions, except when the mother's life was at stake. This case therefore affords us no occasion to revisit the holding of *Roe*, which was that the Texas statute unconstitutionally infringed the right to an abortion derived from the Due Process Clause, *id.*, at 164, and we leave it undisturbed. To the extent indicated in our opinion, we would modify and narrow *Roe* and succeeding cases.

Because none of the challenged provisions of the Missouri Act properly before us conflict with the Constitution, the judgment of the Court of Appeals is *Reversed.*

**JUSTICE O'CONNOR, concurring in part
and concurring in the judgment . . . .**

In its interpretation of Missouri's "determination of viability" . . . the plurality has proceeded in a manner unnecessary to deciding the question at hand. . . .

Unlike the plurality, I do not understand these viability testing requirements to conflict with any of the Court's past decisions concerning state regulation of abortion. Therefore, there is no necessity to accept the State's invitation to reexamine the constitutional validity of *Roe* v. *Wade*. Where there is no need to decide a constitutional question, it is a venerable principle of this Court's adjudicatory processes not to do so for "[t]he Court will not 'anticipate a question of constitutional law in advance of the necessity of deciding it.' ". . . Neither will it generally "formulate a rule of constitutional law broader than it required by the precise facts to which it is to be applied." Quite simply, "[i]t is not the habit of the court to decide questions of a constitutional nature unless absolutely necessary to a decision of the case." The Court today has accepted the State's every interpretation of its abortion statute and has upheld, under our existing precedents, every provision of that statute which is properly before us. Precisely for this reason reconsideration of *Roe* falls not into any "good-cause exception" to this "fundamental rule of judicial restraint . . . ." When the constitutional invalidity of a State's abortion statute actually turns on the constitutional validity of *Roe* v. *Wade*, there will be time enough to reexamine *Roe*. And to do so carefully. . . .

**JUSTICE SCALIA, concurring in part
and concurring in the judgment. . . .**

The outcome of today's case will doubtless be heralded as a triumph of judicial statesmanship. It is not that, unless it is statesmanlike needlessly to prolong this Court's self-awarded sovereignty over a field where it has little proper business since the answers to most of the cruel questions posed are political and not juridical—a sovereignty which therefore quite properly, but to the great damage of the Court, makes it the object of the sort of organized public pressure that political institutions in a democracy ought to receive. . . .

The real question, then, is whether there are valid reasons to go beyond the most stingy possible holding today. It seems to me there are not only valid but compelling ones. Ordinarily, speaking no more broadly than is absolutely required avoids throwing settled law into confusion; doing so today preserves a chaos that is evident to anyone who can read and count. Alone sufficient to justify a broad holding is the fact that our retaining control, through *Roe*, of what I believe to be, and many of our citizens recognize to be, a political issue, continuously distorts the public perception of the role of this Court. We can now look forward to at least another Term with carts full of mail from the public, and streets full of demonstrators, urging us—their unelected and life-tenured judges who have been awarded those extraordinary, undemocratic characteristics precisely in order that we might follow the law despite the popular will—to follow the popular will. Indeed, I expect we can look forward to even more of that than before, given our indecisive decision today. And if these reasons for taking the unexceptional course of reaching a broader holding are not enough, then consider the nature of the constitutional question we avoid: In most cases, we do no harm by not speaking more broadly than the decision requires. Anyone affected by the conduct that the avoided holding would have prohibited will be able to challenge it himself, and have his day in court to make the argument. Not so with respect to the harm that many States believed, pre-*Roe*, and many may continue to believe, is caused by largely unrestricted abortion. That will continue to occur if the States have the constitutional power to prohibit it, and would do so, but we skillfully avoid telling them so. Perhaps those abortions cannot constitutionally be proscribed. That is surely an arguable question, the question that reconsideration of *Roe* v. *Wade* entails. But what is not at all arguable, it seems to me, is that we should decide now and not insist that we be run into a corner before we grudgingly yield up our judgment. The only sound reason for the latter course is to prevent a plurality and JUSTICE SCALIA would overrule *Roe* (the first silently, the other explicitly) and would return to the States virtually unfettered authority to control the quintessentially intimate, personal, and life-directing decision whether to carry a fetus to term. Although today, no less than yesterday, the Constitution and the decisions of this Court prohibit a State from enacting laws that inhibit women from the meaningful exercise of that right, a plurality of this Court implicitly invites every state legislature to enact more and more restrictive abortion regulations in order to provoke more and more test cases, in the hope that sometime down the line the Court will return the law of procreative freedom to the severe limitations that generally prevailed in this country before January 22, 1973. Never in my memory has a plurality announced a judgment of this Court that so foments disregard for the law and for our standing decisions.

Nor in my memory has a plurality gone about its business in such a deceptive fashion. At every level of its review, from its effort to read the real meaning out of the Missouri statute, to its intended evisceration of precedents and its deafening silence about the constitutional protections that it would jettison, the plurality obscures the portent of its analysis. With feigned restraint, the plurality announces that its analysis leaves *Roe* "undisturbed," albeit "modif[lied] and narrow[ed]." *Ante*, at 23. But this disclaimer is totally meaningless. The plurality opinion is filled with winks, and nods, and knowing glances to those who would do away with *Roe* explicitly, but turns a stone face to anyone in search of what the plurality conceives as the scope of a woman's right under the Due Process Clause to terminate a pregnancy free from the coercive and brooding influence of the State. The simple truth is that *Roe* would not survive the plurality's analysis, and that the plurality provides no substitute for *Roe's* protective umbrella.

I fear for the future. I fear for the liberty and equality

of the millions of women who have lived and come of age in the 16 years since *Roe* was decided. I fear for the integrity of, and public esteem for, this Court.

I dissent. . . .

Thus, "not with a bang, but a whimper," the plurality discards a landmark case of the last generation, and casts into darkness the hopes and visions of every woman in this country who had come to believe that the Constitution guaranteed her the right to exercise some control over her unique ability to bear children. The plurality does so either oblivious or insensitive to the fact that millions of women, and their families, have ordered their lives around the right to reproductive choice, and that this right has become vital to the full participation of women in the economic and political walks of American life. . . .

For today, at least, the law of abortion stands undisturbed. For today, the women of this Nation still retain the liberty to control their destinies. But the signs are evident and very ominous, and a chill wind blows.

I dissent.

Missouri Law Upheld in *Webster*

HOUSE BILL NO. 1596
83rd General Assembly

AN ACT

Be it enacted by the General Assembly of the State of Missouri, as follows:

1.205. 1. The general assembly of this state finds that:

(1) The life of each human being begins at conception:

(2) Unborn children have protectable interests in life, health, and well-being:

(3) The natural parents of unborn children have protectable interests in the life, health, and well-being of their unborn child. . . .

188.029. Before a physician performs an abortion on a

woman he has reason to believe is carrying an unborn child of twenty or more weeks gestational age, the physician shall first determine if the unborn child is viable by using and exercising that degree of care, skill, and proficiency commonly exercised by the ordinarily skillful, careful, and prudent physician engaged in similar practice under the same or similar conditions. In making this determination of viability, the physician shall perform or cause to be performed such medical examinations and tests as are necessary to make a finding of the gestational age, weight, and lung maturity of the unborn child and shall enter such findings and determination of viability in the medical record of the mother.

188.039. 1. No physician shall perform an abortion unless, prior to such abortion, the physician certifies in writing that the woman gave her informed consent, freely and without coercion, after the attending physician had informed her of the information contained in subsection 2 of this section and shall further certify in writing the pregnant woman's age, based upon proof of age offered by her.

2. In order to insure that the consent for an abortion is truly informed consent, no abortion shall be performed or induced upon a pregnant woman unless she has signed a consent form that shall be supplied by the state department of health, acknowledging that she has been informed by the attending physician of the following facts:

(1) That according to the best medical judgment of her attending physician whether she is or is not pregnant:

(2) The particular risks associated with the abortion technique to be used;

(3) Alternatives to abortion shall be given by the attending physician.

3. The physician may inform the woman of any other material facts or opinions, or provide any explanation of the above information which, in the exercise of his best medical

judgment, is reasonably necessary to allow the woman to give her informed consent to the proposed abortion, with full knowledge of its nature and consequences. . . .

Section 2. It shall be unlawful for any public funds to be expended for the purpose of performing or assisting an abortion, not necessary to save the life of the mother, or for the purpose of encouraging or counseling a woman to have an abortion not necessary to save her life.

Section 3. It shall be unlawful for any public employee within the scope of his employment to perform or assist an abortion, not necessary to save the life of the mother. It shall be unlawful for a doctor, nurse or other health care personnel, a social worker, a counselor or persons of similar occupation who is a public employee within the scope of his public employment to encourage or counsel a woman to have an abortion not necessary to save her life.

Section 4. It shall be unlawful for any public facility to be used for the purpose of performing or assisting an abortion not necessary to save the life of the mother or for the purpose of encouraging or counseling a woman to have an abortion not necessary to save her life. . . .

"Abortion Rights: Anatomy of a Negative Campaign"
by Marvin N. Olasky

This paper analyzes a highly successful negative public relations campaign carried on by major pro-choice organizations during the 18 months from October 1985 through March 1987.

Throughout that period, public relations women employed by the pro-choice organizations called, visited, and sent pitch letters and press kits to hundreds of reporters and editors at newspapers, magazines, and television and radio stations.

Their activities led to stories attacking the pro-life centers in USA Today, *the* New York Times, *the* Detroit Free Press, *the (Portland)* Oregonian, *and many other newspapers throughout the United States.*

Magazines such as Vogue, Glamour, Self *and* Cosmopolitan, *and many television stations also developed and angled stories as the public relations professionals suggested.*

The effectiveness of the negative public relations campaign is explored, and the ethics of such a campaign is questioned.

Olasky is a professor in the Department of Journalism, at the University of Texas at Austin.

Many recent articles have discussed the growth of negative political advertising.[1] The tendency of the National Conservative Political Action Committee (NCPAC) to run ads attacking the views and integrity of liberal politicians has received frequent mention.[2] Little attention has been paid, though, to opportunities for *negative public relations* activity on controversial issues, i.e., campaigns by employees of one organization to decrease public confidence in another. The concept of negative public relations is especially unheard of in the nonprofit field. Cutlip, Center and Broom list five common nonprofit public relations objectives:

1. To win public acceptance of an agency's mission, new ideas, and new concepts,

2. To provide a favorable climate for agency, health, or hospital fundraising campaigns,

3. To broaden and maintain volunteer participation in a time when more and more women are leaving volunteer work for full-time careers,

4. To promote programs and services so those who need them can get them, and

5. To develop channels of communication with those who are disadvantaged.[3]

But, for some nonprofits, should a sixth objective be listed? This could be: To eliminate or reduce the effectiveness of organizations with a different philosophy.

This paper is based on: a) newspaper and magazine articles provided by two pro-life groups, the Christian Action

Council and the Pearson Institute, and by three pro-choice groups, Planned Parenthood, the National Abortion Federation, and the Religious Coalition for Abortion Rights (RCAR); b) telephone interviews with key individuals at the five organizations; c) press kits provided by the three pro-choice organizations;[4] d) interviews and correspondence with reporters and pro-life center directors and counselors; and e) articles found through computer searches and through general reading.

The organization of this paper follows the classic four-step public relations process: Defining the public relations problem, planning and programming, taking action and communicating, and evaluating the program.[5]

First Step: Defining the Public Relations Problem

Early in the 1980s, the abortion battle was stalemated. The Supreme Court continued to strike down laws attempting to reduce abortion opportunities. Opinion polls and occasional state referenda revealed a sharply-split American public. Pickets and counter-pickets battled.

Pro-life forces tried to break the deadlock in two ways—one violent, one peaceful. A few of the most frustrated pro-life individuals bombed abortion clinics. That strategy was attacked on ethical grounds by most pro-life groups, and public reaction rendered it counter-productive. The peaceful strategy emphasized establishment of counseling centers for pregnant women, centers at which women could receive information on fetal development, abortion consequences, and abortion alternatives. The pro-life hope was that when pregnant women received such information, some would decide not to have abortions.

A few such centers existed during the 1970s, but they were designed to appeal mostly to women already determined to continue their pregnancies. The early pro-life counseling centers often were affiliated with Birthright, an organization providing social services to pregnant women. Other pro-life forces applauded what Birthright was doing but saw their mission differently: They would appeal to those still undecided, or leaning toward abortion.

The new strategy caught on around the United States during 1985. In 1986, *USA Today* reported the existence of up to 3,000 such centers in this country.[6] These centers typically were small, with one low-paid director, volunteer counselors, and no public relations expertise. Most funds were raised from individual donors. The typical center received no government, corporate, or foundation support, and only small amounts from churches.[7]

From the standpoint of pro-life forces, the peaceful strategy worked in two ways during 1985. First, thousands of women who had been undecided or leaning toward abortions were deciding not to have abortions.[8] Second, counseling centers often received favorable media publicity for their "helpful" contribution to the process of developing "informed choice" on abortion.[9] One center director commented that by the end of 1985 her organization had "established credibility in the community as a very caring, responsible, helpful ministry."[10]

Pro-choice organizations initially responded with open protests such as picketing. That produced some publicity but often seemed to rouse the pro-life side to greater efforts. At the end of 1985, the director of one counseling center said she was looking forward to 1986 because she had heard that Planned Parenthood members were planning to picket her center; she planned to "take advantage of the free publicity."[11] Another director questioned at the end of 1985 said, "We're just helping pregnant women make an informed choice. The abortionists don't like it, but I don't think they're going to find an effective way to mount a big campaign against us."[12]

The pro-choice public relations problem was: How to find that effective way.

Second Step: Planning and Programming

Pro-choice public relations professionals chose "deception" as the key angle for their campaign. That choice made sense because of practices followed by many of the 140 counseling centers (less than 5% of the total of 3,000) affiliated with the Pearson Institute, a St. Louis nonprofit organization. According to Pearson director Michael Byers, a woman who plans to "kill her unborn child" is like a Nazi during World War II knocking on a door and asking if there are any Jews inside: "We don't want to help her do evil."[13] Pearson affiliates were supposed to use aggressive and ethically controversial techniques designed to attract women planning abortion to a Pearson center. Those techniques included insinuating over the telephone that a center performs abortions. Receptionists at Pearson affiliates were told to practice "mental reservation," which means that they were not to lie outright when asked about the availability of abortion at their center, but were to talk around the subject and mislead the caller so she would come for counseling. Byers said, "On the use of the telephone we do everything we can to get her into a center."[14]

Pro-life individuals from other groups said in interviews that they generally agreed with the Pearson end but disagreed with the means. The majority of counseling centers offer free pregnancy tests to draw clients, as many pro-choice groups and abortion businesses do, but they tell callers that they do not perform abortions. Centers affiliated with Birthright, the Christian Action Council, and other organizations are encouraged to emphasize, in the words of one director, "the Christian duty of telling the truth." Interviews show that in order to obey one commandment against killing (with the implication that Christians should attempt to save the lives of others), most pro-life volunteers are not willing to disobey the commandment about bearing false witness.[15]

Regardless of the majority opposition to deception, the

minority Pearson stance provided pro-choice public relations workers an opportunity. They had a chance to strike a blow against all counseling centers that tried to attract the undecided, particularly since the "deception" issue would be an easy one for journalists to grasp and explain. Amy Sutnick, public information associate for Planned Parenthood of New York City, was one of the professionals, who in October 1985, began planning an "anti-deception" campaign. By February 1987, she estimated that she had spent close to one thousand hours on the campaign, and "some weeks it's all I do."[16]

Planned Parenthood's two goals in beginning the campaign, according to Sutnick, were 1) "to make women aware of what was going on, and 2) to stop those clinics from deceiving people." Initial media contacts were carefully considered in the light of those goals. Sutnick said: "For goal number one, we wanted a story in the *New York Daily News*. Readers of the *Daily News* might be more likely to go to a center than to a private doctor. Later, you go to the *New York Times* for influence on decision makers who might be able to enforce the second goal. Another advantage of beginning with the *Daily News*," Sutnick said, "was that the *Times* wouldn't have done as dramatic a job."[17]

Third Step: Taking Action and Communicating

New York City's Planned Parenthood officials discussed the approach with colleagues in other cities. Sutnick approached a pro-choice reporter at the *New York Daily News*. The *Daily News* story, published in January 1986, was written along the lines of one of Sutnick's press releases, even to the extent of sometimes using the same words ("plush" in a sentence describing the counseling center).[18] Sutnick then used the article to get the attention of other media outlets. With the *Daily News* article, her press kit, and telephone calls to pro-choice journalists, she soon had stories hitting the "deception angle" on virtually every New

York television station, including the local network affiliates, and in many other New York newspapers.[19]

Sutnick did not stop there. She sent the *Daily News* article and her other materials to Planned Parenthood officials throughout the United States, so that many would contact local reporters they knew and pitch a local version of the story at them. Sutnick also sent out a magazine pitch letter to women's magazines and spent considerable time on the telephone. "I did a lot of mailings at first," she said, "but I find that it's a real verbal story. When I call people and talk, it's very effective." As an example of her work, Sutnick pointed to a July 1987 *USA Today* article. "I thought they'd be interested," she said, "so I called a reporter I had worked with once before. I had a sense she'd be sympathetic. I told her the story and she flew up the next day."[20]

Sutnick was not the only pro-choice public relations professional taking action. Fredrica "Freddie" Hodges, executive director of the Religious Coalition for Abortion Rights (RCAR),[21] hosted a "bogus clinic" press conference in Washington, D.C., on January 22, 1986. The press conference received extensive coverage and led to articles in *Vogue* and other publications. At the press conference William Schulz, president of the Unitarian Universalist Association, called counseling centers "a new and insidious stage" of the anti-abortion movement: "Like spiders, they lure their victims into their webs and then apply psychological terror." The expressions "bogus clinics" and "lure" soon became standard in media coverage of the counseling centers. Hodges said local affiliates of RCAR were encouraged to attack counseling centers in their own cities, or preferably, "get reporters to go undercover to expose them."[22]

The National Abortion Federation (NAF), a trade association for abortion businesses, also took action, according to the association's executive director, Barbara Radford.[23] NAF tried several tactics. "What worked best was to find someone in the local media who was interested, put them on to it, and let them do the work," Radford said. Almost all reporters are sympathetic, in Radford's experience. "You don't come right out and ask them if they are [pro-choice]," she said, "but you get a sense that you can work with them."

How to Take Action
in a Negative Public Relations Campaign

The practice of negative public relations requires great skill, because even reporters who are ideologically predisposed to believe a story are suspicious of "one group attacking another."[24] Development of the "deception" article that probably had the greatest impact, the one in *USA Today*, shows the care needed in planting a negative story.

Marlene Perrin, author of that story, is regularly a reporter on the Gannett chain's *Iowa Press Citizen* in Iowa City.[25] She was on loan to *USA Today* in Washington, D.C., for the summer of 1986. Sutnick and Perrin had talked when Perrin wrote a story on birth control, and Sutnick thought that Perrin would be useful on the counseling center story.[26] According to Perrin, "I didn't get a chance to do much with big stories that summer. The good stuff went to the regular staff. Amy called and said, 'Would you be interested?' "[27]

As Perrin describes her research for the story, "I went to New York to pick up materials from Amy . . . I didn't get to talk to any of those fake abortion people. I got a lot of help from the Religious Coalition . . . I couldn't get to the fake clinics, but I talked to clients who had been there . . . The Planned Parenthood people were very helpful in providing them for me. . . . Amy had a lot of materials, like the Pearson manual . . . I talked to someone from Pearson, but he said the press hadn't been fair, he didn't want to talk . . . [28] I talked to other people. I talked to the [American] Civil Liberties Union."[29]

Perrin said that at first she thought the story was mainly about Pearson-affiliated centers. She said she interviewed Curt Young, executive director of the Christian Action Council, which advises its affiliates not to engage in any deceptive activities. According to Perrin, "He talked a lot about how he wasn't one of them. He said they [centers affiliated with his organization] were up front. They always told people what was going on." Perrin said she came to distrust Young's words when she "talked to a client who had gone to one of those centers. Amy [Sutnick] tracked her down . . . I don't know how she found her. The client said she was lied to. I didn't use the Curt Young material in my story . . . It was a matter of space."[30]

The July 23, 1986, *USA Today* story could hardly have been better from the standpoint of those opposed to pro-life efforts. Following a short story on the front page of the lifestyle page, the major story played on page 4D under a headline, "Anti-abortionists masquerade as clinics." The article led off with a story of one individual who did not like the counseling she received at a center affiliated with the Christian Action Council; this was the client "tracked down" by Sutnick, although the story did not mention the Planned Parenthood connection. One-fourth of the story was direct quotation and paraphrase from Sutnick, who described her visit to two Manhattan counseling centers, where she was "overwhelmed by the brain-washing techniques and the lies."[31]

Sutnick had developed the *USA Today* story with great skill. First, she had found a reporter not on regular staff who would see the story as a major opportunity. Second, she had supplied that reporter with dippings of local stories previously prompted by Sutnick, so that the reporter could use those stories as supposedly independent verification of the Planned Parenthood position. Third, she had produced hand-picked witnesses to provide an additional source of supposedly independent verification. Fourth, there was a

safety valve in case those first three touches were insuffi-
cient; Sutnick said she knew from previous contact that the
reporter was predisposed to accept the Planned Parenthood
position.

Interviewed seven months after the story was published, Perrin recalled, "The leads were provided by Planned
Parenthood. I wouldn't call them an objective source, but a
lot of what they sent were newspaper reports, and they had
people I could talk to. They didn't give a hard sell. They
provided leads, they didn't dictate the whole thing." Sutnick
had created what public relations pioneer Edward Bernays
called a "situation of reality," an opportunity for the reporter
to see for himself exactly what the public relations professional wanted seen.[32] Perrin was left with the memory that,
in a summer without much major action, she had been able
to "initiate something."[33]

Overall, the *USA Today* story suggested that counseling
centers in general are deceptive, with the exception of those
affiliated with Birthright (the older organization that sees its
purpose as helping women who have already decided to
continue their pregnancies, not those who still are undecided). Sutnick, when asked if the use of Birthright as an
exception took away some impact from the story, said, "No.
I'm the one who got Birthright mentioned. I always point
that out. It gives our main message even more credibility,
because it shows that we have no axe to grind."[34]

Fourth Step: Evaluating the Program

The pro-life side was harmed in 1986 when newspapers began running stories implying that virtually all counseling centers established by pro-life individuals, not just the
5% associated with the Pearson Institute, were "deceptive."
That *USA Today* article, for example, started off with the
story of a visit by an individual supplied by Sutnick to a
counseling center affiliated with the Christian Action

Council, not with the Pearson Institute. The *USA Today* headline was a general "Anti-abortionists masquerade,"[35] rather than one pointed at a specific organization. A *Newsday* editorial prompted by the pro-choice campaign was headlined, "Deception: It's No Way of Life/But Right-to-Lifers Use It."[36] Other articles similarly followed the blanket-attack theme of a December 1985, RCAR newsletter: "Abortion Alternative Centers—Beware!"[37]

Was the central goal of the campaign actually an attack on all pro-life counseling efforts, with the exception of those designed only for clients who already are anti-abortion? Sutnick said that women who go to a Christian Action Council affiliate "that's not as blatantly deceptive" still "don't get facts, they get lies."[38] Radford said:

> Counseling centers generally are opened and maintained out of fanaticism. Very single-minded, narrow-minded people with only one view of the world . . . It's a control issue for all of those people. It's very powerful for those people to say, "You will have this baby, you will do this." It's control over people's sex lives. 'If women are going to be sexual, then they'll pay. And the one way we can make them pay is to make them stay pregnant.'. . . It's a real control issue. The people in power in the anti-abortion movement are men. Very few women. It's men. They are men trying to control women's lives.[39]

"That's an incredible charge," said Sandra Hayes, director of the Austin (Texas) Crisis Pregnancy Center. "What motivates us is a concern for the woman and her unborn child."[40] Barbara Hammond of the Christian Action Council noted that over 90% of the centers affiliated with her organization are directed by women. Hammond also said there are many pro-life feminists, but "for financial and ideological reasons the abortion businesses and the feminists allied with them are trying to shut us down."[41]

Sutnick denied such allegations. "Our goal is not to shut them down," she said. "If they provide support services for women who have already decided, such as prenatal care and baby clothes, that's fine."[42] Radford said that she would not object to centers that "tell people they do not provide information on abortion."[43] Hayes noted that her crisis pregnancy center "provides some baby clothes, but our main goal is to provide accurate information that women will not get anywhere else. They're not going to get it from businesses that profit from abortion. If they say we can't exist unless we accept a very limited welfare role, then they're using the press to *try* to kill the only real competition they have."[44]

The charge that pro-choice groups were using the "deception" issue to attack pro-life centers in general gained credibility in January 1987, when the Planned Parenthood Federation of America issued a press release and brochure listing 300 pro-life centers. The press release said of centers, "if their true purpose were known, they would lure few women through their doors." Among the centers listed were those with names such as "Sav-A-Life," "Abortion Alternatives," "Lifeline," "Family Life Services," "Life Alternative," and "Mother and Unborn Child."[45]

Sutnick did say that a positive result of the pro-choice campaign was that "It has alienated a lot of people from the anti-abortion movement." The evidence indicates that the implicit goals of the campaign were the mirror image of those outlined by Cutlip, Center and Broom as typical for nonprofit organizations. The objectives evidently were:

1. To reduce public acceptance of the goals of any counseling center that did not conform to the Birthright emphasis on assistance to those who already had decided against abortion,

2. To provide an unfavorable climate for those counseling centers' fundraising campaigns,

3. To reduce volunteer participation at those centers in a time when more and more women are leaving volunteer work for full-time careers,

4. To attack counseling center programs and services so they did not get to those who might otherwise make use of them, and

5. To restrict counseling centers' channels of communication with women undergoing crisis pregnancies.

The success of the first objective is very difficult to measure in the absence of poll data. Sutnick, Hodges and Radford all saw a reduction in public acceptance of the counseling centers, and their judgment seems intuitively right in the light of all the negative coverage the centers received.

The second and third points are more measurable. Hammond reported that "At quite a few locations supporters have been upset. We've received letters from people saying they are withdrawing support for centers because of what they've read in newspapers. Many people naively believe that if the media says we're being deceptive we are. Unless they're familiar with us, they tend to believe the reports."[46]

The negative public relations campaign may have been particularly effective in that concern about deception would weaken support for centers among their core group of supporters, Christians who believe very strongly in obeying what they see as God's commands, including the proscription against lying. The deception issue could hit hard in a way that a broadside attack based on explicit pro-life vs. pro-choice differences could not.

Concerning the fourth and fifth points, Hammond reported that "Some centers have seen a drop, but others have more clients than ever. Many women don't want to be pressured into an abortion. They want another point of view."[47] Some centers report that newspapers no longer allow them the brief notices of activities that other nonprofit organizations receive. Ironically, when the Austin *American-Statesman* did give the Austin Crisis Pregnancy Center a brief listing, it left out key words that the center included in its requested notice: "The CPC does not perform or refer for abortions."[48]

Final Evaluation:
The Ethics of Negative Public Relations

A successful negative campaign can be a pleasure to run. Sutnick boasted of the stories she had seeded and was also pleased with the personal publicity she had received: "A friend of mine was on vacation in Indonesia and read about me in one of the international papers. I was very interested in that."[49]

The negative campaign, however, does raise three ethical questions; two are specific to the campaign and one is general. The first specific ethical question involves guilt by association. Pearson analysis of the ends/means problem was clearly a minority position among pro-life groups; for example, a Christian Action Council affiliate is to be "committed to integrity in dealing with clients, earning their trust, providing promised information and services, and eschewing any form of deception in its corporate advertising or individual conversations."[50] There is no reliable evidence that Christian Action Council affiliates are departing from those standards.[51] Yet, the negative campaign made it seem like the Pearson position was a majority one. [52]

A second specific ethical question arises out of the way in which pro-choice groups combined to implement the campaign against counseling centers. Radford admitted freely that she worked on the campaign with Planned Parenthood, RCAR, and the Reproductive Freedom Project of the American Civil Liberties Union. Other interviewees agreed that there was great collaboration among the leading pro-choice groups. "We're all working together," Sutnick said. Hodges of RCAR said that her group had divided up responsibilities with Planned Parenthood and the National Abortion Federation.[53] Planned Parenthood is a large organization that receives millions of dollars from foundations and $30 million annually from the federal government. The National Abortion Federation is a trade association. Should there be concern about such organizations banding together to attack relatively small nonprofits?

One general question about the ethics of negative public relations also needs to be asked: If nonprofit organizations devote their time not to building up their own practice but using top-notch public relations skills to attack that of others, will public discourse in this country become increasingly harsh?[54] The "low blows" of negative political advertising are rightfully criticized. If we are to have open debates on social issues, rather than beneath-the-surface campaigns that cause advocates of one position or another to believe that they cannot get a fair hearing, public relations practitioners should be cautious about the use of negative public relations.

Notes

1. See Gina M. Carramone, "Effects of Negative Political Advertising," *Journal of Broadcasting & Electronic Media*, Spring 1985, pp. 147-159; Fred Barnes, "The Snit Brothers," *New Republic*, November 10, 1986. p. 13; Steven W. Colford,"Polls Accentuated Negative," *Advertising Age*, November 10, 1986, p. 3, William A. Henry III, "Hard sell, Soft sell: New Political Ads Cast Aspersions and Spells," *Time*, June 11, 1984, p. 27; Melissa Healy, "The elections' best and worst," *U.S. News & World Report*, November 17, 1986, p. 25; John J. Failka, "Intense Mudslinging," *Wall Street Journal*, November 13, 1986, p. 62.

2. Recent articles reviewing NCPAC's history while report on the death of the organization's founder included Jonathan Alter, "Death of a conservative: Terry Dolan's legacy," January 12, 1987, p. 23, and Irvin Molotsky, "John T. Dolan, founder of group that

backed conservatives, dies," *New York Times,* December 31, 1986, p. 38. See also "A mother's plea," *Harper's,* September 1986, p. 18, and Fred Man, "Bobby Dole Loves Paulie Weyrich," *National Review,* November 29, 1985, p. 22.

3. Scott Cutlip, Allen Center and Glen Broom, *Effective Public Relations,* 6th edition (Englewood Cliffs, N. J.: Prentice-Hall, 1985), p. 22.

4. The two pro-life organizations did not have press kits.

5. Cutlip, Center and Broom, p. 200

6. July 23, 1986, p. 1D.

7. This information is based on a survey conducted by the author of centers associated with the Crisis Pregnancy Center.

8. Estimates by pro-life organizations. Government statistics show that the number of abortions, after rising steadily for two decades, has decreased during the past two years. Abortion statistics are notoriously unreliable, and the decrease may be due to changes in the population cohorts, but the centers do appear to have had some impact.

9. Survey of center directors, and examination of 35 articles on centers prior to December 1985; 33 were positive.

10. Letter to the author, January 1986.

11. Letter to the author, December 1985.

12. Ibid.

13. Author's interview with Michael Byers, February 20, 1987.

14. Byers said, "If you don't use every tool at your disposal, that mother can be left to the abortuary. 90% of the women who come here come in looking for an abortion. 80% leave deciding to continue their pregnancies. That's what the abortionists are afraid of. We estimate that 35,000 babies were saved by centers affiliated with us in 1985, at a cost of $9 million to the abortion industry."

15. Author's interviews with pro-life leaders and with volunteers at one "crisis pregnancy center" affiliated with the Christian Action Council. In many ways, the difference among pro-life groups arose out of the classic question, "Do the ends justify the means?" (Or, more precisely, "Which ends justify which means?")

16. Author's interview with Sutnick, February 5, 1987.

17. Interviews with Sutnick, February 5 and February 27, 1987.

18. *New York Daily News*, January 28, 1986, p. 27.

19. Clippings received and statements from Sutnick during our February 5 interview. The author has not seen the television reports, but everything Sutnick said about coverage that the author was able to check proved to be reliable.

20. Sutnick says that due to her work, "We've gotten in everywhere," with the exception of the *New York Post*, which she had not approached, "because they're very unpredictable." Sutnick said, "I've been able to be so successful because I have a wide range of information—some from the ACLU [American Civil Liberties Union], some from community activists. The more you know, the more you can do. It's been great." Judging by the evidence of clippings across the country, Sutnick's appraisal of her effectiveness seems accurate. She is quoted approvingly in many articles, but her fingerprints are obvious in many more. For example, she obtained a copy of the Pearson Foundation manual and distributed copies of it to reporters throughout the country; quotations from the manual figured prominently in many stories. Copies of the manual were passed around from reporter to reporter. Sutnick said she had to "keep from laughing" when a *New York Times* reporter interviewing her held out a copy of the manual and asked if Sutnick had seen it. "The copy had come from me originally," Sutnick said, "although the reporter didn't know it. I knew it was one of our copies because it has a number of our duplicating department on it."

For a full examination of the actual press coverage of "deceptive clinics," see article by the author and a colleague (citation temporarily deleted to preserve blind judging).

21. RCAR is composed of members of theologically liberal groups who "have joined together to preserve the legal option of abortion." RCAR, according to a fact sheet included in its press kits, "has maintained a professional lobbying program on Capitol Hill since 1973. A national legislative alert, DISPATCH, is mailed to 25,000 key activists around the country whenever necessary."

22. Interview, January 29, 1987.

23. Author's interview, February 27, 1987.

24. Author's interview with reporter Marlene Perrin, February 25, 1987.

25. Interview with Marlene Perrin, February 25, 1987.

26. Interview with Amy Sutnick.

27. Perrin interview.

28. Pearson director Byers said he had "given up on the press," because "98% of the time, no matter what we say to them, they're going to twist it and turn it. Until they print the truth about the real victims of abortion, the babies who are disemboweled and burnt raw, we're not going to have anything more to say to them."

29. Interview, February 25, 1987.

30. Interview.

31. *USA Today*, July 23, 1986, p. 4D.

32. See Bernays's books *Propaganda* (New York: Liveright, 1928) and *The Engineering of Consent* (Norman, Okla.: U. of Oklahoma Press, 1955). For examples of Bernays's work see his autobiography, *Biography of an Idea* (New York: Simon and Schuster, 1985).

33. Interview, February 25, 1987.

34. Interview, February 5, 1987.

35. July 23, 1986, p. 4D.

36. December 29, 1986; article supplied by Amy Sutnick.

37. The author and a colleague have analyzed the news coverage in detail in another article (footnote temporarily omitted to preserve blind judging).

38. Interview, February 27, 1987.

39. Author's interview, February 27, 1987. Sutnick also attacked the "fundamentalism" of many pro-life groups. The RCAR press kit included a booklet complaining that "Religious fervor now combines with reactionary politics, resulting in a type of neofascism that threatens the very foundations of American life."

40. Author's interview, February 27, 1987.

41. Author's interview, March 5, 1987. Along with different views of each others motives, pro-choice and pro-life women had

vastly different assumptions about the ethics of abortion counseling. The new, pro-life centers argued for what they called *informed choice*. They argued that a woman should not make a decision about abortion until she was aware of what was growing inside her and what would happen to the creature inside if abortion was chosen. Often, pro-life centers would show pictures of an unborn baby (fetus) and perhaps even pictures of what happens to a fetus (unborn baby) during and after an abortion. But what was *information* in the eyes of the pro-life forces was *emotional pressure* in the view of pro-choice organizations. Each side accused the other of dishonestly loading the decision-making process.

42. Interview.

43. Interview.

44. Interview.

45. Press Statement by Faye Wattleton, President, Planned Parenthood Federation of America, January 22, 1987. Wattleton argued that the development of counseling centers was one indication that pro-life "extremists have sunk to new depths in an effort to harass and punish women who seek abortion services." She charged that the 300 centers on her list used "manipulative tactics." The list itself, however, had a disclaimer: "Inclusion on this list is not a representation that a facility has engaged in any particular deceptive practice."

46. Interview.

47. Interview.

48. Notice sent by Austin Crisis Pregnancy Center to the Austin *American-Statesman*: clipping from February 1987, provided by that center.

49. Interview.

50. Memo to affiliates provided by the Christian Action Council.

51. At its January 22, 1986, press conference, the Religious Coalition for Abortion Rights presented testimony from a woman who had visited a counseling center; the woman was an employee of an abortion facility. Evidence against Pearson affiliates has accumulated, and Pearson policy statements are now widely available. To show deception among non-Pearson centers, though, it would

be necessary to show that counselors at those centers are going against the express policy of their organizations. Such evidence has not been forthcoming, except occasionally from those with a financial or extreme ideological reason to make such charges.

52. Journalists themselves were, of course, responsible for what they printed and broadcast, but pro-choice public relations professionals skillfully played upon their susceptibilities and presuppositions.

53. Interviews.

54. On the abortion issue specifically, it should be noted that abortion has been the most divisive social issue in this country since the debate over slavery. Whenever there are such tensions, some people will take the positive route—let us reason together—and some will try to impose their will on others through violence and coercion. Pro-choice individuals should encourage those on the pro-life side to take the route of peace rather than the route of warfare.

Public Opinion and Abortion Restrictions

Recent public opinion polls indicate public support for the following kinds of legislative endeavors which would decrease the annual abortions in America drastically:

Parental Consent/Notification

The *Los Angeles Times* poll of 10 March 1989, asked 2,406 respondents:

"How about this statement: 'Minors should have to get their parents' permission before they get an abortion.' Do you agree or disagree with that?"

Agree	81 percent
Disagree	14 percent
Don't know	5 percent

The Gallup poll of 6-9 July 1989, asked 1,253 respondents:

> "As I read some restrictions on abortion that are being considered in some states tell me if you would favor or oppose such a restriction in your state:
>
> Requiring that women under 18 years of age get parental consent before they are allowed to have an abortion."

Favor	67 percent
Oppose	29 percent
Don't know	4 percent

The Yankelovich/Clancy/Shulman poll of 6 July 1989, undertaken for Cable News Network and *Time* magazine, asked 504 respondents:

> "Which of these legal restrictions on abortion would you favor in your state and which would you oppose?
>
> Requiring parental consent before a teenager could obtain an abortion."

Favor	72 percent
Oppose	25 percent
Not sure	3 percent

The *Boston Globe's* poll of 27-29 March 1989, asked its 1002 respondents:

> "In this case, do you think it should be legal or illegal for a woman to obtain an abortion?
>
> A woman is a minor."

Illegal	50 percent
Legal	35 percent
Don't know	15 percent

A Gallup/*Newsweek* poll of 6-7 July 1989 asked 751 respondents:

"Would you support or oppose the following restrictions on abortion that may come before state legislatures?

Teenagers must have parents' permission."

Support	75 percent
Oppose	22 percent
Don't know	3 percent

A *USA Today* poll found that 72 percent of its respondents supported a law which requires a girl under the age of eighteen to notify her parents before obtaining an abortion. The poll also found that 63 percent of those asked supported a twenty-four-hour waiting period before a woman could obtain an abortion.

Informed Consent

The Yankelovich/Clancy/Shulman poll cited earlier asked:

"Which of these restrictions on abortion would you favor in your state and which would you oppose?

Requiring doctors to inform abortion patients about alternatives to having an abortion."

Favor	81 percent
Oppose	16 percent
Not sure	3 percent

The Gallup/*Newsweek* poll cited earlier asked:

"Would you support or oppose the following restrictions on abortion that may come before state legislatures?

Women seeking abortions must be counseled on the dangers, alternatives."

Support   88 percent
Oppose   9 percent
Don't know   3 percent

Fathers' Rights

The *Los Angeles Times* poll cited earlier asked:

"Generally speaking, are you in favor of requiring a woman to get the consent of the natural father before she has an abortion, or are you opposed to that?"

Favor   53 percent
Oppose   37 percent
No opinion   10 percent

The *Boston Globe* poll cited earlier asked:

"In this case, do you think it should be legal or illegal for a woman to obtain an abortion?

Mother wants abortion—father wants baby."

Illegal   72 percent
Legal   14 percent
Don't know   14 percent

The *USA Today* poll cited earlier asked respondents if they supported a law requiring that a husband or partner be notified that his spouse is seeking an abortion. The majority of men responding (64 percent) and 50 percent of the women approved of such a law.

Public Spending

The Gallup/*Newsweek* poll cited earlier asked:

"Would you support or oppose the following restrictions on abortion that may come before state legislatures?

No public spending for abortion, except to save a woman's life."

Support   61 percent
Oppose   34 percent
Don't know   5 percent

"No abortions in public facilities, except to save a woman's life."

Support   54 percent
Oppose   41 percent
Don't know   5 percent

A separate Gallup poll on 6-9 July 1989, asked 1,253 respondents:

"As I read some restrictions on abortions that are being considered in some states tell me if you would favor or oppose such restrictions in your state.

Not allowing abortions to be performed in public hospitals unless the abortion is required to save a woman's life."

Favor   54 percent
Oppose   43 percent
Don't know   3 percent

Abortion as a Means of Birth Control

The *Los Angeles Times* poll cited earlier asked:

"Generally speaking are you in favor of abortion when it is used as a form of birth control, or are you opposed to that?"

Favor   13 percent
Oppose   80 percent
No opinion   7 percent

The *Boston Globe* poll cited earlier asked:

"In this case, do you think it should be legal or illegal for a woman to obtain an abortion?

As a means of birth control."

Illegal	89 percent
Legal	6 percent
Don't know	5 percent

Alternatives to Abortion

The *Los Angeles Times* poll cited earlier asked:

"If abortion were to become illegal again, would you be in favor of using public funds to support the adoption of the babies that would result from that policy, or would you be opposed to that?

Favor	64 percent
Oppose	28 percent
No opinion	8 percent

"Do you think the solution to abortion is adoption, or not?"

Yes	54 percent
No	35 percent
Not sure	11 percent

Political Impact

The importance of the abortion issue is underscored by several polls which indicate that those holding a pro-life viewpoint are more likely to vote for or against a candidate solely because of that candidate's position on abortion. The Gallup/*Newsweek* poll cited earlier asked:

"If state legislatures are permitted to make abortions illegal, would you:

Consider a candidate's position on abortion one of many important factors when voting?"

Yes	56 percent
No	17 percent

Always vote for a pro-life candidate	14 percent
Never vote for a pro-life candidate	9 percent
Not sure	5 percent

A poll commissioned by the National Republican Congressional Committee in July 1989 found that pro-life supporters are more likely, by a 2:1 margin, to base their vote solely on the abortion issue than pro-choice proponents. Of those responding to the poll, undertaken by American Viewpoint, Inc., 48 percent of those holding a pro-life view stated that they would vote against a candidate who didn't share their views on abortion while only 21 percent of those holding a pro-choice viewpoint responded the same.

Model Legislation

MODEL BILL FOR INFORMED CONSENT

Woman's Right to Know Initiative

AN ACT Relating to protecting the health of women considering or having an abortion; adding a new chapter to Title 70 RCW; creating a new section; prescribing penalties; and declaring an emergency.

BE IT ENACTED BY THE PEOPLE OF THE STATE OF WASHINGTON:

NEW SECTION. Sec. 1. This act shall be known and cited as the Woman's Right To Know Act.

NEW SECTION. Sec. 2. This act is necessary for the immediate preservation of the public peace, health, morals, or safety, or the support of the state government and its existing public institutions, and shall take effect immediately.

NEW SECTION. Sec.3. The legislature finds that:

(1) Individuals have a fundamental right to ensure that the choices they make are fully informed, that they take into account both the immediate and long-term consequences of their actions, and that they possess information essential to their well-being before a physician's exercise of his or her medical judgment concerning their health;

(2) The medical, emotional, physiological, and psychological consequences of abortion can be substantial, serious, and long-lasting; and

(3) An informed decision-making process is in the best interest of all women considering or having an abortion.

NEW SECTION. Sec. 4. It is the intent of the legislature to further the legitimate and compelling state interests of:

(1) Protecting the fundamental right of individuals to ensure that their choices are fully informed;

(2) Protecting the health and safety of all women considering or having an abortion; and

(3) Ensuring that a woman's consent to an abortion is the result of an informed decision-making process.

NEW SECTION. Sec. 5.

(1) Only a person licensed under chapter 18.57 or 18.71 RCW may lawfully perform an abortion. A physician shall not perform an abortion unless, before such performance, the physician:

(a) Certifies in writing that the patient voluntarily gave her informed consent after she was given the exact language contained in subsection (2) of this section and the information required to be provided under subsection (2) of this section in a manner that was not biased or misleading and that was understood by the patient;

(b) Certifies in writing that the patient voluntarily waived her right to receive any or some of the information required to be provided under subsection (2) of this section after she was given the exact language contained in subsection (2) of this section in a manner that was not biased or misleading and that was understood by the patient; or

(c) Determines that a medical emergency exists that so complicates the pregnancy as to require an immediate abortion to preserve the life or health of the patient or the embryo or fetus.

(2) In order to ensure that consent for an abortion is truly informed consent, the physician performing the abortion shall inform the patient, or ensure that she is informed by the physician's designated representative, of the exact language contained in this subsection and the information required to be provided under this subsection in a manner that is not biased or misleading and that will be understood by the patient:

(a) That according to the best medical judgment of the physician the patient is or is not pregnant, and the approximate age of the embryo or fetus considering the number of weeks elapsed from the probable time of the conception of the embryo or fetus, based upon the information provided by the client as to the time of her last menstrual period, her medical history, a physical examination, or appropriate laboratory tests;

(b) The general anatomical and physiological characteristics of the embryo or fetus at the time that the abortion is to be performed, including distinct photographs of the actual embryo or fetus or of an actual embryo or fetus at a stage of development approximately equal to that of the patient's;

(c) The particular risks to the patient associated with pregnancy and child birth;

(d) The particular immediate and long-term physical,

emotional, and psychological dangers to the patient associated with the abortion;

(e) A description of the abortion technique or procedure to be used and its consequences, and the particular risks to the patient associated with the abortion technique or procedure to be used;

(f) Alternatives to abortion such as child birth and adoption and information concerning public and private agencies registered with the state that will assist in those alternatives; and

(g) In addition, the physician shall answer any questions or concerns of the patient, including those regarding her health, the embryo or fetus, or the abortion technique or procedure, or may inform her of any other material facts or opinions, or may provide any explanation of the above information that, in the best medical judgment of the physician, is reasonably necessary to allow the patient to give her voluntary informed consent to the proposed abortion with full knowledge of its nature and consequences.

(3) Before the performance of an abortion the patient shall sign a consent stating that she received and understood the exact language contained in subsection (2) of this section and the information required to be provided under subsection (2) of this section, and that she consents, freely and without coercion, to the abortion. The consent shall specify the general areas of information required to be provided under subsections (2) (a) through (g) of this section. The physician shall certify the consent and provide the patient with a duplicate copy. The requirements of this subsection do not apply in the following circumstances:

(a) When the patient has been provided the exact language contained in subsection (2) of this section and does not want to receive any or some of the information required to be provided under subsection (2) of this section, before the performance of an abortion she shall sign a waiver stating that she received and understood the exact language contained in subsection (2) of this section and that she does not want to receive any or some of the information required to be provided under subsection (2) of this section. The waiver shall specify the general areas of information required to be provided under subsections (2)(a) through (g) of this section that were waived or not waived. The physician shall certify the waiver and provide the patient with a duplicate copy. In order to ensure that the waiver is a truly informed waiver, the physician performing the abortion shall inform the patient, or ensure that she is informed by the physician's designated representative, of the exact language contained in subsection (2) of this section in a manner that is not biased or misleading and that will be understood by the patient.

(b) When a medical emergency exists that so complicates the pregnancy as to require an immediate abortion to preserve the life or health of the patient or the embryo or fetus.

(4) The department of social and health services shall publish a list of agencies, including a brief description of the services offered by such agencies, that assist in alternatives to abortion, such as child birth and adoption, and that register with the department. The department shall also ensure that facilities and physicians providing abortion services are provided with the list and shall make the list available to the public upon request. A physician performing an abortion may inform the patient that he or she is not an agent of the state and that the provision of information concerning public and private agencies registered with the state does not indicate his or her approval or disapproval of such agencies. An agency may register with the department of social and health services by providing the following:

(a) The name of the agency;
(b) Phone number, including the area code;
(c) Address, including the county, where services are provided; and

(d) A brief description of the services offered.

NEW SECTION. Sec. 6. To develop statistical data relating to informed consent and the protection of the health and safety of women considering or having an abortion, a report shall be filed with the department of social and health services on a form prescribed by the department whenever an abortion is performed. The report shall be signed by the physician who performed the abortion and shall be transmitted to the department no later than ten days following the end of the month in which the abortion is performed. The report forms shall not identify the patient by name but by an individual number to be noted in the patient's permanent record in the possession of the physician.

The report shall indicate the following:

(1) That an abortion was performed and the date and place the abortion was performed.

(2) The age of the patient and the approximate age of the embryo or fetus.

(3) That consent was obtained under the requirements of this chapter. If consent was obtained under this chapter, the physician shall provide the patient with a copy of this report.

(4) That consent was not obtained under the waiver exception of section 5(3)(a) of this act. If consent was not obtained under this exception, the report shall specify the general areas of information required to be provided under section 5(2)(a) through (g) of this act that were waived or not waived.

(5) That consent was not obtained under the medical emergency exception of section 5(3)(b) of this act. If consent was not obtained under this exception, the report shall include the medical indications on which the physician's judgment was based.

(6) Any medical complications that occurred as a result

of the abortion, the physician's resolution of the complications, and the prognosis for the patient.

NEW SECTION. Sec. 7. Unless the context clearly requires otherwise, the following definitions apply throughout this chapter:

(1) "Abortion" means the use or attempted use of any substance or device with intent to terminate a woman's pregnancy.

(2) "Perform" or any of its derivatives means perform or induce, or the attempt to perform or induce, or any of their derivatives.

NEW SECTION. Sec. 8. A physician performing an abortion has an affirmative duty to comply with this chapter. Any physician who willfully or negligently fails to comply with any of the provisions of this chapter is subject to a fine not to exceed five thousand dollars and an action for suspension or revocation of the physician's license in addition to any other disciplinary action deemed appropriate under chapter 18.130 RCW.

NEW SECTION. Sec.9. If any provision of this chapter or its application to any person or circumstance is held invalid, the remainder of the chapter or the application of the provision to other persons or circumstances is not affected.

NEW SECTION. Sec. 10. The provisions of this chapter are to be liberally construed to effectuate the policies and purposes of this chapter. In the event of conflict between this chapter and any other provision of law, the provisions of this chapter shall govern.

NEW SECTION. Sec. 11. Sections 3 through 10 of this act constitute a new chapter in Title 70 RCW.

MODEL BILL BANNING SEX-SELECTION ABORTIONS

Section 1.

Prohibition.

(a) No physician shall intentionally perform an abortion with knowledge that the pregnant woman is seeking the abortion solely on account of the sex of the fetus.

Exceptions.

(b) Nothing in this section shall be construed to proscribe the performance of an abortion on account of the sex of the fetus because of a genetic disorder linked to that sex.

Severability.

(c) If the application of this section to the period of pregnancy prior to viability is held invalid, then such invalidity shall not affect its application to the period of pregnancy subsequent to viability.

Penalty.

(d) Any physician who intentionally, knowingly, or recklessly violates the provisions of this section shall be guilty of a class _____ felony.

LEGISLATION SPONSORED BY SENATOR GORDON HUMPHREY (R-NH) MAKING SEX-SELECTION ABORTION A VIOLATION OF CIVIL RIGHTS

Be it enacted by the Senate and House of Representatives of the United States of America in Congress assembled,

SECTION 1. SHORT TITLE.

This Act may be cited as the "Civil Rights of Infants Act."

SEC. 2. DEPRIVING PERSONS OF THE EQUAL PROTECTION OF LAWS BEFORE BIRTH.

Section 1979 of the Revised Statutes (42 U.S.C. 1983) is amended by adding at the end thereof the following new section:

"SEC. 4. For purposes of section 1979 of the Revised Statutes of the United States (42 U.S.C. 1983), and for purposes of other provisions of law, it shall be a deprivation of a 'right' secured by the laws of the United States for an individual to perform an abortion with the knowledge that the pregnant woman is seeking the abortion solely because of the gender of the fetus. No pregnant woman who seeks to obtain an abortion solely on the basis of the gender of the fetus shall be liable in any manner under this section."

MODEL BILL
REQUIRING PARENTAL OR SPOUSAL CONSENT

Sec. 1. Definitions. As used in this act:

(1) "Abortion" means the purposeful termination of a human pregnancy after implantation of a fertilized ovum by any person with an intention other than to produce a live birth or to remove a dead, unborn child.

(2) "Abortion facility" means a clinic, physician's office, hospital, or any other place or facility in which abortions are performed.

(3) "Family unit" means persons living together in a single household, including husband, wife, children, other related persons, and foster children.

(4) "Minor" means a person under eighteen years of age who is not married or emancipated.

(5) "Physician" means a person licensed to practice medicine in this state.

(6) "Unborn child" means the unborn offspring of a human being from the moment of conception, through pregnancy and until live birth, including the human conceptus, zygote, morula, blastocyst, embryo, and fetus.

Sec. 2. A physician shall not perform an abortion unless he or she first determines the age and marital status of the person seeking an abortion.

Sec. 3. A physician shall not perform an abortion upon a minor unless he or she first obtains the written consent of the minor as provided for in [cite the public act] and that of her parents, except as provided in Sec. 5 of this act. In deciding whether or not to grant such consent, a minor's parents shall consider their child's and their family unit's best interests and may also consider the interests of the unborn child. If one of the minor's parents has died or is unavailable to the physician within a reasonable time and in a reasonable manner, consent of the remaining parent shall be sufficient. If both parents have died or are otherwise unavailable to the physician within a reasonable time and in a reasonable manner, consent of the minor's guardian or guardians shall be sufficient. If the minor's parents are divorced, consent of the parent having custody shall be sufficient.

Sec. 4. The state department of public health shall supply appropriate forms to be used for parents or guardians to give consent to their minor child to have an abortion.

Sec. 5. If one or both of the parents or guardians of a minor refuse to consent to the performance of an abortion, or if a minor elects not to seek the consent of one or both of her parents or guardians, a court may grant permission for the abortion pursuant to the following procedures:

(1) The minor or next friend shall make an application to the juvenile court which shall assist the minor or next friend in preparing the petition and notices required pursuant to this section. The minor or the next friend of the minor shall thereafter file a petition setting forth the initials of the minor; the age of the minor; the names and addresses of each parent, guardian, or, if the minor's parents are deceased and no guardian has been appointed, any other person standing in *loco parentis* of the minor; that the minor has been fully informed of the risks and consequences of the abortion; that the minor is of sound mind and has sufficient intellectual capacity to consent to the abortion; that, if the court does not grant the minor majority rights for the purpose of consent to the abortion, the court

should find that the abortion is in the best interest of the minor and the family unit of the minor and give judicial consent to the abortion; that the court should appoint a guardian *ad litem* of the child; and, if the minor does not have private counsel, that the court should appoint counsel. The petition shall be signed by the minor or the next friend.

(2) A hearing on the merits of the petition, to be held on the record, shall be held as soon as possible within five days of the filing of the petition. If any party is unable to afford counsel, the court shall appoint counsel at least twenty-four hours before the time of the hearing. At the hearing, the court shall hear evidence relating to the emotional development, maturity, intellect, and understanding of the minor; the nature, possible consequences, and alternatives to the abortion; and any other evidence that the court may find useful in determining whether the minor should be granted majority rights for the purpose of consenting to the abortion or whether the abortion is in the best interests of the minor.

(3) In the decree, the court shall for good cause:

(a) Grant the petition for majority rights for the purpose of consenting to the abortion; or

(b) Find the abortion to be in the best interests of the minor and give judicial consent to the abortion, setting forth the grounds for so finding; or

(c) Deny the petition, setting forth the grounds on which the petition is denied.

(4) If the petition is allowed, the informed consent of the minor, pursuant to the court grant of

majority rights, or the judicial consent, shall bar an action by the parents or guardian of the minor on the grounds of battery of the minor by those performing the abortion. The immunity granted shall only extend to the performance of the abortion in accordance herewith and any necessary accompanying services that are performed in a competent manner. The costs of the action shall be borne by the parties.

(5) An appeal from an order issued under the provisions of this section may be taken to the court of appeals of this state by the minor or by a parent or guardian of the minor. The notice of intent to appeal shall be given within twenty-four hours from the date of issuance of the order. The record on appeal shall be completed and the appeal shall be perfected within five days from the filing of the notice to appeal. Because time may be of the essence regarding the performance of the abortion, the supreme court of this state shall, by court rule, provide for expedited appellate review of cases appealed under this section.

Sec. 6. A physician shall not perform an abortion upon a married woman who is not legally separated from her husband unless he or she first obtains the written consent of the woman as provided for in [cite the public act] and that of her husband, except as provided in Sec. 8 of this act.

Sec. 7. The state department of public health shall supply appropriate forms to be used for a husband to give consent to his wife to undergo an abortion.

Sec. 8. If the husband of a woman seeking an abortion refuses to consent to the performance of an abortion, or if the woman elects not to seek the consent of her husband, a court may grant permission for the abortion pursuant to the following procedures:

(1) The woman shall make an application to the superior court [or specify some other state court]. The woman shall file a petition setting forth her initials; whether she is filing the petition because her husband has refused his consent or because she has elected not to seek her husband's consent; whether she is currently living with her husband; that she has consented to the abortion under the terms of public act [cite the public act]; and that the court should find that the abortion is in her best interests and the best interests of her family unit and give judicial consent to the abortion.

(2) If the petition filed by the woman seeking an abortion indicates she is filing the petition because her husband has refused his consent, he shall be informed by the court of the fact that his wife has filed the petition.

(3) A hearing on the merits of the petition, to be held on the record, shall be held as soon as possible within five days of the filing of the petition. The pregnant woman may attend the hearing, and, if her husband has refused his consent for the abortion, he also may attend. If any party is unable to afford counsel, the court shall appoint counsel at least twenty-four hours before the time of the hearing. At the hearing the court shall hear evidence concerning why the pregnant woman believes she is unable to go to her husband to secure his consent or why she should be able to obtain an abortion irrespective of her husband's wishes, and any other evidence the court may find useful in determining whether the abortion is in the best interests of the woman and her family unit and whether or not to grant the petition.

(4) In the decree, the court shall for good cause:

> (a) Grant the petition, finding the abortion to be in the best interests of the woman and her immediate family and give judicial consent to the abortion setting forth the grounds for so finding; or

> (b) Deny the petition, setting forth the grounds on which the petition is denied.

(5) An appeal from an order issued under the provisions of this section may be taken to the court of appeals of this state by the pregnant woman or her husband. The notice of intent to appeal shall be given within twenty-four hours from the date of issuance of the order. The record on appeal shall be completed and the appeal shall be perfected within five days from the filing of notice to appeal. Because time may be of the essence regarding the performance of the abortion, the supreme court of this state shall, by court rule, provide for expedited appellate review of cases appealed under this section.

Sec. 9. A physician performing an abortion in violation of this act shall be guilty of a misdemeanor and subject to a fine of up to $1,000 for each violation. An abortion facility found in violation of this act shall be subject to a fine of up to $1,000 for each violation.

This is one model bill from a package of eight prepared by Just Life Education Fund, 10 Lancaster Avenue, Philadelphia, PA 19151. This package contains a broad approach to pro-life legislation seeking both to restrict abortion and to provide meaningful alternatives. For the complete package write to Just Life.

LEGISLATION BANNING ABORTION AS A MEANS OF BIRTH CONTROL

Section 1. Legislative Findings and Purpose.

Comment: This section could include an assertion of a compelling state interest in unborn life throughout pregnancy, and profess an intent to reasonably regulate abortion in accordance with the views of the majority of the Supreme Court.

Section 2. Definitions.

(a) "Abortion" means the use or prescription of any instrument, medicine, drug or any other substance or device to terminate the pregnancy of a woman known to be pregnant with an intention other than to increase the probability of a live birth, to preserve the life or health of the child after live birth, or to remove a dead fetus. . . .

(b) "Attempt to perform an abortion" means to do or omit to do anything that, under the circumstances as the actor believes them to be, is an act or omission constituting a substantial step in a course of conduct planned to culminate in an abortion. Such substantial steps include, but are not limited to, 1) agreeing with an individual to perform an abortion on that individual or on some other person, whether or not the term "abortion" is used in the agreement, and whether or not the agreement is contingent on another factor such as receipt of payment or a determination of pregnancy; or 2) scheduling or planning a time to perform an abortion on an individual, whether or not the term "abortion" is used, and whether or not the performance is contingent on another factor such as receipt of payment or a determination of pregnancy. This definition shall not be construed to require that an abortion procedure actually be initiated for an attempt to occur.

Section 3. Abortions as a method of birth control. It shall be unlawful to perform or to attempt to perform an abortion when it is being used or sought as a method of birth control.

Section 4. Abortions for other reasons. An abortion is not used or sought as a method of birth control when and only when:

(a) in the professional judgment of the attending or a referring physician, which is a medical judgment that would be made by a reasonably prudent physician, knowledgeable about the case and the treatment possibilities with respect to the medical conditions involved, the life of the mother would be endangered or severe and long-lasting physical health damage would result if the fetus were carried to term;

(b) the pregnancy is the result of rape [criminal sexual conduct] as defined in [forcible rape statute citation], and the incident is reported within 48 hours after the incident occurs to a valid law enforcement agency for investigation, unless the victim is physically unable to report the rape [criminal sexual conduct], in which case the incident is reported within 48 hours after the victim becomes physically able to report the rape [criminal sexual conduct];

(c) the pregnancy is the result of incest, and the incident and relative are reported to a valid law enforcement agency prior to the abortion; or

(d) in the professional judgment of the attending or a referring physician, which is a medical judgment that would be made by a reasonably prudent physician, knowledgeable about the case and the treatment possibilities with respect to the medical conditions involved, the child would be born with profound and irremediable physical or mental disabilities incompatible with sustained survival.

Section 5. Injunctions against abortions as a method of birth control. (a) A person with standing may maintain an action against the performance or attempted performance of abortions unlawful under section 3. Those with standing are [public officials: specify proper titles for prosecuting attorneys, attorney general, child abuse and neglect authorities, etc.], a woman upon whom an abortion unlawful under section 3 has been performed or attempted to be performed, the parent of a minor upon whom an abortion unlawful under section 3 has been or is about to be performed or attempted to be performed, and the father of the unborn child subject to an abortion unlawful under section 3 that has been or is about to be performed or attempted to be performed. It is an affirmative defense that the defendant performed or attempted to perform an abortion for a reason or reasons set forth in section 4.

(b) Actions against the performance and attempted performance of unlawful abortions may seek temporary restraining orders, preliminary injunctions and injunctions in accordance with the [state] rules of civil procedure [except that there shall be no requirement that a showing be made of injury, loss or damage to the applicant for the order or injunction].

(c) Any person knowingly violating the terms of an injunction against the performance or attempted performance of unlawful abortions shall be subject to civil contempt, and shall be fined $10,000 for the first violation, $20,000 for the second violation, and for each succeeding violation, shall be fined twice the amount levied for the immediately preceding violation, which shall be the exclusive penalties for such contempt. Each performance or attempted performance of an unlawful abortion in violation of the terms of an injunction is a separate violation. These fines shall be cumulative. However, no fine shall be assessed against the woman on whom an abortion is performed or attempted.

(d) If judgment is rendered in favor of the plaintiff in any action for an injunction or if a defendant is adjudged in contempt of a temporary restraining order, preliminary injunction, or injunction, the court shall also render judgment for a reasonable attorney's fee in favor of the plaintiff and against the defendant. The attorney's fee shall be taxed and collected as other costs of the action, and when collected shall be paid to the attorney for the plaintiff. If the attorney is a public official, the attorney's fee shall be paid into the state or county treasury.

Section 6. Civil damages for abortions as a method of birth control. Any person upon whom an abortion unlawful under section 3 was performed, the father of the unborn child who was the subject of such an abortion, or the grandparent of such an unborn child [Alternate wording A: Any person with standing under section 5(a), other than a public official; Alternate wording B: Any person with standing under section 5(a)] may maintain an action against the person who performed the abortion for $10,000 in punitive damages and treble whatever actual damages the plaintiff may have sustained. No person shall be estopped from recovery in such a suit on the ground that either the plaintiff or the person upon whom the abortion was performed gave consent to the abortion. In such a suit, it is an affirmative defense that the defendant performed or attempted to perform an abortion for a reason or reasons set forth in section 4.

Section 7. Privacy of woman upon whom an abortion is performed or attempted. In every proceeding or action brought under this Act, the anonymity of any woman upon whom an abortion is performed or attempted shall be preserved from public disclosure unless she gives her consent to such disclosure. The court, upon motion or sua sponte, shall issue orders to the parties, witnesses, and counsel, and shall direct the sealing of the record and exclusion of individuals from courtrooms or hearing rooms, to the extent necessary to safeguard her identity from public disclosure.

In the absence of written consent of the woman upon whom an abortion has been performed or attempted, anyone, other than a public official, who brings an action under section 5 or 6 shall do so under a pseudonym.

Section 8. Severability. If any provision, word, phrase, or clause of this Act or the application thereof to any person or circumstance is held invalid, such invalidity shall not affect the provisions, words, phrases, clauses or applications of this Act which can be given effect without the invalid provision, word, phrase, clause, or application and to this end, the provisions, words, phrases, and clauses of this Act are declared to be severable.

This proposal was first drafted by the National Right to Life Committee. A subsequent version of this legislation was passed by the Idaho State Legislature in March 1990, only to be vetoed by Governor Cecil Andrus.